Lifeboat Sailors

The U.S. Coast Guard's Small Boat Stations

DENNIS L. NOBLE

Brassey's
Washington, D.C.

Portions of Chapter 1 appeared in a different form in United States Naval Institute *Proceedings*.

Portions of Chapter 2 appeared in Dennis L. Noble, *That Others Might Live: The United States Life-Saving Service, 1878–1915*. Annapolis, Md.: Naval Institute Press, 1994.

Portions of Chapter 8 appeared in a different form in *Wreck & Rescue: Journal of the U.S. Life-Saving Service Heritage Association*.

Title page photo courtesy of BMI John Joffe, USCG.

Editorial Offices:
22841 Quicksilver Drive
Dulles, VA 20166

Order Department:
P.O. Box 960
Herndon, VA 20172

Brassey's books are available at special discounts for bulk purchases for sales promotions, premiums, fund-raising, or educational use.

Library of Congress Cataloging-in-Publication Data

Noble, Dennis L.
   Lifeboat sailors : inside the U.S. Coast Guard's small boat
stations / Dennis L. Noble.
     p. cm.
   Includes bibliographical references and index.
   ISBN 1-57488-200-7
   1. United States Coast Guard—Search and rescue operations.
  I. Title.
VK1323.N6297 1998
363.12'381'0973—dc21

                                     98-38679
                                         CIP

First Edition

10 9 8 7 6 5 4 3 2 1

To:

Boatswain's Mate Second Class David A. Bosley (1960–1997)

Machinery Technician Third Class Matthew E. Schlimme (1973–1997)

Seaman Clinton P. Miniken (1974–1997)

They crossed the bar to help strangers in peril

and

To all the crews of the U.S. Coast Guard's small boat stations, past, present, and future, who have done so much for so long, so that others might live.

"We ask so much of our young people in uniform and they so freely give it."

Master Chief Boatswain's Mate George A. LaForge, Officer-in-Charge, U.S. Coast Guard Station, Quillayute River, Washington

"There were times that the only thing that kept us from turning back because we were so cold, wet, sick, and miserable was the fact that we were too damned scared to realize we were all of those other things."

Comdr. Michael C. Monteith, Former Commanding Officer, U.S. Coast Guard Station, Cape Disappointment, Washington

Contents

Contents

Preface

There are over 15 million registered boat owners in the United States. As Sebastian Junger put it, any "weekend boater knows the Coast Guard will pluck him out of whatever idiocy he gets himself into" no matter what the weather. Usually, it is a small, white boat from a Coast Guard small boat rescue station that will appear. In 1993, for example, the Coast Guard received 52,445 calls for assistance, 9,914 of which were rated as moderate or severe incidents, and saved 4,689 lives. This volume of response came from an organization that had only 38,832 active duty personnel in 1993. Despite these amazing statistics, very few Americans know anything about the people who serve at the small boat stations of the Coast Guard. This book attempts to give recognition to these men and women who have, over the years, silently carried out a humanitarian tradition.

Since 1878, Coast Guard personnel, and their predecessors of the U.S. Life-Saving Service, have rammed small boats into very large seas with a single purpose: to save strangers from the cruel sea. Most Americans, however, have no idea what it takes to be a professional maritime lifesaver. Their perceptions are influenced more by the television series "Baywatch" than by anything else. As is usually the case, the difference between reality and the flickering images on the living room screen is huge. One has only to see the tired, sun- and wind-burned faces of a crew, after fighting the pounding of a motor lifeboat or 41-footer for hours, making their way wearily up the dock, carrying their SAR (search and rescue) bags, and bundled in their bulky Mustang exposure suits, to understand the difference between make-believe and reality. This book will show the lives and service of these forgotten people who daily face the real possibility of dying so that others might live.

The story of the Coast Guards small boat rescue stations is an emotional roller coaster for those who serve at the units. A chief warrant officer best described the range of feelings: "I remember the first time I jumped into the water off Northern California and helped pull two 14-year-old girls out from under a capsized boat. I will never forget the feeling of floating in the Pacific with one girl hugging me, telling me how much she loved me. It's funny. They both had cut their feet and were bleeding pretty bad, but when they got on our boat they would not sit down and let us bandage them until they had kissed every guy on the boat." The chief warrant officer then paused a moment and added: "I also remember as a young crewman staring into the lifeless eyes of a 13-year-old that I'd been doing CPR on for 2 hours and literally wanting to get hold of someone and beat him to death for putting me into that situation."

As in any human organization, there is friction in the Coast Guard. It is always easy to blame district headquarters, or headquarters in Washington, D.C., for all problems. In the interests of objectivity, I visited both Coast Guard headquarters and a district office so they could give me the "big picture" as they see it. I hope the results of my research will allow the reader to balance the comments of the stations and headquarters in forming their own opinions concerning the future of the units.

I served in the Coast Guard and retired as an enlisted man, a senior chief petty officer (E-8), but not in the small boat community. I began at a small boat station, however, at Michigan City, Indiana, which I revisited while researching this book almost 40 years after first reporting aboard. Upon retirement, I returned to school and earned a doctorate in history. From the beginning of this book project, I realized that, if I wanted to understand the people who serve at the Coast Guard's small boat rescue stations as fully as possible, I would have to live aboard the units. To enable the reader to capture the feel of living and working aboard the units, I have strapped into a 30-foot surf rescue boat, which tossed me about as I looked *upward* at the tops of the swells. I have been aboard a 47-foot motor lifeboat as its bow pointed downward toward the bottom of a trough and I wondered if it ever would rise again. I have sat on a boat during a torrential rain shower and felt like either quacking like a duck or squawking like a sea gull. Ashore, I endured hours in communications rooms during long, boring watches, with watchstanders trying to pass the time away by doing such exciting things as giving me their impression of a chicken, along with sound effects. I also observed watchstanders under the stress of working cases that literally meant life or death and spent a long night with a crew that lost three shipmates. I think my accumulated insights of almost 40 years, coupled with the experience of having actually lived aboard the modern-day stations, will provide a good understanding of the people and their duties. I could not visit every station, so I selected stations from various geographical locations, as the cases are somewhat different in each region. I also sent out questionnaires.

As a historian, I had originally thought I should provide copious footnotes to document my sources. A quick glance through the pages ahead will reveal only a few. I wanted people at the stations to feel free to talk to me. I found a disturbing trend among senior petty officers. Many were worried about retribution from senior commissioned officers if they stated their views. Some even asked me: "Aren't you worried they might still be able to do something to you?" One of the reasons for this attitude is illustrated by the incident I describe in Chapter 9. Therefore, I decided to protect my sources. I use few names, and I do not identify many stations.

The bibliography is very small, because no one has appeared to have written a book on the Coast Guard's small boat stations until now. Indeed, only recently have a few books appeared about the U.S. Life-Saving Service, the predecessor to the small boat stations.

There is an old saying among sailors that, even at the best unit, there is always someone who is never satisfied. To maintain objectivity, therefore, I do not include any observation in the book, except where noted, unless two or more people have made the same comments to me. I believe my method helps to weed out the lone chronic complainer. For those of you who think they know who is being quoted in unidentified passages, you are wrong. But I do use real names when I am satisfied doing so will in no way harm anyone, for example, in the passages about Quillayute River.

In researching this book, I have tried to give decision-makers their chance to respond to any charges made by people in the small boat community. If senior officers failed to respond, perhaps this speaks volumes. I leave it for the reader to make up his or her mind where the truth may lie. Some of the statements have the ring of "sea stories," because these are, after all, the perceptions of the person relating the incident, and perceptions can be as important as "facts."

I will confess to two sins a writer should not possess: I am not unemotional and I have certain prejudices in relation to the topic of this book. My heart is for the small boat community. The reader should be aware that, after over 20 years of enlisted service in the Coast Guard, and even though I have a Ph.D. and have been on the retired list for very close to 20 years, I am still an enlisted sailor. This fact has been brought home to me many times.

The period during which I conducted much of my research and writing was dominated by the loss of three Coast Guardsmen at the Quillayute River station while attempting to rescue people on a sailboat. It is not hyperbole to say that the shock waves from this event are still reverberating through the stations and will continue to do so for many years to come. This project was no longer fun for me after Quillayute River.

Over the period I worked on this book, I received a number of suggestions from people who served at the units. Two suggestions that repeatedly surfaced at various stations are worth repeating: don't be a crusader, as you are an outsider, and don't think you are going to change anything. To respond to these points, I approached this book from the perspective of acting as the Boswell for the stations. What you read is what I actually observed or what people at the stations told me. This is a book about the small boat rescue stations by those who now serve, or who have served, at the units. Quotation marks, unless otherwise noted, denote information given directly to me by station personnel or published material about or by station people. Some quoted conversations may not be grammatically correct, but most sailors do not speak in proper English, and I wanted their story in their language, not mine. Readers may note that, contrary to the stereotype of all sailors, there is not much swearing in the book. I think people watched their language when they told me their stories. I did not clean the language up in any way. To ensure that this book reflected the small boat community, I asked people of various ranks from that community to read the manuscript to see that it reflected the viewpoints and life at the stations. Again, to protect my sources, these people are not identified in the acknowledgments.

The stations are commanded either by senior enlisted men—all in the boatswain's mate (BM) rating, in the top three enlisted grades of chief petty officer (E-7), senior chief petty officer (E-8), or master chief petty officer (E-9) (some smaller units are commanded by boatswain's mate first class [E-6])—or they are commanded by chief warrant officers in the boatswain speciality in the ranks CWO-2, CWO-3, or CWO-4. A few stations, such as Cape Disappointment, Washington, now have commissioned officers at their helm. See Appendix 2 for the military ranks of the Coast Guard and of other services.

Technically, when enlisted people are in charge of stations, their official titles are Officer-in-Charge (OIC) and their executive officers are called Executive Petty Officers (XPO). When commissioned officers or warrant officers are in charge, their title is commanding officer. I believe people are more aware of commanding officer and executive officer as the titles of the two senior people at a unit and, therefore, in most cases, I have used these terms. An OIC is still commanding a station and an XPO is still the second in command.

The two primary enlisted ratings (petty officers) on a small boat station are boatswain's mates and machinery technicians (MK), formerly called engineman (EN). Other ratings exist at some of the larger units. Those crewmembers who have not yet made petty officer and who are in the deck branch are seaman recruit (SR) (E-1), seaman apprentice (SA) (E-2), or seaman (SN) (E-3) or they are in the engineering department, the position titles of which include fireman recruit (FR), fireman apprentice (FA), and fireman (FN). The Coast Guard now calls anyone who is not a petty officer a nonrate or nonrated. Appendix 2 compares the Coast Guard nonrates with those of the other armed forces. There is a brief description of the various ratings assigned to the small boat stations in Appendix 3.

A few words about the two primary ratings at the station. There are other rates attached to a small boat station and I do not mean to minimize their work aboard a unit, but, in fact, most stations have larger numbers of BMs and MKs. For the more than 20 years I spent on active duty, a rivalry existed between the "deckies" of the BM rating and the "snipes" of the MKs. I am not without guilt; I joined in on the bantering. This trait continues today. Most of the time the comments are friendly. However, at times they are not so friendly. One of the aspects of the comments deal with the BM rating. The rate has been known as a "jack of all trades" position. A good BM, in fact, must be able to do a little bit of everything. Unfortunately, what many translate this into is: If you cannot do anything else in the Coast Guard, you can always be a boatswain's mate. This is about as true as the old civilian saw that those that do, do; those who can't, teach. This has led to the stereotyping of BMs as unthinking and unfeeling people. Even some senior commissioned officers have played upon this stereotype when trying to make changes at the small boat stations, as will be shown in Chapter 9. Readers will note some comments of "knuckle-dragging surfmen" and others that even some BMs make as a result of hearing the comments so often. The attitude toward the BM rating is one of those intangible concepts that have helped prevent the public from increasing its knowledge of the stations. Many of the BMs I met during my active duty days and during this project felt they "were not good enough to write." Yet, when you discuss rescues, they can be as articulate as any officer and, in most cases, prove to be much more articulate. Having heard the comments for a long time, many now believe the stereotype. Perhaps this proves Joseph Goebbels right: repeat a lie long enough and people will believe it. In cases where I did not use a boatswain's mate's name, I call him the sobriquet all BMs go by: "Boats."

The first link in the military chain of command for the stations is the group, such as Coast Guard Group Astoria, Oregon. Many groups are commanded by a captain (O-6) and many of these are aviators, as several groups are located at Coast Guard air stations. However, I visited stations within groups that were under the direction of commanders and lieutenant commanders who were not aviators.

The next link up the chain is the Coast Guard district, commanded by a rear admiral (O-8). Usually, the stations are supervised by the Office of Search and Rescue (OSR) in the district, which is headed by a captain. However, since the stations' missions are quite diverse, many other offices, such as law enforcement, also conduct activities at the units.

The final link in the military chain of command is Coast Guard headquarters, located in Washington, D.C. The Coast Guard is commanded by a commandant, a full four-star admiral (O-10). At the time this book was written, in 1997 and 1998, Adm. Robert E. Kramek, a 1961 graduate of the Coast Guard Academy, held the post of commandant. Admiral Kramek reports to the secretary of transportation. In time of war, or at the direction of the president, the Coast Guard operates under the U.S. Navy. Within head-quarters, the stations are supervised by a number of offices, but the primary one is the Office of Shore Activities, headed by a captain, under the Division of Operations, which is headed by a rear admiral.

The latest idea from headquarters is to call the units "multi-mission stations." I will use "small boat rescue stations" throughout this book, as it is the more recognizable term to most people. The Coast Guard now has divided the units into stations (large) and stations (small). The main boats for stations are either motor life-boats or utility boats. Some units have both types. Most units now have rigid-hull inflatable boats (RHIB), but these are not considered standard boats. At the time of the writing of this book, motor lifeboats were mainly 44-footers. The new 47-footers that are slowly coming into the fleet tend to be assigned to units where there is apt to be high seas and surf. The primary boats of many of the stations from Georgia southward and along the Gulf of Mexico and in southern California are the 41-foot utility boats. I visited almost every type of unit.

This book will reflect courage, discouragement, anger, laughter, intelligent thinking, less than intelligent thinking, sadness, and frustration. In short, it will show human beings in a dangerous profession, and it will show some of their dangers, some of their frustrations, and some of their bravery. It should never be forgotten that the reality of the work these little-known people perform every day is reflected in what happened at Quillayute River. If, when finished with this book, the reader appreciates the efforts put forth by the dedicated lifesavers of the Coast Guard's small boat rescue stations and has an understanding of the people who make up the crews of the units, then the book will have accomplished its mission.

I finished this book where I began it: at the "Guardian of the Graveyard of the Pacific": the U.S. Coast Guard Station, Cape Disappointment, Washington.

Acknowledgments

The acknowledgments for this work of nonfiction are somewhat different than most. As discussed in Chapter 9, I needed to ensure the anonymity of those who gave me information, thus I cannot list the names of most of the people at the stations who were my primary sources for this book. A number of senior people at the units read the manuscript for accuracy. I chose to protect them, but I want to thank all those who took the time to read the material.

One would expect an organization whose commandant says his policy "is to provide appropriate assistance to those who are helping to tell the Coast Guard story" to have many acknowledgments listing the higher levels of the Coast Guard. Instead, I have never experienced so much obfuscation from senior people of the service in the preparation of a book. Letters, telephone calls, and requests went unanswered, including those to the commandant, which perhaps proves policy may not mean too much in some organizations. There were exceptions to this statement, and they are listed below.

At Coast Guard headquarters, I received a great deal of assistance, as usual, from the Historian of the U.S. Coast Guard, Dr. Robert M. Browning, Jr., and his assistant, Mr. Scott T. Price. These two people provided information and material quickly and professionally. If the rest of the Coast Guard headquarters and districts were as efficient and helpful, more would probably be written about the service.

Dianne Porter, Chief, Medals and Awards Branch, was very helpful in obtaining citations, and Comdr. T. J. Martin, chief of the Auxiliary Operations Division, responded quickly to inquiries. Wayne Paugh of the Audiovisual Section helped in the selection of photographs. Two captains and a commander took time out of their busy schedules for interviews. The questioning was probably not enjoyable to them, but they accomplished the task as professionals. As with the people at the stations, I decided not to use their names.

Acknowledgments

I especially want to thank three Coast Guardsmen for allowing me to show their service lives in detail. I wish, in particular, to acknowledge the help of Master Chief Boatswain's Mate Thomas McAdams, U.S. Coast Guard (Retired), for sharing a part of his career. CWO4 Mark Dobney and CWO2 Thomas Doucette—promoted from BMCS during the writing of this book—both were extremely helpful and courteous in putting up with my continuous questions and requests about their careers.

At the U.S. Coast Guard National Motor Lifeboat School, I received help and assistance from CWO3 Paul D. Bellona, the commanding officer; his staff of instructors, especially BM1 Tim Stentz, now transferred to Guam; and BM1 Darrin Wallace. I agree with CWO Bellona: the "best of the best" are instructors in a very hostile environment.

Throughout this project, I received a great deal of support from Capt. Philip C. Volk, Commander, U. S. Coast Guard Group Port Angeles, Washington. Captain Volk made the way easier in many ways. I wish to thank all of the Group Commanders who gave me permission to visit the stations under their command. I want to give special mention to Comdr. Hank Haynes, then at Group Astoria, and now at Coast Guard headquarters, for smoothing my access to the units under the group. His assistance is the type any researcher greatly appreciates.

At Commander, Atlantic Area, PAC Keith Spangler provided me with needed photographs; Lt. Comdr. M. E. Woodring and PA3 Scott Carr of the Seventh Coast Guard District provided great assistance; and PAC John Moss of the 13th Coast Guard District provided me with photographs.

BM3 Angela Renee Buzinski went out of her way to provide me with additional information that helped in another research project, and FN Jessie Charleton can come up with great titles.

This book could not have been written without the help of the commanding officers/officers-in-charge and especially the crews of the small boat rescue stations of the Coast Guard. It was a pleasure and an honor visiting with them or exchanging information by mail.

William Wilkinson, director emeritus of the Mariners' Museum, graciously shared his vast amount of knowledge on Coast Guard small boats and offered a great deal of encouragement during this project. Peggy Norris, as usual, performed outstanding

Acknowledgments

work of reading the manuscript for my inevitable misspellings and for content. Tom Beard provided information from both the aviation aspect and as a sailor. Greg Shield again assisted me with his critical eye and encouragement. Loren Noble helped in the proofreading.

Susan Browning deserves thanks for her artistry in producing the maps in this book.

I wish to thank the North Olympic Library System and my supervisor, Peggy Norris, for allowing me the time off to do the needed research for this book.

A very special thanks goes to BMCM George A. LaForge, BM1 Jon Placido, and the crew of the Quillayute River station. I will never forget the early morning hours of February 12, 1997. The crew could well have shut me out after the tragedy, but they continued to help in their normal thoughtful way.

At Brassey's I owe a great deal of gratitude to Don McKeon, editorial director, for his enthusiasm and editing. Linda Ridinger Smith shepherded the book through the publishing process, and I benefited from Gary Kessler as a copy editor.

This book is based upon my observations and information provided to me by the crews of the small boat stations, but I am responsible for the final conclusions.

prologue

February 12, 1997

Seven months into my research for this book, I received permission to visit the U.S. Coast Guard Station at Quillayute River. The station is located on the Quillayute Indian Reservation, and within the reservation's village of La Push, along the isolated, rocky northwestern coast of Washington State. Bald eagles whirl among the steep rocky islands no more than a mile from the station. The station lies squarely in the migration path of the Pacific Flyway, during which time huge skeins of waterfowl can be seen. When the winds pick up, as they always do in the winter months, heavy surf can be heard crashing on the rocky beach less than half a mile from the station. Forks, the closest town to the reservation, is about 20 minutes away by car and has a population of about a thousand. The nearest movie theater is at least an hour and a half away by car in the city of Port Angeles, which has a population of around 17,500. In winter, Pacific low pressure systems entering the United States come directly over the area, bringing gray skies, strong winds, heavy surf, and rainfall that is measured in feet, not inches. One of the former commanding officers of the station dubbed the unit "The Fortress of Solitude."

The Quillayute River station is small. At the time of my visit on February 11, 1997, Master Chief Boatswain's Mate (BMCM) George A. LaForge commanded the unit, with Boatswain's Mate First Class (BM1) Jonathan Placido as the second in command. Twenty-two Coast Guard men and three Coast Guard women made up the station's complement. The unit has two 44-foot motor lifeboats and a rigid-hull inflatable boat.

Even though the unit did not have much room, they went out of their way to make me feel at home, as did all the stations I visited while working on this book. After I had settled in, BM2 David A. Bosley, of Coronado, California, the officer-of-the-day (OOD), assigned BM3 Paul Lassilla to show me around the station. At any small boat station that has pride, the crew is extremely anxious for visitors to see their boats. Petty Officer Lassilla took me to the boathouse and showed me through all of the compartments of one of the motor lifeboats. In the engine room, I saw gleaming brass and could run my finger around fittings and find no dirt.

Lassilla and I sat in the forward compartment and discussed his background and mine and the "new" and "old" Coast Guard. Eventually, it was time for the noon meal, and I faced my largest hazard on this project. The meals are designed for young people with an appetite, not someone who is shaped like a pear.

After lunch, Petty Officer Bosley assigned BM2 Brent Cooking-

An aerial photograph of La Push, Washington, and the mouth of the Quillayute River, taken shortly after the CG-44363 tragedy. The surf continues high. The Coast Guard boathouse is in the upper right, the largest white structure at the top of the protected area off the river. To the right of the boathouse is the station building. James Island is the largest one pictured. The cove that CG-44363 entered is visible on the island's left side. *U.S. Coast Guard*

ham to fit me out with the necessary survival gear in anticipation of riding a boat during the station's ever-constant boat drills (practice). Petty Officer Cookingham gave me all of the necessary paraphernalia to survive in the cold waters of the North Pacific, including a Mustang survival suit, a bulky orange coverall that also is a flotation device. I received warm thermal underwear, socks, rubber boots, a cap, gloves, and a helmet to protect my head from heavy surf and heaving lines. All of this is stowed in a nylon flight bag carried by boat crewmen and which they call either the "ready bag" or the "SAR bag." The ready crews keep their SAR bags in compartments at the docks so they are not slowed down while running toward their boat.

Cookingham and I talked about how the Coast Guard now spends so much time on environmental practices which, while a good policy, places additional paperwork on already overburdened senior petty officers. Cookingham picked up a very thick manual. "We're required to post these anywhere there are hazardous materials. Even the cleaning locker in the barracks has to have one of these, so everyone knows what is in the cleaning material."

Today, Cookingham informed me, the nonrates (those people below noncommissioned officer grade—petty officer grade) think nothing of donning a respirator when opening a can of paint. This is a far cry from the Old Guard.

By evening, I was doing what I most enjoyed about researching this book: talking to crewmembers about their lives, their likes and dislikes, and their hopes for the future. I talked to one petty officer, who said he was slowly becoming disillusioned with the Coast Guard because of the number of hours he worked. Just as many others said during my interviews at other stations, he said he was so tired by the time liberty came, all he wanted to do was go home and sleep. He really did not have much time for his family.

Then machinery technician third class (MK3) Matthew E. Schlimme, of Whitewater, Missouri, sat down next to me and, as usual, we traded backgrounds. There are some people you meet who seem most natural with a smile on their face. Schlimme fit into this category. As a civilian, Schlimme had worked on tugboats on the lower Mississippi River. As luck would have it, his first duty assignment after graduating from boot camp was on a small buoy tender on the upper Mississippi River. He told me that one of the things the tender did was stop every evening and tie up at a small town. Schlimme enjoyed walking along the river and visiting the small river towns. "I really liked the small, clean towns," he said.

I told Schlimme of my forays along the Mississippi River in Iowa, and he immediately hurried off the mess deck and came back with a road atlas. We sat and looked at the names of towns along the river, seeing if we had been in the same ones. When I mentioned that I needed the address of someone who had been stationed at Quillayute River, he called his wife and obtained the information for me. This service was in keeping with the helpful and friendly nature of most people at the stations.

In the meantime, BM2 Bosley had sat down near us. Bosley, I learned, had received orders to the cutter *Point Hobart*, an 82-foot patrol boat, homeported in Oceanside, southern California. "These are my wife's orders," said Bosley. He explained that she was from southern California, that he had wanted to come to the Quillayute River station and that now it was time to go to southern California.

By now it was time for me to turn in. I said goodnight to Bosley and Schlimme. I learned two additional things before leaving the mess deck: They both had the ready boat (the first boat the crew would use for an SAR case) for the night and Schlimme now had fewer than 16 days to serve in the Coast Guard. He gave me one of his smiles and said, "I'm going home."

I looked through the window at the weather on the way to my room. Wind shook trees in strong, gusty bursts. Visibility seemed low, and I could hear the surf crashing on the beach a quarter of a mile away. I dozed off wondering if I should reconsider riding the 44-footer if the surf was too high. Riding a motor lifeboat is a young person's game, not one for someone in their late 50s. Most people do not realize how much the pounding of a motor lifeboat punishes your back and knees. A few months earlier I had ridden a 47-foot motor lifeboat for 3½ hours in moderate seas and was sore for days.

A short few hours later, I was jolted awake. The Search and Rescue alarm was blaring off the barracks wall. Then the announcement: "Sailboat on the bar taking on water!"

I waited a few minutes for the ready boat crew to race to their motor lifeboat. When an SAR alarm rings, and you are not a crewmember, it is always best to stay out of the way as the crews race toward the docks. I made my way to the operations room.

Near operations, I looked out the double-glass entry door and saw that the wind was still whipping the trees.

Unlike in most movies or cable television programs, radio transmissions between sea and shore are never crystal clear, and this is especially true when a storm strikes in the midst of an SAR case. Transmissions are usually bad; static and other stations compete with stress-filled voices. Adrenaline surges and voices rise, making transmission even more difficult.

Two watchstanders, a woman and a man recently out of high school, handled the radio traffic, intercom traffic, and telephone messages from Group Port Angeles, Washington, 80 miles to the east, which was Quillayute River station's immediate supervisor.

The ready 44-foot motor lifeboat, CG-44363, with BM2 Bosley; MK3 Schlimme; Seaman (SN) Clinton P. Miniken of Snohomish, Washington; and Seaman Apprentice (SA) Benjamin F. Wingo of Bremerton, Washington, was in the process of leaving the dock, while the second motor lifeboat crew was being mustered. Master Chief LaForge arrived from home just after I came to the operations room. Petty Officer Placido donned his survival gear and listened to the reports filtering into operations.

The group advised the station to hold the 44-foot motor lifeboat from crossing the bar, always a hazardous and dangerous operation in high seas and when visibility is limited, as the distress call might be a hoax. The watchstanders began calling the motor lifeboat. No contact.

LaForge called the CG-44363 and received a "we're busy." LaForge could tell from the tone of Bosley's voice that he was busy, perhaps crossing the bar, and that this was not a good time to distract him with radio traffic. LaForge told the watchstander to get the second boat underway as soon as it had a full crew. LaForge then turned to me and said, "Come on with me, Dennis, while I check the bar."

We drove in a four-wheel-drive Jeep, with a radio. LaForge heard Bosley say in a more reassured voice that they were across the bar and the seas were running 16 to 18 feet. LaForge felt that Bosley had turned the CG-44363 away from James Island and had headed toward the sea buoy and deep water.

We arrived at the observation point and peered through the driving mist. Then I heard a faint transmission that sounded like: "We rolled the boat." LaForge and I discussed what the transmission sounded like. LaForge tried to raise the CG-44363. He heard "disoriented." The station confirmed this. LaForge then saw a spotlight pointed toward the south, from what looked like the seaward side of James Island. Glimpsing it only momentarily, the beam swept rapidly through the night. LaForge knew the CG-44363 was in trouble. LaForge again told the station to get the second boat underway. He also told the station to have Port Angeles launch a helicopter. The station called LaForge. The duty officer at Port Angeles wanted to talk to him directly. The officer still felt this might be a hoax.

We will never know what BM2 Bosley had in mind when he pushed the throttles of the CG-44363 forward and maneuvered out into the river, as he did not brief his crew. Did he think the sailboat was right on the bar and taking on water? If so, this accounts for his haste in getting underway. In retrospect, listening to the tapes of the radio transmissions, it is easy to reach this conclusion. It may also account for how Bosley decided to make his track line after crossing the bar.

Wingo, aboard the CG-44363, recalled the weather as "rainy and nasty." Once under way, Schlimme came over to the starboard side of the coxswain flat and adjusted the radar. He then returned to his normal position to the left of Bosley. Miniken operated the spotlight on the port side. Bosley ordered Wingo to use the starboard spotlight. Bosley wanted Wingo to light up Wash Rock, near the bar.

Wingo recalled Bosley as being impatient. When Schlimme reminded Bosley to be careful of the oil pressure getting too high, Bosley said, "Yeah, yeah, I got it."

Somewhere before they reached Wash Rock, near the bar, Schlimme said to Bosley, "Let's get the fuck out of here!" Bosley said something that sounded like: "Fuck that!"

By the time they reached Wash Rock, near the bar, Wingo, dripping wet, became nervous at the size of the waves. He had never seen so much water go over the boat as it plunged into the swells.

Bosley told Wingo to put the light on James Island. He wanted the island on the starboard beam. Wingo recalls that the island seemed 100 to 150 yards in the distance.

The CG-44363 crossed the bar, and someone said the group wanted them to hold off, that this might be a hoax. Bosley replied, "I hope not."

The boat moved along the island. Wingo spotted a rock and said to Bosley, "Rock! Starboard side, 10 feet!" Then the boat hit something. Bosley asked, "What was that?" Then a shout: "Wave,

6

port side!" The boat rolled at least 180 degrees. When it came up, the bow was pointed toward James Island. Bosley grabbed the radio microphone and called in that they had rolled the boat and that the crew was disoriented. Wingo found himself wrapped in a canvas dodger, which was used to help protect the crew in foul weather. He quickly freed himself. Schlimme said they were still on the bar. Wingo reached for the spotlight. Gone. Bosley yelled out to look for buoy number 3. Wingo could see the lights of the village of LaPush, but not number 3.

Another shout. The boat rolled again. When they came up, the boat rested on rocks. Wingo could tell by the engine noise that the boat was out of the water. The entire top of the forward cabin was gone, as was the mast. So were Bosley—the man who loved to drive boats and fish—and Miniken, a hard-working kid who always tried to do his best.

MK3 Schlimme now took command of the boat. Wingo started to unbuckle. He said, "We've got to get out of here!" Schlimme made Wingo get back into his belt. They needed to get inside the boat. Schlimme tried to call the station. Then Schlimme yelled, "Hold on!" A wave knocked the boat off the rock. When it came up, Schlimme—the kid with the ready smile—was gone. Wingo saw a body go by the boat, but he could not throw a life ring, as both were gone.

Wingo then realized the CG-44363 was moving backward into the cove on the south side of the island. The boat banged along the rocks. He turned on the strobe light in his pyro vest (the pyrotechnic vest containing signaling devices).

Wingo started to pray. He thinks he then put the engine throttles into neutral. He reached into his pyro vest, took out five flares, and shot them off. He used his last two flares to help illuminate the beach area. The boat swung stern to the beach, and its navigation lights lit up the area.

Wingo remembered that Schlimme had told him to stay with the boat. He attempted to get into the forward cabin, hoping to get the emergency radio and battle lantern located there. The hatch could not be opened.

Wingo then unclipped his safety belt and leaped from the boat. He landed in knee-deep water. He reached the beach and activated a personal marker light. He eventually worked his way up a cliff and awaited rescue.

Meanwhile, LaForge and I had returned to the station. La-

Forge called the officer at Port Angeles and told him he had a serious situation. He said he still needed an HH-65 helicopter—a machine that is short-ranged—and also requested an HH-60, a medium-range helicopter, from Astoria, Oregon, over 100 miles away. I watched both LaForge and Placido becoming uneasy.

"Flares."

"What color?" asked LaForge.

"Red." Red means distress.

"I'm going!" Placido shouted back, as he ran toward the second 44-footer.

"Let's go back to the bar," LaForge said to me.

Parking again at the observation point we had taken before, I could see a red flare arcing through the sky. I have participated in a number of cases involving flare sightings, all of which proved to be false. This is the first instance of actually seeing one fired in distress.

Suddenly, a bright light moved through the darkness, up, down, and sideways, indicating a roiled sea. The 44-footer, with Petty Officer Placido and his crew of three, came into sight. The boat pitched and rolled, as only a motor lifeboat can in a heavy sea. It then turned from the protection of the river to make its run across the bar.

I will always carry with me the sight of Petty Officer Placido's 44-foot motor lifeboat as it entered the waves on its passage—waves that were later estimated to be at least 20 feet. A searchlight probed the darkness and the waters ahead, looking for obstacles. The small white boat was rising. Rising. Rising. Rising, until it seemed to stand on its stern. White water almost enveloped the small boat. Then it plunged downward.

Master Chief LaForge kept up a radio conversation with the second lifeboat. Meanwhile, the call from the sailboat was now definitely proven not to have been a hoax. Transmissions were being received from a frightened woman, who was having a hard time understanding the Quillayute River station's instructions. This complicated a situation that was becoming more and more anxious.

Then everyone lost communication with Petty Officer Placido's boat. Calls from Master Chief LaForge and the station went unanswered.

A woman's nervous voice asked: "Are you coming out to help us?"

LaForge again called for helicopter assistance, which entails a long flight from Port Angeles in heavy wind.

More calls ensued.

Finally, Petty Officer Placido reported: "We are on hand-held [radio]. Our antenna was damaged by a breaker." Master Chief LaForge advised Placido to remain in deep water. He would have to remain out until daylight, at least 6 hours hence.

LaForge and I returned to the station.

I recall further impressions of a very long, sleepless night: "Better put out beach walkers"; off-duty crewmembers coming in without being called; a badly shaken woman on a sailboat, barely able to communicate. LaForge saying to radio watchstander, "Keep off the air, if possible. If the pilot gets into trouble, he may have only one chance to broadcast for help"; the Port Angeles helicopter transmitting to the sailboat, "You have 30 seconds until you hit the rocks. Prepare yourselves"; only moments later a report of both people aboard the sailboat somehow hoisted to safety; two beach party crewmen injured; a speeding truck approaching the station, lights flashing, horn blasting; a crewman running in shouting, "We need an EMT! We need an EMT!". BM2 Cookingham calming the man down, obtaining information; this is not someone from the beach party; LaForge off to the beach; two crewmen brought into the station, one just barely able to hobble, the other with his arm bound against his body; CPR being administered to a crewman from the missing 44-footer washed upon the beach; a woman radio watchstander almost crying, but still working.

Everyone now knows something very bad has happened; an injured crewman on the mess deck in pain, his shipmate, a woman, trying to support him while she fights her own grief; another crewmen on the mess deck starting to cry; two other crewmen grabbing him and supporting him with embraces; everyone now knows that only one man in the first lifeboat has survived; Master Chief LaForge, drawn, haggard, close to tears, "I should have trained them more. I should have trained them more"; Petty Officer Placido's lifeboat finally able to make it back across the bar; Comdr. Paul A. Langlois, after an amazing hoist of the two people from the sailboat, the only Coast Guard helicopter pilot I have ever heard say, "I was scared!"; a helicopter rescue swimmer swearing, "Someone was watching out for us"; a crewman from Petty Officer Placido's lifeboat, "I was scared!"; four crewmen sitting exhausted

The CG-44363 after the night of the loss of three crewmen. The top of the cabin has been sheared off. *U.S. Coast Guard*

on the deck, fighting tears, then embracing each other; a burly career Coast Guardsman starting to say something about Matthew E. Schlimme and then suddenly moving into a closet.

Once Wingo's location on a steep cliff on James Island was known, Comdr. Michael Neussl and his crew, flying an HH-60 helicopter from Astoria, Oregon, and knowing rescue could not be undertaken until daylight, remained in a hover close to the rocky precipice until daylight, despite heavy buffeting winds. Along with my shipmates, I had often made disparaging remarks about "airdales" and their flight pay. On this night, I saw an officer and his aircrew place themselves in harm's way to provide psychological comfort for an enlisted man and fellow Coast Guardsman.

In the light of early morning, the rescue team brought Ben Wingo into the Quillayute River station so his shipmates could see him before he was taken to the hospital. His face, with many cuts, held an expression many veterans of combat would recognize. Wingo's eyes focused on something only he could see. I do not know how he had survived.

In the early morning hours of February 12, 1997, three crewmen of a Coast Guard motor lifeboat died in an attempt to save two people they did not know. Their shipmates from the Coast Guard Quillayute River station cried, comforted each other, and suffered.

In the early phases of researching this book, a petty officer said, "When a police officer or fireman is killed in the line of duty, there is a coming together of fellow officers or firemen to pay honor to the fallen comrade. In the Coast Guard, it seems we want to point the finger at someone and blame them."

In a very short period of time after the Quillayute River incident, amid a flurry of media hype, the Coast Guard released its investigation into the causes of the tragedy. The report noted that, while BM2 David A. Bosley went into harm's way for all the best of reasons, the finger of blame still pointed squarely at him for the loss of the CG-44363 and three of its crew. The Coast Guard saw fit to release Bosley's service record. It contained damning documents. Bosley had been warned about being too reckless and, most importantly, had lost his coxswain qualifications. According to the investigation, Bosley did not wish to advance beyond the coxswain stage to the next higher level of boatmanship, to surfman—this at a station that has a bar that needs the skills of surfmen to cross during bad weather. Yet, Bosley had been reinstated as a coxswain. In the conditions on that awful night, Coast Guard policy clearly states that no coxswain will take a motor lifeboat out in such fierce weather. The winds and swells required the skills of a surfman to operate in the environment present on

SN Benjamin F. Wingo, the only survivor of the CG-44363, nine months after the tragedy. Wingo received a promotion to seaman in October 1997. *Dennis L. Noble*

that night. What Bosley planned or thought will never be known, as he did not brief his crew, for which he also received censure.

The news media, which, along with the American public, knows very little about the men and women of the Coast Guard's small boat stations, rightfully noticed that everything in the investigation pointed to the fact that BM2 Bosley seemed unable to be trusted and at one time lost the right even to command a motor lifeboat. In their lights, the Quillayute River incident was an open and shut case.

Perhaps because of their lack of knowledge, no one attending the news conference in Seattle commented upon why at least 86 percent of the people stationed at Quillayute River on February 12 had been there less than a year. No commentator mentioned a very telling statement the commander of the 13th Coast Guard District, Rear Adm. J. David Spade, made about a change in policy concerning the transfer of surfmen, even though the admiral said it was important. After having listened to and having viewed the taped news conference, no reporter seemed willing to ask a very important question: If Bosley was relieved of duty as a coxswain and stated he did not want to be a surfman at a station that badly needs surfmen, then why was Bosley still a coxswain at the Quillayute River station? The question would have opened the door to a number of responses that would have called into question the Coast Guard's personnel policies. Quite simply, BM2 David A. Bosley remained at the Quillayute River station because of poor personnel policies set by an officer corps that has, at best, a very poor understanding of what takes place at their own service's small boat stations. The personnel policies and poor comprehension of the units has caused a deterioration of the stations despite the best efforts of commanding officers and officers-in-charge. The policies of the Coast Guard have caused one commanding officer to make this very frightening comment: "You have to work with what you've got. You may qualify a marginal person, but try to make sure that person is never put into a bad situation."

In short, in the early morning hours of February 12, 1997, three Coast Guardsmen paid with their lives for a very flawed system. To understand the genesis of this statement, it is necessary to know about the men and women who crew the stations—their daily routine, their duties, their frustrations, and their heroism.

chapter one

That Others Might Live

On Thursday afternoon, April 15, 1993, at the U.S. Coast Guard Station, Yaquina Bay, Newport, Oregon, Chief Boatswain's Mate F. Scott Clendenin was working on the bane of an executive officer of a small boat rescue station—paperwork. Chief Clendenin, a 16-year veteran of battling the high surf of the West Coast and an expert surfman, is described by other surfmen "as born to do search and rescue." Other senior chief petty officers have told me he is only alive when trying to rescue someone from the sea. On this day, Chief Clendenin would come alive again.

Less than 2 miles away from Chief Clendenin and his dreaded paperwork, the fishing charter boat *Rain Song* began to make the approach to Yaquina Bay, with 15 customers and a crew of 7 aboard. The skipper of the 42-foot *Rain Song* was returning early because of rain squalls and low visibility. The sight confronting the crew of the charter boat did not comfort them. The surf was breaking at least 16 to 20 feet in height on the Yaquina bar. It would be rough for the passengers, but the charter craft could handle the passage. Then, as so often happens in heavy surf, without warning, a tremendous breaker hit the *Rain Song*, and the boat immediately capsized. Twenty-two people were now in high-breaking surf. The 46-degree temperature of the water added to the danger. Hypothermia would quickly set in.

When the *Rain Song* went over, seawater activated the vessel's emergency position-indicating radio beacon (EPIRB). A patrolling Coast Guard aircraft received the beacon's signal and relayed the information to both the Yaquina Bay station and a helicopter unit at Newport. At almost the same time, BM1 Will Johnson, a surfman at the station who was driving a watchstander to the lookout tower, caught sight of the *Rain Song's* overturned hull. He immediately grabbed the radio microphone in the vehicle, called the station, and told them to light off all boats. The SAR alarm blared. Chief Clendenin, with MK3 Jon P. Busier as boat engineer, got underway with a 30-foot surf rescue boat (SRB), the CG-30618. The chief's boat led the 52-foot motor lifeboat *Victory*, with BM1 Johnson at the helm and BM1 Steve True, another surfman, at the wheel of CG-44400, into the surf. Once near the reported area, Chief Clendenin, using a radio, assigned the motor lifeboats to two different search patterns, while he maneuvered through seas almost as high as his boat was long.

In the rain, blowing spray, and plunging surf, MK3 Busier

Chief F. Scott Clendenin put the bow of a thirty-foot surf rescue boat into the waves. *U.S. Coast Guard*

spotted the bow of the *Rain Song*. Chief Clendenin then gingerly maneuvered the SRB in the high breakers and came alongside the wreck. Busier looked into the cabin and yelled into the pilot house for survivors. He then saw a large breaking wave headed toward the SRB and yelled to Chief Clendenin, who immediately moved the Coast Guard boat clear of the *Rain Song*. The wave struck the wreck and smashed it to pieces. Chief Clendenin then began searching north of the bar for survivors. MK3 Busier yelled out that he had spotted an orange float in the surf line to the north reef. Five survivors were clinging to the float. The five survivors were desperate. Two had serious hip injuries and all were hypothermic and barely clinging to the flotation device. Clendenin needed to act quickly. He began to maneuver the 30-footer toward the life ring. Later, even in the detached tone of the official report, the skill that was required to approach the survivors comes through. "The slightest mistake in maneuvering," reads the report, "could have caused the boat to crash down onto the victims."

Somehow, Chief Clendenin brought the 30-footer alongside the helpless survivors. MK3 Busier shouted out instructions to the people in the water and then pulled the first person aboard. The SRB then took a 12-foot break (a breaking wave). Chief Clendenin maneuvered the single-screw (propeller) boat back to the float and somehow managed to go to the side of the boat to help bring the five victims aboard the small craft. The last two survivors who were recovered weighed over 250 pounds each. As the last of the people were brought aboard, the SRB took a large break, which slammed the crew and survivors to the deck.

The chief knew the seas were too rough for a helicopter hoist, so he now set about getting the survivors to shore. He started the boat across the tempest of the bar.

Meanwhile, BM1 True maneuvered the twin-screwed 44-foot motor lifeboat alongside seven terrified people who were clinging to a life float at the edge of the surf line. True's crew worked at their highest speed. The Coast Guardsmen knew the changes of survival of the people in the water would be minimal if they entered the surf zone. Somehow, all seven people were pulled from the ocean in one pickup. Normally, this would have taken several passes.

BM1 True then set course for the station and radioed: "Seven people recovered. Medical attention needed. Inbound!"

Out from the motor lifeboat's speaker came the station's reply:

"Chief is in the breaks on the bar with five survivors." BM1 True responded: "The bar conditions have increased. Huge breaks, 20 to 25 feet. I will back up the chief. Inbound! Inbound! Tower. Keep an eye on us, no time for additional radio traffic today." Normally, the tower and boat would communicate often in a rough bar crossing.

Chief Clendenin, who was approaching the bar, saw a series of large waves bearing down on the 30-footer. To keep from broaching (becoming sideways), Clendenin turned into the breakers. Once clear, the surfman again maneuvered to cross. Another series of 16-to-22-foot waves rushed at the boat. The surfman once again put the bow of CG-30618 into the high waves. Clendenin turned the surf rescue boat for the third attempt over the bar. Several 22-foot breakers came over the top of his 30-foot rescue craft. Clendenin continued on. He made it.

The survivors were taken to waiting ambulances.

While the survivors were rushed off, BM1 Johnson, on the motor lifeboat *Victory*, had been searching in the north reef area, which was known to surfmen as "no man's land," especially when breaks reach 18 to 20 feet. This is an area of large breaks and shallow water. Only the 52-footer can work in this area. A huge 22-foot break struck the *Victory*, standing the 70,900-pound boat on end. The starboard rudder hit bottom and punched through the hull. BM1 Johnson yelled to his crew, "Hang on! We lost steering!" The crew clung to the boat, but still yelled out the series of breaks to Johnson. They knew they needed the same skills in surfmanship that the other two boats had displayed just to survive.

Chief Clendenin and BM1 True learned of the *Victory*'s casualty. True maneuvered the 44-foot motor lifeboat out to the 52-footer and towed it out of the breaks. Without hesitation, Clendenin again turned his 30-foot boat out toward the bar. He crossed the crashing waves and met up with the motor lifeboats. The chief then helped the two boats by escorting them and using the radio to call out the location of large waves to the other coxswains. Chief Clendenin then maneuvered his boat to the location where a rescue swimmer had been deployed to help other survivors of the *Rain Song*, and MK3 Busier assisted the swimmer into the boat. The chief returned to the station, dropped off the swimmer, and refueled. After obtaining fuel, for the *third* time Chief Clendenin and MK3 Busier crossed the storm-tossed bar to search for other survivors.

The overall dedication to saving lives of small boat sailors is best illustrated by events happening away from the just-described heroic actions. Retired former officer-in-charge of the station, Master Chief Thomas McAdams, helped with the beach crew, while another retired officer-in-charge, Master Chief Ron Garrison, assisted in the lookout tower by calling out the series of breaks as the boats crossed the bar. Retired Chief Warrant Officer Wit Patrick assisted in the busy communications room.

For his work on this Thursday afternoon, Chief Boatswain's Mate F. Scott Clendenin won the Coast Guard Medal, the highest award in peacetime an enlisted person at a small boat rescue station can receive for heroism. The Coast Guard Medal is such a high award that it is given very sparingly. In 20 years of active service, I never saw it presented. MK3 Jon P. Busier received the Coast Guard Commendation Medal, with O device (to indicate the award was for an operational incident). The Coast Guard Commendation Medal is the sixth highest medal a person at a small boat station may receive for an operational incident. During the entire *Rain Song* incident, 12 lives were saved and five Coast Guard Commendation Medals, with O device, were awarded to crewmembers. In one instance, SA Todd A. Meir, aboard the 52-foot motor lifeboat *Victory,* took a breaking wave that knocked off his safety helmet and unsnapped one of the clips of his surf belt (safety belt). The force of the break threw SA Meier over the lifeline and he was continually dunked under the water, hanging by the one strap, until he could be helped back aboard by his shipmates. Even though injured, SA Meier continued to work until the *Victory* reached calm water, where he could be evacuated to a hospital by helicopter.

What happened next would have left audiences in disbelief if Hollywood had presented it on the screen. Rear Adm. John W. Lockwood; the commander of the 13th Coast Guard District; the mayor of Newport; and Capt. Michael McCormack, Yaquina Bay station's immediate senior officer, were all assembled and about to present the award, when the wail of the SAR alarm sent the duty boat crews into action. Witnesses later reported they thought Admiral Lockwood would have to grab Chief Clendenin to keep him from running to the surf rescue boat instead of completing the awards presentation.

Why do crews of the Coast Guard push off into howling gale

and pounding surf? Who are the men and women who make up the crews of the small boat rescue stations? What are their duties, and how do they live aboard their stations? To begin to answer these questions, it is necessary to know how rescue operations by small boat evolved in the Coast Guard.

Seaborne trade played an important role in the economy of the fledgling United States. In addition to trade goods, a flood of humanity entered America, as emigrant packets brought the huddled masses to the shores of the New World. The large number of ships plying the waters of the United States also brought about a somber reality—the death of sailors and passengers due to shipwreck. Many family Bibles register the names of relatives lost along the United States' coastline, but several generations have passed without the dreaded cry "Ship Ashore!"

Today, it is difficult to imagine the loss of hundreds of lives when a ship ran into the beach. However, this was not an uncommon occurrence during the 19th century. Those who go down to the sea in ships have always faced danger. Windjammers faced their greatest danger when they came onto soundings (to come inshore sufficiently to reach the bottom with a hand lead, a device to measure depth). In the 18th century and most of the 19th century there were few aids to navigation in this country. For example, in 1852 only 331 lighthouses dotted our coastline. Thus, skippers of sailing ships could not depend on a network of lighthouses or buoys to help guide them into port. In addition, many captains of sailing ships that engaged in the coastal trade navigated by coasting. That is, they sailed close to shore and sought out landmarks to fix their position. A sudden gale could catch a careless skipper unawares and drive his ship onto the beach.

The topography of the East Coast added to the dangers. On the approaches to busy New York City's harbor, for example, are many sandbars of various directions and depths that lie at least 300 to 800 yards offshore. A wooden ship that was driven onto one of these bars would go to pieces in a few minutes during a typical gale. Few people can survive a 300-yard swim in 40-degree, storm-tossed surf. Even those strong enough, or lucky enough, to make the beach stood a good chance of perishing from exposure on the largely uninhabited shore. The dangers to early-day sailors and passengers are well illustrated by the fate of the American bark *Mexico*.

The *Mexico*, after a long and stormy passage from Liverpool, England, arrived off the New Jersey coast on New Year's Day 1837, with 112 seasick emigrants aboard. Capt. Charles Winslow signaled for the pilot, as the *Mexico* began to work past Sandy Hook, New Jersey. But this was the Sabbath; there would be no pilot.

The winds of an approaching blizzard began buffeting the *Mexico*. Captain Wilson fought to keep his ship in deep water, but by dusk he knew his ship badly needed assistance. He fired off his distress rockets.

Would-be rescuers on the shore spotted the distress signals but did not want to risk the now-violent sea. Toward dawn, with the seas at their greatest height, the *Mexico* began her inexorable drift toward shore. At 5:00 A.M., on January 2, 1837, she struck heavily at what is now Hempstead Beach, New York. All aboard were lost.

The dreaded cry of "Ship Ashore!" usually brought volunteers to the scene from seaside communities. Very early, some recognized the need for an organized group of people to help in case of shipwreck. The first U.S. shore-based lifeboat station that was designed to launch small boats for those in distress close to the beach was built in 1807 at Cohasset, Massachusetts, by the Massachusetts Humane Society, a volunteer lifesaving organization. The stations, however, were located only in Massachusetts; thus large gaps of the coastline remained without lifesaving equipment.

The federal government entered the shore-based lifesaving business in 1848 through the efforts of Congressman William A. Newell of New Jersey's Second Congressional District. Several years earlier, while Newell, a physician, was on a call in the beach area of Barnegat Inlet, New Jersey, he witnessed the aftermath of the wreck of the bark *Terasto* and the death of 13 crewmen. The ship had been stranded on a bar too far away from the beach for the local populace to assist the doomed sailors.

The wreck apparently made a deep impression on Newell, for, shortly after he was elected to Congress in 1847, he began entering resolutions calling for the House Committee on Commerce to investigate whether the federal government might assist those in distress along the coasts of his district. Finally, in 1848, after a "vigorous and victorious" appeal to Congress for $10,000 to provide "surf boats, rockets, carronades, and other necessary apparatus for the better preservation of life and property from shipwrecks on the coasts of New Jersey," the Massachusetts Humane Society also requested, and received, funds for stations on the coastline. The stations were to be administered by the U.S. Revenue Marine (later called the U.S. Revenue Cutter Service), within the Treasury Department. Actually, once the stations were built, they were run like a volunteer fire department, but without either someone in charge or any inspection system to ensure that men and equipment could perform their work.

The lifesaving system managed to continue under this type of organization for the next 6 years. Then, a strong storm swept the East Coast in 1854. Many sailors died, because there were not enough lifesaving stations, and equipment had not been properly cared for. One town, in fact, had used its lifeboat "alternately as a trough for mixing mortar and a tub for scalding hogs."

Again, Congress appropriated funds for more stations. This time, however, some of the money was used to employ a full-time keeper at each station. Also included was money to hire two superintendents to supervise the stations along the New Jersey and Long Island coasts. The problems, however, continued. As one old salt recalled, the "only person on duty was a keeper who received $200 a year, and if he discovered a vessel in distress he had to collect a volunteer crew." This also caused problems. Along the then wilds of Barnegat Beach, New Jersey, a keeper would have to tramp miles before he could get a crew together, and perhaps by the time they reached the station, the vessel would be broken up and all hands would have been lost.

The higher priorities of the Civil War subsequently caused the neglect of the government's shore-based lifesaving network. This neglect continued until 1870, when another vicious storm ripped into the East Coast and many lives were lost. Newspaper editors began to call for reform to "check the terrible fatalities off our dangerous coasts" and to revamp the lifesaving system so that sailors could depend upon help "in the future."

The year 1871 marked a turning point in the history of shore-based federal lifesaving efforts. That year Sumner Increase Kimball, a young lawyer from Maine, was appointed as the chief of the Treasury Department's Revenue Marine. One of his first acts was to send Capt. John Faunce, of the U.S. Revenue Marine, on an inspection of the lifesaving network. Faunce noted that rescue "apparatus was rusty for want of care and some of it ruined," some keepers were too old and few were competent, and politics had more influence in the selection of keepers than did qualifications for handling boats. In short, the report painted a dismal picture.

Kimball, using his own political know-how and reinforced with Captain Faunce's report, proceeded to completely remake the lifesaving network. He succeeded in gaining an appropriation of $200,000, and Congress authorized the secretary of the treasury to employ crews of surfmen wherever they were needed and for as long as they were needed. Kimball instituted six-man boat crews at all stations, built new stations, drew up regulations with standards of performance for crew members, set station routines, set physical standards, and, in short, set the organization on the road to professionalism.

The number of stations grew. In 1874, the stations were expanded to include the coast of Maine and 10 locations south of Cape Henry, Virginia, including the Outer Banks of North Carolina. The next year, the network was expanded to include the Delmarva Peninsula, the Great Lakes, and the coast of Florida. Eventually, the Gulf and West Coasts would be included, as well as the coast near Nome, Alaska.

In 1878, the growing network of lifesaving stations was finally organized as a separate agency of the Treasury Department and was named the U.S. Life-Saving Service. Sumner I. Kimball was chosen as the general superintendent of the service. Kimball held tight rein over the service and, in fact, remained the only general superintendent of the organization. The law that created the Coast Guard in 1915 also provided for the retirement of Kimball. The service's reputation for honest, efficient, and nonpartisan administration, plus performance of duty, can be largely attributed to the efforts of this one man.

The stations of the service fell into three broad categories: lifesaving, lifeboat, and houses of refuge. Lifesaving stations were staffed by full-time crews during the periods when wrecks were most likely to occur. On the East Coast this was usually from November to April and was called the "active season." By the turn of the century, the active season was year-round in some locations. Most lifesaving stations were in isolated areas, where the topography forced crewmen to perform open-beach launchings. That is, crews needed to drag boats over sandy beaches and launch their boats from the beach into the surf, one of the most difficult of all operations. This is the reason the heavy lifeboat did not see service on the East Coast during the U.S. Life-Saving Service era.

Lifeboat stations were located at or near port cities. Here, deep water, combined with piers and other waterfront structures, allowed the launching of heavy lifeboats directly into the water by marine railways on inclined ramps. In general, lifeboat stations were located on the Great Lakes, but some also were located on the West Coast. On the Great Lakes, the active season stretched from April to December.

Houses of refuge made up the third, and last, class of U.S. Life-Saving Service units. These stations were located on the coasts of South Carolina and Georgia and on parts of the Florida coast. A paid keeper and a small boat were assigned to each house, but the service did not include active manning and rescue attempts. It was felt that shipwrecked sailors would not die of exposure to the cold in the winter along this stretch of coastline as they would in the north. Planners also took into account the topography of the East Coast. Beaches in many locations in the north were rocky, whereas beaches in the south tended to be sandy. It was felt that sailors who were shipwrecked in the south stood less chance of being killed in the wreck and had an excellent chance of being able to walk to a shelter. Thus, only shelters would be needed.

The first stations consisted of only one building, measuring 42 by 18 feet. As the service grew, so did the size of the stations. The early buildings were strictly utilitarian, but by the 1880s they were becoming more elaborate and usually were made up of two or three structures. The main building contained the offices, boathouse, and berthing area for the crew. It usually had a lookout tower on the roof. Some were built to resemble a Swiss chalet, and one was even designed with a clock tower. By the 1890s, the architect A. B. Bibb designed stations that looked much like beach resort homes with lookout towers.

The U.S. Life-Saving Service operated under a dual chain of command. The district superintendents reported directly to Kimball and were responsible for most of the administrative matters of the stations, including such matters as pay and supply. The other channel of command was the inspector assigned to lifesaving stations, who held the rank of a captain in the U.S. Revenue Marine Service. The inspector appointed assistant inspectors, usually lieutenants of the U.S. Revenue Marine Service, to each district. These officials were responsible for the operational matters concerning the service. The assistant inspectors held drills, investigations, and so forth. The inspector of the U.S. Life-Saving Service also reported to Kimball, thus creating a system of checks and balances.

The U.S. Life-Saving Service had two means of rescuing those aboard ships stranded near shore: by boat and by a strong line stretched from the beach to the wrecked vessel. The service's boats were either a 700-to-1,000-pound, self-bailing, self-righting surfboat pulled by six surfmen with 12-to-18-foot oars, or a 2-to-4-ton lifeboat. The surfboat could be pulled on a cart by crewmen or horses to a site near a wreck and then launched into the surf. The lifeboat, following a design originated in England, could be fitted with sails for work further offshore and was used in heavy weather. Some crews at first viewed the lifeboat with skepticism because of its great weight and bulk. The skepticism soon changed, and crews began to regard it as "something almost supernatural," for it enabled them to provide assistance "when the most powerful tugs and steam-craft refused to go out of the harbor." The heavy lifeboats were generally used only on the Great Lakes and along the West Coast, where they could be launched directly into deep water by an inclined ramp.

One of the service's more amazing rescues by small boat came on December 21, 1885. The captain of the *Ephraim Williams*, of Providence, Rhode Island, was fighting for the life of his ship and crew. A severe gale had damaged the ship near Frying Pan Shoals, in the area of "Graveyard of the Atlantic"—the Outer Banks of North Carolina. The captain ordered the anchor dropped, hoping it would hold the ship. The storm was so strong the ship dragged its anchor and the *Ephraim Williams* headed toward the shoals.

The crews of four U.S. Life-Saving Service stations had spotted the ship, but "such a fearful surf was thundering in" and the ship lay so far offshore that "it was absolutely impossible for them to do anything." The crews followed the drifting ship throughout the night. Dawn's light revealed that the barkentine had missed the shoals and "fetched up" in surf that, in the judgment of old-time Cape Hatteras surfmen, was the "heaviest and most dangerous they had seen for years." At 10:00 on the morning of December 22, the lifesavers had no indication that anyone was alive aboard the *Ephraim Williams*. Then the crews of two stations, the Cape Hatteras and Big Kinnakeet, spotted a distress flag flying from the ship.

Both lifesaving crews began to make preparations for the seemingly impossible pull of at least 5 miles in mountainous seas.

The two crews lashed down everything that might break loose in their boats, and, despite the piercing wind, they stripped off any clothing that might impede them in the event of a capsize. The men then donned their cork lifejackets and shoved their boats into the waters of the inner bar. Keeper Benjamin Dailey and his lifesavers from the Cape Hatteras station were the first to shove into an "almost unbroken wall of tumultuous water."

Keeper Dailey's surfboat managed to get over the breakers of the inner bar, which were "immense in themselves"; then the surfboat's crew faced the full fury of the sea at the outer bar a half mile farther out. Witnesses on the shore felt that for any boat to withstand the pounding seas was a "forlorn hope." But Dailey held his boat in check, while he waited for what residents of the Outer Banks call a "slach," a brief period when the seas slacken. After a short period, the slach arrived and Dailey gave the order for his crew to give way together. The boat shot past the bar. The Big Kinnakeet station's surfboat and crew arrived at the bar and waited for a slach, but none came and the boat was forced to turn back.

Meanwhile, Keeper Dailey's crew continued to fight the seas in their long pull to the *Ephraim Williams*. The waves were so steep that at times witnesses on the beach could see the entire interior of the boat, and there was a real danger of the surfboat's pitchpoling, that is, being flipped end-over-end. The lifesavers rowed for approximately 2 hours to reach the stranded ship. The effort and endurance required of the seven men to pull the 5 miles is difficult to imagine.

Once near the *Ephraim Williams*, Keeper Dailey faced the task of getting the nine sailors from the ship into the plunging surfboat. The high seas made it impossible to lay the boat alongside the barkentine, so Dailey dropped the boat's anchor off the *Ephraim Williams's* quarter. He then shouted for the ship's captain to pass a line to the surfboat. With the anchor line played slowly out from the small boat and the boat pulled by the line from the ship, Dailey was able to place the surfboat close enough to take the sailors aboard one at a time. As soon as the *Ephraim Williams's* crew were in the surfboat, Dailey weighed anchor and started for shore. The boat, with 16 men aboard, was so heavily laden that it was down almost to the gunwales. On the run to the beach, Dailey rigged a sea drogue to steady the deeply laden boat. The return, with the high following seas, went faster than the outbound struggle, and lifesavers and rescued sailors were soon being helped out of the boat and onto the shore.

The U.S. Life-Saving Service called the efforts of Keeper Benjamin B. Dailey and his crew "one of the most daring rescues by the Life-Saving Service since its organization" and awarded the entire boat crew the Gold Life Saving Medal, the highest civilian award for the saving of life at sea.

When a ship wrecked close to shore and the seas were too rough for boats, the service could use another method to reach the stranded mariners by stringing a strong hawser (line) from the shore to the ship. To propel the line to the ship, a cannonlike gun, called the Lyle gun, named after its inventor, U.S. Army Maj. David Lyle, was used. This shot a projectile up to 600 yards. The projectile carried a small messenger line by which the shipwrecked sailors were able to pull out the heavier hawser.

Once the line was secure, a life car could be pulled back and forth between the wreck and the safety of the shore. The life car looked like a tiny, primitive submarine. It could be hauled over, through, or even under the seas. After the hatch in the top of the car was sealed, there was enough air within the device to accommodate 11 people for 3 minutes. It is hard to envision 11 people crowding into the car's small compartment but, as one surfman put it, people "in that extremity are not apt to stand on the order of their going."

Typically, a life car carried four to six people. The devices were heavy and difficult to handle. Also, as those in distress evolved from crowded immigrant packets, with many on board, to small commercial schooners, with fewer than a dozen, the life car was replaced by the breeches buoy.

A breeches buoy resembles a life-preserver ring with canvas pants attached. It could be pulled out to the ship by pulleys, enabling the endangered sailor to step into the life ring and pants and then be pulled to safety much more easily than the heavier life car. A beach apparatus cart carried all the equipment needed to rig the breeches buoy and could be pulled by the crew or horses to the wreck site.

The boats, beach apparatus, and life cars were only as good as the surfmen who served in the U.S. Life-Saving Service. The man in charge of the station, officially known as the keeper, was called captain by his crew and was an expert in the handling of small boats and of men. Keepers were required to be able-bodied, of good character and habits, able to read and write, under 45 years of age at the time of application, and a master at handling boats, especially in rough weather. Most keepers tended to have long experience at fishing or other maritime occupations or had worked their way steadily through the ranks of the U.S. Life-Saving Service. Many keepers tended to stay in one place for long periods of time, thus becoming experts on their region.

The men who made up the crews of the service were known as surfmen, because those on the East Coast, where the service began, launched their boats from open beaches into the surf. To join, surfmen could be no older than 45 and had to be physically fit and adept at handling an oar. A glance at the muster rolls of the service shows that most surfmen listed their occupations before entering the U.S. Life-Saving Service as "fisherman" or "mariner." The number of men composing a crew was determined by the number of oars needed to pull the largest boat at the station. This meant the crews ranged from six to eight, but, by the turn of the century, some stations were staffed with at least 10 men. Because keepers selected the crews from the local area, the U.S. Life-Saving Service, more than any other government organization, remained basically a local service. Surfmen were ranked by order of their experience, with surfman number 1 being the most experienced after the keeper and second in command.

In 1889, the service became uniformed. The idea grew from stations on the Great Lakes, which had adopted a naval uniform. Initially, this did not result in an esprit de corps but, instead, resulted in a shout of outrage; the surfmen were expected to pay for the uniforms out of their meager salaries. Despite the uniforms, the U.S. Life-Saving Service was always a civilian organization.

Each day of the week, except Sunday, the surfmen were expected to drill or clean. On Mondays and Thursdays, for example, the crew practiced with the beach apparatus. The surfmen had to complete the entire procedure of rigging the equipment, including firing the Lyle gun at a practice pole shaped like a ship's mast. When the district inspectors arrived, the entire drill had to be completed within 5 minutes, or the man slowing the operation could be dismissed from the service.

On Tuesdays, the men were expected to practice with boats. The craft were to be launched and landed through the surf. In order to have the men react automatically in an emergency, the boats would be deliberately capsized and righted. This was a great crowd pleaser, one observer noting that "no sight is more impressive."

The remainder of the week was taken up with practice in signaling and first aid. Saturdays were devoted to cleaning the station. All of the drills, while not overly technical, were constantly hammered into the crew. This ensured that the men would react quickly and automatically during an emergency, which would pay large dividends when the surf was running and danger was high.

There remained one other important duty that took up a large portion of the surfmen's routine—lookout and patrol duties. During the daylight hours, a surfman was assigned to scan the nearby water areas from the lookout tower. No seats were kept in the tower in order to prevent inattention to duty.

At night, or when the weather grew foul, the surfmen performed beach patrols. Originally, the patrol distances were set up so that the beach patrol would meet the patrol from its neighboring station, thus providing good coverage for isolated shorelines. As more and more of the coast came under the watchful eye of the service, it became impossible to provide such coverage. In the areas where overlapping patrols could not be maintained, the surfmen patrolled for 5 miles or more. At the end of his patrol, there would be a stake with a patrol clock key attached. The key was inserted into the patrol clock so that the surfman would be able to prove that he had completed the patrol.

Patrolling a beach might seem to be easy, even romantic, duty. Such notions are erased, however, at the thought of making a beach patrol in November along the cold, windswept beaches of Lake Superior or through blizzard conditions along the New Jersey beaches in February. The beaches many times were clad with ice and, at best, were pathless deserts in the night. Oftentimes the soft sand, bewildering snowfalls, overwhelming winds, and bitter cold threatened to stop the men.

Surfmen bundled up in oilskins and carried a patrol clock, if patrols did not overlap, and a pouch of coston signals. The coston signal was much like a flare and was used either to warn ships that were approaching too close to the beach or to let grounded ships know that they had been spotted and help was on the way. Mari-

In 1899, Rasmus Midgett of one of the Coast Guard's forerunners, the U.S. Life-Saving Service, single-handedly saved ten people shipwrecked off North Carolina's Outer Banks. *U.S. Coast Guard*

ners were fortunate that beach patrols were run in all weather. In 1899, for example, surfmen burning coston signals warned off 143 ships in danger of running aground. In fact, one of the most amazing rescues in the annals of the U.S. Life-Saving Service was accomplished by a beach patrolman.

On August 18, 1899, Surfman Number 1 Rasmus Midgett of the Gull Shoal station, on the Outer Banks of North Carolina, spotted boxes, barrels, and other debris coming ashore in the darkness. Two miles further, he stopped and listened. A voice could be heard over the high surf and wind. Midgett had come upon the wreck of the 643-ton barkentine *Priscilla*, which had split in two in the surf. Capt. Benjamin E. Springsteen had already lost his wife, two sons, and the cabin boy to the sweeping, tearing surf. Midgett had indeed found the wreck, but what could he do? If he rushed back to the station to give the alarm, it would be hours before help could return and by that time the remaining 10 crewmen would be dead.

Midgett hesitated only long enough to think things through. He waited, timing the waves as they pounded in and then slowly receded. Having gauged them, he ran into the ocean after the receding waves, coming as close to the hulk as he dared, and shouted for the sailors to "jump overboard, one at a time, as the surf ran back, and that he would take care of them." He then ran back before the rushing surf.

To the men on the *Priscilla*, it must have seemed an insane plan, but what other hope was there? Midgett watched the surf, then screamed for the first sailor to jump. Over the sailor went. Midgett rushed forward, grabbed the man, and dragged him to shore. Seven times he rushed headlong into the jaws of death. Seven times he escaped with his rescued sailors. Now another dilemma confronted the surfman. Three sailors, including Captain Springsteen, were so badly bruised and exhausted that they were unable to move.

Hesitating only a minute, Surfman Midgett plunged into the water again, fought his way through the pounding waves to the side of the hulk, seized one of the ropes, and pulled himself hand over hand to the deck. "Panting for breath from his . . . exertions," he lay there for a few minutes, trying to catch his breath and rest his aching muscles. Regaining his strength somewhat, he put one of the helpless sailors over his shoulder, slid down the rope into the sea, and fought his way through the flaying surf to shore. Twice more Midgett made his harrowing trips. Captain Springsteen proved extremely difficult, as he weighed at least 200 pounds. When Midgett was struggling up the beach under this burden, a wave "dashed over them." Midgett dug his toes in and fought to keep upright. Later, he admitted that he thought his "time had come." Finally, all 10 surviving crewmen of the *Priscilla* lay panting and shivering on the beach. Midgett directed the seven who could walk toward the station. He gave his coat to Captain Springsteen, who had suffered the worst injuries, and then set out to get help. Eventually, all were warming themselves at Gull Shoal station.

The work performed by Rasmus Midgett is the best example of the tenacity and spirit displayed by the crews of the U.S. Life-Saving Service. For his extraordinary work, Rasmus Midgett received the Gold Life Saving Medal.

The greatest days of the U.S. Life-Saving Service cover the years 1871 to 1881. These were the years of its greatest growth and some of its greatest rescues. As the 19th century began to edge closer to the 20th, however, two major problems began to develop for the service. First, with the advent of steam-powered ships, the age of sail was coming to an end. With improved navigational technology, ships were at the mercy of the wind less and were in less danger of being driven into the beach. Secondly, at the turn of the century, the U.S. Life-Saving Service noted the increase of gasoline-powered small boats, especially those used for recreational purposes. For example, the number of cases involving these boats increased 58 percent from 1905 to 1914. The service was not equipped for this type of work. To be sure, it had experimented with motor lifeboats as early as 1899, when Keeper Henry Cleary of the Marquette, Michigan, station tested a 34-horsepower Superior engine. By 1905, 12 power boats were in operation. This effort, however, was too little too late. The service was essentially set up to move boats, or beach apparatus, by cart to the site of a major shipwreck. The procedures required to do this were fast enough for sailing and steamships, but not for large numbers of pleasure boats.

Other problems developed. There was no retirement system, nor was there any compensation for injured crewmen. Salaries became too low to attract new men and, with no retirement system, there was little turnover, so it became difficult to gain promotion. By 1914, there "were instances of keepers in their seventies manning the customary sweep oar while the strokes were manned by men in their sixties." In 1914, after years of trying to obtain a retirement system, Kimball agreed that a merger of the U.S. Revenue Cutter Service and the U.S. Life-Saving Service would be best for both services and for the country.

The law that created the Coast Guard on January 28, 1915 by combining the two services also provided for the retirement of Kimball and many of the older keepers and surfmen. The U.S. Life-Saving Service performed nobly over its 44 years of existence. During this period, "28,121 vessels and 178,741 persons became involved with its services." Only "1,455 individuals lost their lives while exposed within the scope of Life-Saving Service operations."

The legacy of the U.S. Life-Saving Service is a great one. The organization Kimball formed provided the basis for the new Coast Guard's search and rescue operations from shore-based stations. Indeed, one can find little fault with the drills and organization of Kimball's routine. The routines begun in the U.S. Life-Saving Service continued until at least the 1960s, when equipment and policies, as we will see, changed. The good practices of the U.S. Life-Saving Service, however, remain in effect. Today, the men and women of the Coast Guard carry on the traditions of service to others established by the crews of the U.S. Life-Saving Service; but with more sophisticated equipment, they are able to surpass the records of their illustrious predecessor.

chapter two

The Man with the Cigar

Those who serve at the Coast Guard's small boat rescue stations are virtually anonymous. There is one exception. Master Chief Boatswain's Mate Thomas D. McAdams (retired) is arguably the most famous Coast Guard enlisted man on record. In 20 years of research on the service, I know of no other enlisted man who has received as much national press for his exploits. To say McAdams has received more national publicity than any enlisted man in the Coast Guard from 1915 to the present day is no hyperbole. He has appeared in *Life, National Geographic, True,* and other national media. CBS's Charles Kuralt featured the master chief on network television. A motor lifeboat with McAdams at the wheel even made an episode of the television series "Lassie." I heard from another old salt that, after the show aired, sometimes when McAdams received telephone calls and he identified himself, the caller would say, "Woof! Woof!" and hang up.

McAdams earned the reputation of being the service's best boatman. His major military decorations include the Legion of Merit (only the second Coast Guard enlisted man from a small boat station to receive this award, which ranks highest in any medal a Coast Guardsman can earn in peacetime), the Coast Guard Medal, the Gold Life Saving Medal (2nd highest), the Coast Guard Commendation Medal, the Coast Guard Achievement Medal (8th highest in peacetime), and the Coast Guard Unit Commendation Ribbon. His civilian awards include an Oregon Governors Award;

the City of Newport, Oregon, Valor Award; and the Newport Chamber of Commerce Award for Civil Achievement.

The master chief is important to the story of the small boat stations for a number of reasons. When McAdams entered the Coast Guard in 1950, the 36-foot motor lifeboat was the mainstay of the small boat stations, as it had been since at least 1907, and he remained in the service long enough to be consulted in the design of the service's new 47-foot motor lifeboat. Thus, he represents a transition from the "Old Guard" to the new era. Through his comments, we are able to see the remarkable changes in training, boatmanship, and even just what it took to go ashore on liberty. McAdams represents the transition from small crews to large. The master chief epitomizes the chief petty officer who I recognize from 40 years ago. McAdams is one of the old breed who spent most of his career in a limited geographical area, much like the old keepers of the U.S. Life-Saving Service. For those who look for subtext in any book, this chapter on Master Chief McAdams highlights almost everything that frustrates people at small stations today. This may prove, among many things, that the more things change, the more they remain the same. Or it may prove another thesis of the book covered in Chapter 9: most officers still do not understand what is happening at the stations.

McAdams developed two distinctive trademarks. One was a modified aircraft pilot's helmet he wore while on a lifeboat to both protect his head and keep his ears warm and the other was a cigar. The ever-present cigar became a part of the mythology that grew up around the master chief, something that McAdams did little to scotch. CBS's Charles Kuralt learned of it while riding a lifeboat with the master chief. The standard refrain heard up and down the coast was "As long as the cigar is lit, you can relax. But when it begins to get soggy, that's when you have to pay attention. If he takes the cigar out, turns it around and sticks the lit end in his mouth, then you know you're going to get wet. But if you ever see him spit it out, then you better take a deep breath, because you'll have to hold it a long time as the boat rolls over." There are very few, if any, photographs of McAdams in his active duty days that depict him on his lifeboat without his cigar.

I interviewed Master Chief McAdams at the U.S. Coast Guard Station, Yaquina Bay, Newport, Oregon. It was an appropriate site. McAdams began his career at the station, made chief petty officer

Master Chief Boatswain's Mate and Coast Guard legend Thomas McAdams prior to his retirement in 1977. *Thomas McAdams*

at the unit, and retired as officer-in-charge of the station in 1977. Thomas D. McAdams enlisted in the Coast Guard on 7 December 1950 in Seattle, Washington. He attended boot camp at Alameda, California, and then received orders to the Coast Guard's 13th District (Washington and Oregon). After a short stay at a base in

Seattle awaiting assignment, he and three others received orders to a lifeboat station at Yaquina Bay.

Sailors carry two seabags. One of these, which is imaginary, is full of stories that salts will bring out at a moment's notice. There are sea storytellers and then there are sea storytellers who make an art of the tradition. McAdams is also a master chief of storytellers. You have only to sit for a few minutes, watching his hands gesturing, making the movements of a pitching, rolling lifeboat, and listening to his voice rising to a crescendo at the proper places to know you are in the presence of a natural storyteller. A reporter once described McAdams as resembling "the actor Jimmy Cagney in looks, stance, and staccato speech":

"After checking in, we went down to the Pip Tide [a bar]. We were all of 19 or 20 years old. The old Pip Tide with the old fishermen was different than it is now. We went in there and, of course, the old fishermen said, 'There's some Coasties. Buy them guys a beer.' I think we each had a beer or two and we asked them about the station.

"'So, you're going up there and be with old "Fancy Pants."'

"'What do you mean?'

"'*You'll* find out!'

"The commanding officer was a warrant officer. Well, a warrant officer to a seaman apprentice out of boot camp is God. At least one of his disciples. The warrant officer in charge of the station at that time was something else. He was called 'Fancy Pants,' because he always wore his uniform and was straight-laced. If he drove downtown in his car and you were on the street, you'd better salute him. But he had no, *no* experience in small boats. At the time you thought he did because he talked it up. If you went out in a lifeboat and got seasick—he never went out to sea in a lifeboat—one of the questions he would ask when you came back in with the lifeboat was 'Who got seasick?' He would then say, 'I want them to make every call until they get over seasickness.'

"I think when I got here there was 12 men and 4 of us reported aboard. They couldn't believe they got that many men. They went up to 16. We received on-the-job training in boats. At that time we had duty for 8 days—24 hours a day duty—and then 48 hours off.

"Beside the boat training, down below in the basement, 5 days a week, we'd have an hour a day of drills, including Morse code. We still had wig-wag signals, semaphore, and knots. We'd get a little bit of training out of the book: the old blue book, [*Manual for Lifeboatmen*], which was about half an inch thick.

"The CO was a stickler for training. He knew nothing about actual sea duty and small boats and the misery of going to sea in the small boats, but he was a stickler for training. You had to learn the blue book and you had to learn it by heart. We didn't have a chief petty officer at the time. What you had was a man in a chief's uniform, but the pins were different: he was a surfman. We called him chief, but he was officially called Number One."

This is a holdover from the old U.S. Life-Saving Service days, when ranks were by numbers. The man who held the number one position would be second in command.

Today, most people at the stations who are ready to go on liberty simply ask the OOD if they can go ashore. As McAdams described it, at his first station the procedure entailed something quite different.

"You would walk into Number One's office at 10:00 in the morning. You'd say: 'Request permission to attend complaint and request mast.'

"He already had your sheet and he'd say, 'What's it about?'

"'To see the commanding officer about my liberty.'

"He'd check, and if you'd missed a punch on the watchman's clock or had been late in a punch in the lookout tower, he'd say, 'Refused.' Anything over 15 minutes was considered late. If you were 17 minutes late on a punch for the tower, you'd lost your liberty. You didn't even get into the commanding officer's office.

"If everything was clear and free, then you'd come into the commanding officer's office. You'd stand at attention. The old man would shuffle papers while you stood there for a minute or two minutes, just to leave you standing at attention with your hat under your arm, in your dungarees. He'd look up and say, 'What is it?' You'd give your name, rate, and serial number and say, 'Request liberty, sir. This is the day of my liberty.'

"He'd check the sheet and say, 'Very well, you meet all requirements. You haven't missed any punches in the tower. That's very good. We have no complaints against you on your work and your drills. This week is distress signals. Give me number three and number eight from the book.' You'd better repeat them by heart. If you could, he'd say, 'Very well, you have permission to go on liberty.'

"If you could not recite it, he'd say, 'Come back and see me.

I'm going home at 1600 [4:00 P.M.] this afternoon. See the Number One and tell him you will be in here at 1600.' Then, the rest of the afternoon you could go study the book. You didn't have to go back to work. You went up and studied until you knew it by heart. At 1600, you'd come back and recite it by heart. If you didn't, he'd say, 'Tomorrow at request and complaint mast.' Well, you'd already lost 24 hours of your liberty, so you'd go back and study.

"So you had to learn signals and then there was the beach cart [also known as the beach apparatus]. You had to learn all the numbers, the assignments for each of the crew's position in the beach cart drill. 'What's your number in the beach cart?' 'I'm number six, sir.' You had to recite the duties of your number and the one aft of you. If there was no one aft of you, then you had to repeat the one forward of you.

"That's how you got your liberty and that's how you got your training. But most of the boat training was actually done on the boats.

"The second warrant officer I had at Yaquina Bay was Mr. Harold Lawrence. He was an old lifeboat station man right down the line. He was one of the men I always looked up to. He was here at a reunion, after I had been out for a couple of years, and he was still Mr. Lawrence to me. His teaching was great. He would tell stories. Sit at the table and tell sea stories. I would pick up things from those that I would use later. I would incorporate them into the motor lifeboat school when I took over and they became part of the procedures."

McAdams next served at the Coos Bay station and then went to a cutter. He then received orders to Yaquina Bay again, this time as a BM1. About these years, he told me:

"You know, the dividing line between glory and loosing a stripe is very thin. I found this out on my second time at Yaquina Bay. In 1956, we got the 52-foot motor lifeboat here at Yaquina Bay. Whole new concept in boat handling. Twin screws, single rudder. Whole new concept, but, boy, does it work.

"On this day in June 1957, everybody had a boat call and all the boats were out. It was foggy. The bar was good. A little swell. I'd just towed in a boat. I was back to the bell buoy, not even to the whistle buoy, when the tower called me and said, 'I have a boat. I can just see it through the fog and he is coming over the north reef.'

"The tower says, 'He's inside the reef! He's inside the reef!'

"By the time I got to the reef, the tower says, 'He's capsized! He's capsized! I have four people in the water! I think there's a dog there, too.' The tower watch is looking right down on it.

"So, we came across the reef. I knew the holes in the reef. You gotta know your rocks and holes. I came right on through.

"The people in the water were still 50 to 100 yards ahead of me. I'm going to hit bottom. The 52-footer draws 6 feet aft and 3 foot forward.

"We hit bottom."

Here McAdams used a storytelling device that startled me the first time I heard it. He would stress the action, or scene, with a very loud voice.

"Boom! The boat hit. I said, 'Oh, shit!'

"Here comes the next breaker. I waited until it picked me up, and I turned the boat broadside. Surfed on the wave. I would ride on the wave broadside and come down on the side and put the people in the water in the lee of the boat. Boom!"

What McAdams was doing was taking a new boat and deliberately going into a shallow area with strong surf.

"I took the 52-footer right up to their small boat. But by this time the people were being carried away by the seas. There were two women and two men."

Pilots are accused of gesturing with hands when speaking about their exploits. Watch a lifeboat sailor sometime. As McAdams spoke, his hands would show the movements of a pitching rolling motor lifeboat so well so you would almost think you would be seasick.

"In those days we did not have the restrictions on wearing lifejackets that we do today. None of us on the 52-footer had lifejackets on. I always considered myself an excellent swimmer. The people in the water had no lifejackets on.

"We hit bottom.

"I said, 'Grab those two people forward!'

"It was a man and his wife. He was in good shape, but he was holding his wife up. They were, I don't know, 20 or 30 feet from the boat.

"I said, 'I'll get them!'

"I ran across the lifeboat and dove completely over their boat that was upside down alongside of us. I hit the surf. Boom! Boom! I swam up to the guy.

The Man with the Cigar

"'How you doing?'

"'Okay, but my wife.' Her head was draggin' in the water. I started to swim them back to the lifeboat. You can go 20 or 30 feet towing somebody kickin'. I got them to the 52-footer's lifelines that hang over the side. I grabbed him and stuffed him in the lifeline, and he's holding his wife. Then I crawled up onto the motor lifeboat. We're being smashed against the other boat. The breakers are coming over the boat. They weren't real big at that time because I'm inside the reef. So I climbed back upon the boat. I hear, 'Helllp!'

"This other guy, he's in bad shape. The woman he's got is floating away from him. He can't handle it anymore. There were four of us as crew on the lifeboat. I turned to one of the guys, name was James Dean. 'Go get 'em!' Then, 'No, you get a lifejacket on!' I'm responsible for him. I got the lifejacket on him in a hurry. I gave him a shove and overboard he went.

"The guy was hanging on the lifelines forward, but Dean went and got the woman. He's coming back to the boat with her.

"Meanwhile, now there's three of us and we go get the guy in the lifeline. We drag this guy onto the deck. God! He's 200-some pounds. We get him on deck, and he's breathing. So, I tied him onto the towing bit.

"By this time Dean is back with the woman, so we grab the woman.

"The guy aft, meanwhile, is going under every time the boat goes down in the breakers. And his wife is going under, too. He's losin' all his strength. We grab the woman and we pulllll the woman on board. I think she was almost out of it by this time. Barely breathing. I told my guy, 'Start artificial respiration.' In those days we used the back pressure arm lift method. He starts working on her a little bit. Then I go back and get the woman from this other guy.

"I now got one guy in the water, one guy working artificial respiration, and so two of us go back to get this other woman. My crewman was the first colored guy at this station. Big guy. Good man. Good seaman. We really have to pull. On deck, she needs help. I yell, 'Start on her! Start on her!'

"The other woman's moaning and groaning. So the crewman comes over. We tie her in the towing bit. Then we go for the guy.

"All this time we're being hit broadside and being driven in.

Well, it had been foggy. Here is where you talk about your fine line of getting a medal or loosing a stripe. Either you're falling in glory or you're falling in shit.

"We get the guy back up on board. The woman starts to breathe. We got the four people aboard. I said, 'Get them down below!'"

"Now, we're all going to be saved, but we're going to be washed upon the beach. Everybody's alive. Even the little dog. The dog had been swimming in circles, and the guys from the beach party have him on the jetty. We got the four people locked down below.

"The fog had burned off in the middle of this operation. We are in bright sunlight. All of this had been going out over our radio. It's an old AM radio and the locals could all hear it. Cars coming across the bridge on Highway 101 were stopped and watching. The bridge was packed. We got hundreds watching this operation of the Coast Guard. They don't know what we're doing. All they see is a boat in the surf and people being pulled up on board and water breaking over the boat.

"The 36-footer from the station is just outside of us. The reef is now breaking pretty good. The 36-footer can't get to us, but they're going to try."

Using his twin screws and rudder, McAdams managed to work the 52-foot motor lifeboat off the beach, but he damaged the rudder.

"The station at that time was run by an E-8 chief. The group was also here, with two warrant officers in charge. The chief was gone, but he got back while all this was happening. The Group Commander just chewed his ass out. 'That boat should not be in there! What's he doing with that boat in there? We're going to rake his ass! We're goin to give you a letter of reprimand!'

"We've done a neat rescue. We've saved four lives. The crew down on the jetty saved a doggie. You should feel pretty good. Jesus! Everyone's getting an ass chewing!

"We had a real good engineer at the station. I said, 'What's the problem with the steering?' The steering was all by cable and when the rudder hit the bottom, it tore all the cable out. The engineer said he could run down to the store and, hell, for $25 he had new brackets, and in less than an hour he came up and said, 'She's ready to go.'

"I said, 'Okay, I'll be down. We got to get her out. We're still running calls.'

"The Group called the chief back in again. Now, the boat's all right. God! There's $25 damage. The warrant officer said to the chief, 'You'll tell him not to do that again! Stay away from the surf!' and on and on. Finally, the chief can't take this anymore, and he wrote me a note and left the station.

"When I came in a couple of hours later, things had quieted down, most of the boats were in. I find the chief's note: 'Really sorry to leave you with this mess, but I had to get out of here or I would say something that would jeopardize my career.'

"One of the warrant officers in the Group was a great old man. He didn't care, but he was a little nervous on this. I walked into the office and I told him, 'You gonna transfer me outta here? You'd better do it right now. If I get another call in the surf in the next 5 minutes I'm taking that boat in there. I don't give a damn if you don't like it. Far as I'm concerned, lives are more important than property. I won't abuse property, but I will use it to save lives. Not only that, I'll get ahold of the news media. I'm going to tell them exactly what you told the chief after we saved these lives. I'm going to tell them everything you said to the chief. You're not going to be talking to me. You're going to be talkin' to the whole damned public!'

"'Well, wait a minute! Before you do that, let's wait until tomorrow and we'll get the chief and we'll all have a nice talk. Settle down!'

"'All right. You give him any crap over this call, and it comes back to me. I'm the guy that made the decision. I'm going to let everyone in the world know.'

"That ended it for the night.

"The next day is Monday. They make up a message. Had to make up a grounding report and this and that. Saved four lives, saved this, saved that. They really downplayed it. It was just nothing.

"Well, one of the people watching from the bridge was high up in the governor's office. The head captain of the Oregon State Patrol was also watching. Lot of visitors. The next morning they're writing letters and calling the district admiral. I never seen such a brave thing. The boat in the breakers. Guys diving over the side. They ought to get medals.

"The admiral's gettin' all these calls. All he's got is this little message. Then the governor's office calls and wants to congratulate the Coast Guard. The admiral calls his aide and says, 'You call the damn Group down there and find out what in the hell is going on!'

"When the Group finds out the admiral is asking about the rescue they say, 'Yes, we're goin' to hang those guys.'"

At this point, I should have known what was coming—another loud comment, this time with a very intense stare from McAdams.

"'Hang those guys? We're going to give them medals! Jesus Christ!'

"Two of us got Gold Life Saving Medals and two got Silver Life Saving Medals. That's a fine line you walk. If the fog hadn't lifted I'd probably been busted."

At this time, before the Coast Guard Medal was authorized, the Gold and Silver Life Saving Medals were the two highest medals in peacetime that Coast Guard personnel at small boat stations could receive for heroism. The Gold and Silver Life Saving Medals were originally established in the U.S. Life-Saving Service era. Today, only Coast Guard personnel on off-duty status can win the awards. They rank in precedence just after the Coast Guard Medal. The awards board ruled McAdams's feat deserved to be called extraordinary heroism, and, thus, he received an extra 10 percent in his retirement pay.

McAdams next went to an 83-foot patrol boat, and, when that was decommissioned, he took command of an 82-foot patrol boat. He then received orders to command the Cape Disappointment, Washington, station. About his time in this assignment, he commented:

"When I had the stations, I trained most of the people to be boat people. I went through people pretty quickly. I could weed out people. As in any job, there are a lot of people who just ride. They're hiding, staying back, riding it out. They do their job, but they don't get into it. Same way in the fire department. You got the guys that really go in and hit the fires and then you got the others. You need those people to get the gear. They're not really into it.

"We had changed finally from the old 36-footer to the new 44-foot motor lifeboat. The 36-footer sat down low. She can't take any bigger break than the 44-footer, but the 44 has 10 times the power. You got more power for working in the breakers. You got twin screws so you got maneuverability, so you won't get near trouble, and you do have a lot of protection for the coxswain. You can sit there now in the coxswain's chair. You have a windshield in front of you and side curtains around you. You're not encountering the weather just raw.

"In the days at the Cape, one time I had turned the garage into a morgue. We were bringing in so many bodies. It was a Sunday and in the little town of Ilwaco, [Washington,] the guy from the funeral parlor was gone for the day, so I had to put the bodies in the garage.

"One woman calls in and she's all balled up. Her husband's missing. She gives a description of the boat he was in. 'Well, ma'am,' I said, 'we've had a lot of bad accidents today. I believe your husband's boat capsized and I believe we've got him.'

"'Oh, my God,' she says.

"'We don't have any identification on him. Do you have friends that can come into the station to identify him?'

"She said no. She came out herself, and she had her 10- and 12-year-old daughters with her. We're talking in the office and this woman looks to be about 35.

"I went out of the office and said to one of the guys, 'I think it's one of the middle ones, go clean him off.' You know, they foam. The guy ran out to clean them up and then came in and nodded his head that they had them all set.

"I'm going to show her the older guy first. Then she will know what a drowned man looks like and make it easier for her when she sees her husband. I undid the blanket.

"'Oh, Henry!' she bawled out.

"The girls are outside and hear their mommy crying and they start crying. But she handled it real well. I give her a minute or so. I said, 'Ma'am, would you like us to leave? I'll be just outside the door.'

"She said, 'No.' She stood up and wiped the tears from her eyes. We stepped outside the door.

"She said, 'You know, I don't know what to do. I've lost everything, everything.' Then she turns to me and puts a hand on my shoulder and says, 'I feel sorry for you.'

"Of course, my crew is standing around and everyone has a lump in their throat. The little girls are crying and holding onto mommy.

"'Ma'am I don't understand. You feel sorry for me?'

"'Yes. I only have to go through this once, you must have to go through this every week.'

"My God, that stuck in my throat! I never forgot that."

McAdams's next assignment took him to isolated duty in Japan, and, when he returned, he received command of the Umpqua River, Oregon, station. He then received a year's duty testing the then new 41-foot utility boats at various locations on the East Coast. By now, McAdams was a master chief petty officer, and he then took over the motor lifeboat school at Cape Disappointment for 2 years. He left this position because of a "difference of opinion" with the commanding officer of the Cape Disappointment station. At this time the school was under the command of the station, later it would be placed under the control of Coast Guard headquarters. From here, McAdams once again received orders to the Yaquina Bay station.

"We were up into the 20s in crew size and even moved up to 30 to 32 men at Yaquina Bay and then dropped back into the 20s.

"When I was at Cape Disappointment, everybody in training picked up the man overboard dummy called 'Oscar.' It was a race to pick up Oscar. 'Man overboard, starboard side!' You're supposed to turn on your starboard side to get your stern away. By the time a guy falls overboard and you get the word, you're already past him. But you swing around, and the guys grab out there with a boathook and throw him on board. Gee whiz! Twenty-three seconds, you got him on board.

"I said, 'Okay, pair yourselves off. Okay, Bill, you jump in the water. Joe, you pick him up.' Five minutes later they got him on board. What happened? Four and a half minutes late.

"'Well, I didn't want to chop him up.'

"Now he gets to pick you up. The whole realism of the arms, legs and in the water. Getting bruised underneath the boat trying to pick him up. It changes. They were picking up a dummy before. If you ran over it, nothing happened. They were going for time.

"Then the Coast Guard comes out and says you can't pick up real people in the water. It's too dangerous. What do you mean it's too dangerous? If you are not going to train people, they are not going to know how to do it. Of course it's dangerous. That's the name of the game. You've got a bunch of people here in the station that's never been out in a lifeboat and you've got others that do it all the time. Now I understand that, if they're out there 8 hours, they get relaxation time, or a day off. Well, bull!

"Nowadays they train like hell in the boat, but not the practical things. You don't want to take the boats into the surf past the reef because it's dangerous. But, if there's a boat call in the middle of the night past the reef, then they lose the boat, because they don't know where every log is and every shoal is. If you're going to train, yes, you're going to have an accident once in awhile. It's just human nature. I call them calculated risks. When I came in, if you rolled a boat, that was it. Now all of a sudden you've got to write a letter and get an investigation.

"One of the reasons I retired began when they wanted to know how many hours you were spending working. When I told them, they said, 'You can't spend that many hours at work.'

"'Well, yes, I can, if you add up total hours on duty.'

"'That's absurd. You can't spend that many hours on duty.' To run that station for that many hours we have to go from 20 men to 50 men, and that's why you got 40 or 50 men at the stations.

"Then they knocked off the salmon season. Then they cut down on this and that, so your private small boats plummeted, as far as ocean-going. At the Cape, there would be 7,000 boats out on a single day. Here at Yaquina Bay in the last few years there'd be 1,000 to 2,000 boats screaming out into the waves to go salmon fishing and all the commercial boats rushing out to sea. You don't have that now. So the calls plummeted on down and now you are left with 40 or 50 men and women.

"They didn't have any women at the stations when I was in [the service]. I say it's lucky I didn't have any. Not that a woman can't do a good job. Some women can run boats better than guys. That's fine. But women do not have the physical strength, I don't care who they are. Oh, you might find one in 200 or 300. But I ask, 'Who do you want to pull you on board if your life depends on it, a 180-pound guy, or a 130-pound gal?' There is a problem with personal strength. And you are going to have problems when you put men and women to-gether when you have physical contact. It's just there.

"Another problem I found just before I got out. Every 6 months they would send an officer down from the district, and that officer would take the crew for half a day. He would tell those people all their rights. He would tell them that chief cannot do this. If that chief does this, you have the right to do this. The chief does not have the right to do this; the chief cannot do this. I listened to several of these talks, and not one time did I ever hear that officer say that you have a responsibility. They always said you have rights and don't let these people get away with anything.

"You have a right to captain's mast. I could hold captain's mast. At captain's mast you are God, jury, and the whole shootin' match. You know your people. So most of the time I would say, 'Okay, you've got 14 days restriction on your own. You take it, you do it, and there's no book work. You're saving money, a whole bunch of paperwork, and you are saving any type of documentation.' This was great and that was it. They knew that. Then, all of a sudden, these officers come along and say, 'you've got rights, take a summary court-martial.'

"Now the guy says, 'I don't want a captain's mast, I'll get 14 days. I want a summary.'

"You couldn't restrict them if they were up for a summary, because that's giving them punishment before the trial. So the guy's off. Hell, he's doin' the same thing again. He don't give a shit. You lost your authority, so the guys didn't give a shit about your authority. Why should I do what he says, because I can do this, this, and this? The officer can get me off and the chief is going to foul up the paperwork anyways. I got my rights and I got an officer backing me up. Pretty soon, you've lost him. Then what did you lose? You started to lose your training. The guy says, 'I don't have to know this, why should I?' You lose this down the line. If you don't have authority, you have chaos, and that's happened a lot. Not just the Coast Guard, all the services, the police, everything. There's no respect anymore for the basics.

"I finally decided to retire. I went out on 1 July 1977.

"Small boat stations do not get the credit they deserve. Most of the officers did not know what went on at the stations, although a few in headquarters and the district did. Most of the warrants in those days—Fancy Pants was the exception—were old lifeboatmen. They'd been around since the Life-Saving Service days. When the Coast Guard took over, the officers wanted nothing to do with these small boat stations. I mean, in the old 36-foot lifeboats you were standing on grates, your feet were under water. The boats were heavy, 10½ tons. You were out in the open. We didn't have the foul-weather gear they have now. We had the worst kind of clothes you could have—denim, the worst thing you could have.

Nobody heard of hypothermia. You were cold. I had crews laying down on the deck. Eighty-five percent of my people got seasick. That meant my two crew members were seasick, so you had double duty. Even if you gave up the wheel, you had to be there to watch. There was no place to huddle. If you went into the engine room, there was just enough room to get in there. It was warm in there. But, the diesel fumes—if you weren't sick, you would be. You were cold. You were wet. You were miserable.

"I had people laying in the well deck so seasick and the water going over them. I remember, coming back from Siuslaw River one time, my crew begged me, 'How long before we get back?' I told them 4 or 5 hours. Oh, the spray and green water pouring over the decks. 'Just run us into the surf,' they said. 'I'll give you my car, my next three paychecks. I'll give you my girlfriend. I'll give you my *wife*! You can have anything you want, just run us into the surf and get us off of here.' There are two stages of seasickness: the first is you think you'll die; the second is you're afraid you won't.

"Officers didn't want to do that type of thing [taking lifeboats out]. So, the enlisted men or the warrant officers would do it. They [officers] should just let them [enlisted men] do their job.

"Helicopter pilots do a wonderful job, but a helicopter pilot is sitting in a warm seat and he's got it right there. Everything is right there. Like I told them one time, give me a chopper and give me 3 months, and I'll fly a chopper as well as anybody. But they're officers and the jealousy thing comes in.

"With the detailer system they have now, they're plugging holes. [Detailers are officers who are responsible for transferring officers and enlisted personnel.] They take a guy that's had so much time here and transfer him there without any reference to his experience. If you have a bad head injury, you wouldn't go to a foot doctor for help just because he's a doctor. No way. Same thing with lifeboat station men that are lifeboatmen. But now there's this mass transfer of people so that no one ever gets it nailed down anymore. I ran this station for my last tour. I still have to run the boats to keep my timing. In fact, I have a boat now, and I go north each year to Alaska and Canada and spend 2 months outside Vancouver Island, British Columbia, just cruising. With the sea, you've got to keep your timing sharp. Professional piano players practice constantly. If you don't do this constantly, you don't stay the best. You lose your timing. One thing about being in the service and getting older and doing your job: as long as you have your health, you can keep that timing, keep those other things going. You can be an asset to the situation. But most of the guys as they get older, they get lazy and start running downhill. They start sending the young guys out. Well, that's good. The young guys got to get the experience. But the old man has to be there too.

"The spirit of the guys today is still there, just give them a chance. Give them that extra training. I could take a group of people and put them to work and weed out 4 or 5 out of, say, the 20, and I would come out with a crew on the other end that would be just so great and they would respect you. They would be a working team. I used to have that here."

McAdams notes that he rolled the 36-foot motor lifeboat at least twice and "rolled the 44-footer nine times." Master Chief McAdams is still fit. He is a lieutenant in the local volunteer fire department and is justifiably proud he now has over 50 years of service in rescuing people.

McAdams still has what the military likes to call a command presence. When he fixes his eyes on you to make a point, he has what I think is better described as "the master chief stare." Any veteran will understand the stare. The only concession to age that I could see is that he no longer smokes cigars, because he "noticed a cough."

Prior to my interview with McAdams, I sat on the mess deck of the Yaquina Bay station and talked with a boatswain's mate. During our conversation, McAdams's name came up and "Boats" told me a few stories he had heard about McAdams. When I told Boats I would be interviewing the master chief, Boats mused, "I wonder if he regrets going in the Coast Guard?" Later, during our interview, McAdams looked out the window and saw a sailboat capsize—I really did not plan this. He jumped up, wondering if the communications watch had spotted the overturned boat. He was out the door in a second and moving toward the operations room. (The boat was okay.) I would say the only thing Master Chief Boatswain's Mate Thomas D. McAdams regrets is hearing the SAR alarm blaring over the station and not being able to run to the lifeboat, don his modified aviator's helmet, stick a cigar in his mouth, and push the throttles forward.

chapter three

Coasties

The SAR alarm sounded throughout the Yaquina Bay station, Newport, Oregon. Then the loudspeaker blared: "Light off the ready boat! Boat sinking near the south jetty!"

Doors slammed open, as the ready boat crew dashed downhill to the 44-foot motor lifeboat. The slow Sunday pace of the operations room over the previous 2 hours shifted to frantic. The watchstander began handling questions from the OOD and the duty surfman, plus responded to the continued calls of the charter vessel *Seven Seas*. Shortly, the scene in operations settled into just hectic, as the watchstander and the OOD began to sort things out and the lifeboat sped away from the dock. At the door of the operations room, the commanding officer, Chief Warrant Officer 3 Dale V. Shepardson, who had recently reported off leave, quietly informed the watchstander that he had reported back for duty and knew what was happening.

Over the next few minutes Shepardson made quiet decisions, but only when asked, never interfering with his crew's working of the case. At one point, one of the boats at the dock needed to be moved to allow the boat bringing survivors to tie up at the station's moorings. With everyone in the duty section occupied, Shepardson, again quietly, said he would take care of it and left for the dock. The watchstander turned to the seaman helping her and said, "I'm sure glad Mr. Shepardson is here. I feel more confident when he's around." The confidence CWO3 Dale Shepardson instills in his crew comes from well over a decade of service aboard small boat stations. What experience do the senior people at the small boat stations bring to their positions? Just as importantly, what causes people to come into the Coast Guard?

The experience level of the commanding officers and of their executive officers in the Coast Guard's small boat community borders on the incredible. Statistics, however, do not do justice to those in the top two slots at a station. A clearer picture can be obtained by examining the backgrounds of a commanding officer and an executive officer in detail. This effort to show the experience of two senior people brought about one of the hardest decisions I made while writing this book: which two people to choose? Everyone I met in the senior positions in the small boat community deserved to be included. I therefore turned to the time-honored scientific method of selection—I put all the names of all the people I met in a box and drew out a name. Traditionally, the small boat stations were commanded by chief petty officers. My selection brought up a chief warrant officer in charge, but he had commanded at least one small boat station as a chief petty officer. I hope this method of selection does two things. First, if a random sampling brings up this level of expertise, it is a good indicator of the credentials of these senior people. Second, I hope it takes me—and the men selected—off the hook as to why they are highlighted.

1

I met Senior Chief Boatswain's Mate Tom Doucette in 1996, while he served as the Executive Petty Officer (XPO) at the Cape Disappointment Station. Tom Doucette was born on August 12, 1959, in Mt. Vernon, Washington, and grew up in Tacoma, Washington. During high school, he held jobs as a lifeguard and caretaker. Tom saw a television program called "Exploration Northwest," which depicted boats at "Cape D crashin' and bashin' in the surf," which made him want to run motor lifeboats.

"I figured I would head to college. I had two brothers in college—one in premed and the other was doing a social services degree and also playing football. But the Coast Guard looked like it would be a lot of fun too. My dad was a high school guidance counselor. He said, 'You may not be ready for college. You might want to think about doing something else. The service sounds like a great idea.' He'd been an air force officer for a few years. So, I'd been sort of thinking about it. I think he knew I would benefit from the self-discipline the service instills in you.

Senior Chief Thomas D. Doucette returns from drills in a 30-foot surf rescue boat. *Brett Powers*

"I was a competitive swimmer on my high school swim team. I knew to go to college with two kids already in school meant money was going to be a problem. So, I knew I'd need some kind of scholarship. I was too small for football. Swimming was my big shot. I was pretty competitive. I knew basically how fast I had to go to get a college scholarship. That was pretty much a given. I can remember in 1978 going to the University of Washington's pool. They have electronic timing, so you know immediately how fast you're going. I swam in the 100-yard butterfly, pulling for all I was worth and hit the timing pad. I remember looking at the time and thinking, I hope the Coast Guard is fun, that's obviously where I'm going.

"That was March 4, 1978, something like that, and on April 4 I went into the Coast Guard on a delayed enlistment. Ten days out of high school I was in the Coast Guard and have been doing it ever since."

Tom also brought out that he came into the service to obtain money for college, but 18 years later, he said, "I still don't have money for college, but I am having a good time."

"I took the entry tests on enlisting. I could have been an electronics technician, a machinery technician, sonar technician, radar technician—they wanted me to do somethin'. I had pretty decent test scores.

"I said, 'Who gets to drive those 44-footers?'

"The recruiter said, 'That's the boatswain's mates.'

"'Okay, that's what I want to be.'"

"'No, no, you don't want to be a boatswain's mate, you got good test scores. You need to do something else.' The recruiter then said, 'I will give you any school you want. I will guarantee any school comin' out of boot camp. You'll be a petty officer right away.'

"'I really want to drive those boats.'

"'Well, we really don't have a school for that.'

"I thought that was kind of unusual, but I said I'll just go to boot camp and go for that boatswain's mate. I said I wanted to drive 44-footers, so what type of unit should I put in for? At that time you picked your unit according to where you placed in the company. I was told to take anything that is a station, except an air station. They'll have boats."

When Doucette graduated from boot camp at Alameda, California, in 1978, no small boat station had an open billet. The openings were largely for high endurance cutters, known as 378s, for their length. The brand new seaman apprentice saw an opening on the cutter *Yocona*, homeported in Astoria, Oregon. "I asked what kind of ship is the *Yocona* and found that it was a seagoin' tug. I knew it was near the Columbia River bar, where I saw those boats on TV, so I said I would take the *Yocona*."

The cutter *Yocona*, a 213-foot seagoing tug, did a great deal of fishery enforcement patrols. "I had a year of Russian in high school and this was more than anyone else on the ship, so I got picked for boarding parties."

Doucette began to "strike" (learn a rating by on-the-job training rather than attend a formal school) for boatswain's mate on the cutter. "Everyone on the deck force was considered a boatswain's mate striker. I was actually on the list for hospital corpsman school. Another school came up, a small arms school at Fort Lewis, and I told the XO I really wanted to go to that school. He said, 'You can't go to that school. You're going to be a corpsman. Corpsmen don't carry guns.' I'd been on the cutter about 15 months.

"'Corpsman? What are you talkin' about?' I'd forgotten I'd put in for it. 'I don't want to be a corpsman, I want to be a boatswain's mate.' That kind of sealed my fate.

"I knew to get off this thing you either go to school or advance by striking. Well, I'd already turned down school. I went from SA to BM2 in just under 2 years. I advanced so much they had to get rid of me.

"I was on the *Yocona* for just about 2 years and then rotated to the Quillayute River station in July 1980. To me that was the end of the earth. I wanted to go to any station in the 13th District, other than Neah Bay [Washington] or Quillayute, so they sent me to Quillayute. It actually ended up being a real good tour."

Even though Tom had run motor surf boats and zodiacs on the cutter, at first he ran into difficulties at the small boat station. "I wanted to run 44s, so naturally I was drawn to anything that had screws and a rudder while on the cutter. I ran them as much as I could. I got pretty good with an MSB [motor surfboat]. When I went to LaPush and ran the 44-footers with twin screws, it was really tough for me to pick up on how to work with this type of boat. I can remember being out with Bert Morris, who is a master chief now, and *trying to get this 44 to do what I wanted it to do*. Put a single screw on it and I could put it anywhere, but the twin screws really confused me. Then one day—I don't know if it was after a week or a month, or whenever—it was like someone threw a switch in my head. All of a sudden I knew how to run the boat. I'm still figuring it out, but at least I sort of can put it where I want it to go most of the time.

"Gerry Boss was my first CO at a small boat station. Then we got Larry Ringenberg, who in the wild days at station Willapa Bay, Washington, operated in that area for 7 years with no radar, lousy electronics, in an unmaintained channel [without aids to navigation], just horrible weather conditions, and with Willapa being one of the roughest bars around. He was quite a guy. He thought if we had surf boats, they should be in the surf every day. Every day there was surf, we did surf drills.

"Larry had *incredible* natural boat-handling ability. He could do just about anything with a boat. I don't know if he was so good at teachin', as he could just do things with a boat you'd think couldn't be done. I remember going out in surf drills with him, and he just loved to lay broadside and get knocked over. He seemed to be able to gauge exactly how far we were going to roll. He could go up to the wave and say, 'Ah, about 80 degrees.' We'd stop, get hit, and roll about 80 degrees and come up. If I ever tried something like that, I'd end up upside down, pounding on the beach, something like that. He just had an eye for it. Incredible boat-handling ability.

"Larry eventually made E-8 and went down to Grays Harbor, became the OPS [operations] boss.

"To me, if you're a coxswain, you're always working toward that qualification of surfman. I got qualified as coxswain when I had about 40 hours underway. I kind of learned as I went. Little different program than we have now. I got qualified as surfman about 2 years after I got to Quillayute.

"The two people who set me straight in the Coast Guard were Gerry Boss and Bert Morris. When I came off the *Yocona* I knew I was a decent boat driver. I knew that way more than I should have. I wasn't near as good as I thought I was. Gerry Boss and Bert Morris had the tenacity to stick with me as I went through my learning process. They took me from being just another BM2 in the Coast Guard, who was more or less along for the ride, to somebody who took responsibility for his actions and realized this wasn't all just a great big game. That it could be fun, but it wasn't a big game.

"Morris had me up against the wall one time and explained to me the facts of life—what I would have to do to succeed in the Coast Guard. I was pretty upset with him to begin with, but those two really got me shifted around as far as in my head, becoming more part of the solution than part of the problem. I'll never be able to pay them back. Gerry went off to the *Campbell*, and I saw him only once or twice again. Bert retires this year [1997]. Both led by example. Both were formidable men. In my mind now I picture them as 6' 4", 300 pounds.

"It is usually plumb peaceful at Quillayute River in the winter, but the first case I ever did as a coxswain came on the 21st of December 1980. Sort of a trial by fire. A big ferrocement hull sailboat got on the wrong side of the jetty and ran aground, right on the edge of the breakers. Remember, this is the dark Northwestern Washington coast—no real lights of any kind."

BM2 Doucette and his crew of the 44-foot motor lifeboat set out into the night. Doucette recalled he began "talkin' to them on the radio, as I tried to find my way out through the little narrow entrance. I worried about getting myself killed, or running aground, or hitting the rocks, or whatever. Brand-new coxswain, second class, 21 years old. I'm talkin' to them on the radio as I head out.

"They said, 'Abandoning ship! Abandoning ship!'

"I said, 'Head out to sea! Just head straight out to sea! Don't go for the beach! Stay out of the breakers!'

"'Roger, Coast Guard. We'll head out to sea.'

"'Head out to sea, and I'll pick you up.'

"First thing they did was launch their little zodiac and they drove right into the breakers, rolled it over and tossed everybody into the water. They were in where it was awful tough for me to get to them in the boat. I hooked up by radio with the beach party.

"There it was in the night. They're on the beach, their mast is fouled in some overhead power lines going to James Island, so every once in awhile there was arcin' and sparkin' off of those.

"Joe Lantz, another engineer, on the beach, ended up in a float coat [a short jacket that can be used as a life preserver], kind of swimmin', wadin' and collarin', and draggin' them into the beach. Managed to save the whole crew.

"I tried to pull the boat off that night. I managed to get a line to our station crew while they were working in the surf. I pulled and pulled and finally parted the tow line. So, we left them for the night and kedged the anchor [placed the anchor high on the beach] up as far as we could and then pulled them off at high water the next morning.

"What a night! What a way to get initiated into motor lifeboats! The sailing vessel *Puda*. I'll never forget the name of the boat or the night.

"I got married in September 1983. I met the girl with the incredible smile when I was on liberty at Forks, Washington. Ellen Claussen and I started dating, and shortly thereafter I got transferred. We weren't really sure we were going to get married, but *I* knew that she was the one for me. I reported in to Grays Harbor in December, and we were married the next September. We have two children—Sean, 11 years old, and Staci is 7.

"By 1982, I really wanted to leave Quillayute. I had enough of the isolation. There was also some personality conflicts. When the detailer asked me in September how soon I could get to Grays, I said it is 1:00 now, it's a 4-hour drive, but I'll hurry and I think I can be there at 3:30. He said, 'Well, I was looking more at December.'

"We agreed on an October departure date, and the orders said to report no later than 1 January. I reported in to Grays Harbor. They gave me my orders to EMT (emergency medical technician) school. I reported into Grays Harbor and then I drove down the coast to Petaluma, California, for the EMT school. I was still second class but had taken the servicewide examination for first.

"Grays Harbor, what a great station. It's really well laid out. Everything you needed for maintenance and taking care of your people is centrally located. At Cape Disappointment we've got about a quarter mile between the station building and the docks. Your command structure gets isolated from the folks out there doing the work.

"Grays Harbor has a nice covered moorage, nice haul-out, the *Invincible* [a 52-foot motor lifeboat], and well-maintained boats. It was a real pleasure being stationed there.

"I had a great boss, Joe Duncan, who was a lieutenant commander when I got there. It was a lieutenant billet, but he'd made 0-4 [lieutenant commander]. What an outstanding individual. He was an academy officer and a great guy to work for. He really cared about the crew.

"The first years I was at Grays I was in charge of training boat crews. I then moved over to deck and became First Lieutenant and ran the deck division.

"I was also working as an EMT in the Coast Guard and realized right away there wasn't enough EMT work in the Coast Guard for me to stay current. So, I hooked up with the local ambulance service, along with a couple of other boatswain's mates. We started doing that and realized there was an awful lot more training available. So, we went to the Coast Guard training folks and said, if you pay for this, the ambulance corps is going to pay for part of it and you guys pay for the rest, I'll get certified in some advanced life-support procedures. Which worked out really well.

"Initially, I went up to Grays Harbor County for defibrillator training. This was back before there was automatic defibrillators, when you had to learn to read heart rhythms off the EKG monitor and make a diagnosis and do electric countershock. All that sort of stuff. After that I kind of got interested in it and went on and got certified as an intravenous therapy technician. As a Grays Harbor tech, you actually carried some cardiac drugs. We were supposed to administer these drugs on standing orders on our ACSL [advanced cardiac systems life-support] protocol before we made contact with the physicians. So, it was actually a very progressive program, and it was making a difference out in the community. We were gettin' some lives saved.

"At the same time, we got a heart monitor from Group Astoria, with a defibrillator. It was a real old one, but it worked. We put together a drug box from the ambulance corporation and carried that with us on the boats when we launched for EMT calls. Things were going really well, and everybody sort of understood what was going on. Well, almost everybody.

"We went out to a charter boat that had called. A guy was having chest pains and the charter boat operators were aware of the program we were running. I was on a 41-footer with another coxswain, another IV tech, John Prentice, who is a BMC now. He came out to the 41-footer in a Boston Whaler, hopped aboard, and we took off.

"The other coxswain put the two of us over, and the guy is presenting the classic myocardia infarction. Textbook. You could tell what was happening. Diaphoretic, rapid pulse, anxious and all this.

"We were pretty sure what we had, so we put him on the

monitor. His heart rhythm seemed normal, and we tried to get a line into him, but we couldn't get it. Meanwhile, the charter boat, *Mac's Effort*, was headin' into Westport, and we're about 20 minutes out. The 41-footer is escortin' us in.

"The guy looked up at us and says, 'You know, I'm feeling better. I'd like to get up and shake it off.'

"I said, 'No. Just stay down.'

"'Okay.'

"As he said okay, his eyes rolled back and he went into ventricular tachycardia at a rate of about 220, from what I could tell, which is a really fast rhythm. There's no time for the heart to refill. Essentially, a pulseless rhythm. He was goin' to die unless we did something. We used countershock, some aggressive drug therapy and whatnot. We made contact with the hospital with the portable radios.

"There was a marine on board the charter boat who just walked up to us and said, 'I know CPR. Can I help?' Just like the trainin' videos. He was doin' CPR and Prentice and I worked him [the patient].

"I remember cardioverting him, and he went to coarse fib [coarse ventricular fibrillation], another bad thing. Okay, I can deal with coarse fib.

"I countershocked that and he went into flat line. Oops, now I'd done it.

"We continued. Had a big crowd around us and the charter boat is still going in. Within a minute and a half we had a pulse, a viable pulse, and the man was regaining consciousness when we got to the dock.

"We went straight from the boat into the ambulance and headed toward the hospital. The guy was treated and eventually released. He'd experienced a full cardiac arrest. Obviously, the direct intervention was what saved his life.

"So, we shot off a situation report message to the district. This is what happened, and this is what we did. This was on a Thursday.

"Friday morning we get this message from the district, K branch I think it was, that says cease and desist paramedic activity in association with SAR mission at Grays Harbor. Something like that. Basically, it was saying don't you ever do anything like that again.

"We thought this was kind of funny. We just saved this guy's life.

We're pretty sure *he* wanted us to continue to do this. We're heading into a busy weekend and the CO was just beside himself. You know, we'd just done somethin' good and he is gettin' chewed out.

"Apparently what happened was a chief corpsman had read the message and said, 'Oh my God! You've got boatswain's mates doing this and my corpsmen are not qualified to do this. This is crazy. You're going to have to stop.'

"Well, things went back and forth, back and forth. Everybody debated the legality of all this. Finally, Comdr. Al Steinman, who is now Adm. Al Steinman, the chief medical officer in the Coast Guard, came into the picture. He said whoever sent this message to stop is out of their minds. You guys are worried about liability. Liability goes both ways. It's doing something you are not trained to do or failing to act the way you were taught. These guys have this training. You're out of your minds, if you think you're going to limit your liability. Why are you going after them for all of this?

"On Monday morning we got a message from the district commander himself, the admiral, that said something like, 'Reference the first message, which was paramedic activity, Grays Harbor, paragraph one: keep up the good work.' The original message was the classic response: don't you ever save another life.

"So, the program went on for a few more years. It was a high-maintenance program, and it took a lot of time with everybody involved in it, but it worked. You had to have 60 IV starts a year and all this and it took time. Ellen and I started to have kids. She was on the ambulance, too. People moved out and the program sort of faded out, but there were some good saves by it. The program was completely out of character for a bunch of knuckle-draggin' surfmen, but it was lifesaving."

Doucette, of course, also responded to boats in distress. "I remember a 35-foot wooden cabin cruiser which started to take on water and tried to get into the Willapa. The bar was breakin', and he got into the breaks. An HH-3 Coast Guard helicopter got there about the same time I got there with a 30-foot surf rescue boat. The HH-3 put a pump on. I put a pump and engineer on him and got him turned around and headed out into the breaks, and he didn't get rolled over.

"Got him headed up toward Westport. The motor lifeboat 44372 came down from Grays Harbor. So now we had an HH-3, a 30-footer, and the 44372.

"The 372 puts another pump on him, and I hauled ass with the 30-footer and went up to Westport and got the *Invincible*. I came out and met him and came across the bar with him. By the time we got him in, we had four pumps and two eductors [another type of pump] running on him, and the station had arranged for haul-out for him. So, we took this guy with all these pumps running water out these 3- or 4-inch discharge hoses everywhere. Must've been pumping a thousand gallons a minute. Took him in an alongside tow with all this stuff runnin'. Ran him into the haul-out at the Westport shipyards.

"When they picked the boat up, there was water pouring out of about every seam. Boat was still full of water. What had happened was he'd just had the boat recaulked and the caulking was just comin' out all over everywhere, so, instead of just having one or two leaks, the whole planked boat was leakin' everywhere. It was one of those responses where I don't know if the Coast Guard would be capable of doin' anymore in some ways, 'cause of the cutbacks on the number of hulls and number of people and everything. At the time, what an impressive response. We had all the resources and all the people and about a 6-hour case, something like that. We ended up saving the boat and people. A great case."

While serving at Grays Harbor, Tom experienced the case he most remembered throughout his career. "In November of 1983, Thanksgiving Day, I had 52-foot motor lifeboat standby. I wasn't on ready boat, but if the 52 was needed, I would go in. At about 0455 in the morning, the telephone rang at my apartment.

"'We need you to get underway. Got a boat taking on water off Point Grenville.'

"I knew the weather wasn't great, but I hadn't been paying that much attention to the weather. Fatal mistake number one—not knowing what the weather was going to be before going out. So, when I got in and was heading in a hurry to the boat I asked, 'What boats are underway?'

"'Nothing. You're going alone.'

"I said, 'You didn't launch?'

"'Naw, you guys got it.'

"They had called in my whole section and we got underway with the 52. Me and Fred Crippen and Bart Pope and I can't remember who else—real good crew. We head out across the

Grays Harbor bar. It was pretty sloppy, but going out in a 52 you can get out in pretty darn near anything.

"I called the boat on the radio and asked, 'Where's the water comin' in from?' The boat, a big steel fishing boat, a dragger, was coming apart, you could hear the welds breaking it was that bad.

"Turned north and had a southwesterly swell of about 15 feet and 30 knots of wind. Wasn't real bad, certainly doable. We're heading up after the fishing vessel *Monk*. An HH-3 flew overhead. They're heading up there too. It was something to see that HH-3 go overhead. Those guys are good at what they do also. About two-thirds of the way up, we had made about 15 or 18 miles up the coast, when finally the fishing vessel *Captain Nice*, out of Coos Bay, located the *Monk* and got everybody off it and left it saying it's sitting low in the water and lights flickering. The HH-3 turned and headed for home.

"I remember *Captain Nice*, when he picked the people up, asked, 'What's the Westport bar look like?' I told him it was rough, it wasn't good. So he said, 'I'm going for Neah Bay, then.' He headed for Neah Bay. As long as the wind was out of the south, he was okay. But it shifted when the front went through, and it started to beat him to death heading for Neah Bay. He then headed back to Westport, and he ended up steaming around out there in an 80-something-foot boat. He managed to weather it out and got in on his own.

"Meanwhile, the Group told me to keep going. 'We need you to go up there and put a light on the hull.'

"I said, 'What light? I don't have a light for that, and it's too rough for that. There's no way I'm going to be able to do that.'

"'We want you to go up there and see what you can do.'

"We're not going to be able to do anything, the boat's sinking. There's nobody on it. There's no distress here.

"The Group said, 'We want you to continue on to this boat to get us a good position.'

"I said, 'Okay, whatever, but it doesn't sound like a great idea to me. Who wants me to do this anyway?'

"'Group ops does.'

"'Okay, fine, I'll go.'

"We went up there. Like I said, I hadn't checked the weather. It started getting worse and worse and worse. Pretty soon we're doin' about 70- to 80-degree rolls and going up and down 25- or

30-foot seas. Winds got up to around 100 knots. Seas were 20 to 30 feet, had to be. That's when I had enough. I said, 'We're going home.'

"By the time we turned and headed home, it was as rough as I've ever seen it in my life. The seas were driven just completely white with spray. Huge swells. We ended up doing about 90-degree rolls from one side to the other. Going through 180 degrees of motion. Going up and down 20 or 30 feet, every swell, and just gettin' the livin' hell beat out of us.

"I made it for about 6 hours—maybe 5½ hours—before I finally got seasick. It got down to where darn near my whole crew was seasick, except for Pope. He was the only one who didn't get sick. We had the autopilot locked in, headed back in, and started to feel a little better. Then we started to get near the bar.

"The Grays Harbor bar had breakers for about 5 miles. From buoy 3 all the way in to almost buoy 11 was breaking. The tide was flooding, which meant the bar wasn't going to get better. We transited a 5-mile zone of breaking surf, the biggest surf zone I've ever transited in my life, ever. I got in and got tied up at 1:00 or 2:00 in the afternoon. We'd been underway in just horrible seas for quite awhile. Then, because they called us in early, we had duty that day. We were on the ready boat. They didn't have a back-up boat, and I just hoped and prayed that we wouldn't be going out again. It was horrible weather. Roughest weather I was ever out in, and we never made a rescue.

"I spent 4 years at Grays Harbor. I was looking for qualifications to advance. I had 6 months' sea time as a petty officer. But you can't make E-8 if you don't have a deck watch officer qualification, and the only way to get that is to be on a ship. I started to look for a patrol boat or something small enough that they would let a first class qualify. Usually, 210-foot and below you can do that.

"Well, we had the 110-foot Island Class patrol boats coming on line. I had an XO at Grays Harbor who was trying to make sure I didn't get anything I wanted. In some ways I don't blame him. He endorsed my dream sheet [form on which Coast Guard people send their requests for duty assignments to the detailers] and said he recommended any 378 or other large floating unit out of district, which made it very clear that he thought the 'surfman club' needed to be broken up. I didn't know there was such a club, but apparently I was a member of it."

Doucette and the detailer discussed the dream sheet. The detailer said, "It sounds as if whoever endorsed this really wants you to go to a 378."

"'I think that's a good read of it.'

"'Yeah, he really wants you to go to a 378. Unfortunately, I don't have any of those. How would you like to have a brand new Island Class patrol boat?'

Years later, Tom recalled, "I thought I was being tricked. I thought we might have those in Antarctica."

"'Well,' the detailer said, 'I've got two coming open. One out of Crescent City, California, and the other out of Eureka, California. Which one do you want?'

"'Sir, it doesn't matter.'

"So, I left Grays in October 1986 and went to New Orleans, where they were building the *Edisto*. Spent 3 or 4 months there, while the ship was completed and did the sea trials and got underway in January from New Orleans and went to Key West for some tactical trials. Then I transited the Panama Canal and came up the west coast of Mexico and the United States to Crescent City, where we were homeported.

"It was really a unique situation at Crescent City. There was no small boat station there, so we were a patrol boat whose program manager was law enforcement, who was doing more search and rescue cases than a lot of the stations. At that time we were doing about 80 cases a year in search and rescue. We maintained a rigid hull inflatable ready to go immediately, known as Bravo-Zero. So, in addition to a patrol schedule, we also had to maintain a Bravo-Zero rescue boat.

"So, I was in seventh heaven. I was underway as an OOD on a 110-foot patrol boat, known as the Island Class, which is just a great ship, I was still running SAR on small boats. I extended for a year there; it was a 2-year tour. I was just starting my extension when I got a phone call from a former CO, Commander Duncan, who said, 'How would you like to come up to Cape Disappointment to be a test coxswain on the new 47-footer?' I said okay.

"Commander Duncan was in charge of acquisition in the 47-footer project and was picking some folks to go up to the school and be test coxswains. It sounded real neat. So, I came up to the school at fairly short notice. Reported in April 1989 and got qualified as an instructor. Didn't get to do a whole lot of teaching.

"We went in on summer break, where we do most of our maintenance. I was assigned from the instructor corps over to the 47-footer project. I started to do the rough drafts of the test plan. Which was neat to do as first class, because I was writing how we were going to evaluate this boat. Went through a whole bunch of rewrites.

"There was a whole bunch of stuff I wanted to test, but those in charge didn't want to test the same things. We went back and forth on that a lot. I wanted to test the boat to destruction eventually, find out what it could do and how to improve it. Their goal was to make sure it complied with the contract, and those are two very different things. If it was built to take 20-foot breakers, they wanted to make sure it met the goal of 20-foot breakers consistently. I wanted to see what would happen if someone overdid it, like they run out in the field, because that's obviously going to happen. They had their marching orders. I had mine.

"Scotty Clendenin was my neighbor. Another guy with incredible boat-handling abilities, besides being one of the hardest working guys in the Coast Guard that I've run into. We'd be down with the students, comin' off the boats, and all the students and instructors would be heading up to eat lunch. We'd pass Scott's group heading down to clean up the boat. They'd go down to scrub down the boat thoroughly between drills, because if anyone saw their boat it would be clean. I can see them shuffling along with their heads down, following Scott who was out front leadin' the way. He sure wasn't afraid to work. He put in incredible hours to make sure things were right.

"When Scott went to a station, if another station sent a boat down to his unit, there'd be an army of people at the dock waitin' to take care of you, to make sure you were taken care of. They'd come aboard your boat with buckets of soap and deck brushes. They'd just pull your crew off the boat and start cleaning up your own boat for you and make sure you headed up to the galley for a hot meal, whatever time it was, day or night. Scotty really knew how to look out for people. He's now in charge of an 82-foot patrol boat and making warrant officer. He's trying to get back to the West Coast again. Maybe he'll have another run at it. [Clendenin was promoted to chief warrant officer in June 1997, and his first assignment was Yaquina Bay station, Oregon.]

"Another neighbor at Cape D was Bob Beck, an engineer, a

warrant now at Seattle. We pay a lot of attention to the surfmen, but someone has to keep them runnin'. To show you some engineers have as much experience as BMs, Bob was stationed at Umpqua River, Cape D, National Motor Lifeboat School, and Engineering Petty Officer at Chetco River. He could easily have been anything he wanted to be in the Coast Guard. He picked engineering, because he's a bit of a motorhead. He qualified as coxswain on some of the small boats. He could have qualified on the 44-footer, if he could have put in the time, but I doubt if anyone in the engineering division wanted to turn him loose.

"He could get you back in out of anything. Things would start to break down and he would bubble gum, spit, and bailing wire it together to get the mission done and you back in. When you got a boat transferred from one of Bob's stations, you knew you were getting a boat in top-notch condition. I remember when he was mowing his lawn. Afterwards, he'd spend a half hour cleaning his motor to make sure his mower was right. If it was mechanical, it had to be perfect. He works in marine inspection now and probably won't be coming back to the motor lifeboat community."

"Terry Smock, now a warrant at Coos Bay, was able to accomplish things that other people wouldn't be able to do if they tried it his way. He could sort of make up stuff as he went. Ended up with some neat rescues. Scared the heck out of me a few times.

"First time I ever rode in a 24-foot rigid hull, made by Osborn, which is a real high-speed boat, Terry took us out in about 10-foot swells. I finally just put my head down, I was just so sure we would end up going end-over-end in the thing I just put my head down. I figured when we blew over, I didn't want to have my head taken off. Terry's just up there laughing away. Maintaining about 25 knots, 8-to-12-foot seas, boat was even in the water a couple of times. He was so good at it, he could just sort of fly from wave top to wave top without getting beat up. Scared the hell out of me, though.

"I was under the impression that when I came up to the Cape that if I was advanced to chief, I was going to stay put. In fact, the word I heard was: 'Oh, if you make chief, don't worry about it, we'll just make it a chief's billet.' Early in December 1989 they faxed a profile letter and I found I was getting advanced. I didn't even put in a dream sheet.

"Middle of March I came back from an evaluation trip of RNLI

[Royal National Lifeboat Institution] lifeboats in Scotland. The chief's detailer called me and says, 'Hey Boats, why don't you have a dream sheet in?'

"'I'm not going anywhere.'

"'Like, hell.'

"'Excuse me?'

"'You're making chief. You're going.'

"'No, no. They're going to adjust my billet. They're going to make it an E-7.'

"He again used some choice words to say, no, you're getting transferred. You need to get a dream sheet in.

"There were a few stations, but nothing I was interested in. But there were some stations in Upstate New York that didn't look too bad. Everything else was ships and I'd just come off the *Edisto* and wasn't lookin' to go back to sea. I got transferred to Station Niagara, New York.

"At the time, the idea of going to New York was like going to the moon. I was from the West Coast. I'd spent 12 years in the Coast Guard west of Highway 101 and north of Crescent City. Almost all of it in Washington State and near Astoria, Oregon. Here they were going to send me to New York. I had visions of the Manhattan skyline and concrete jungle, all this. There was a real short fuse on the orders, so I packed up the house, and my wife stayed behind until I could get everything squared away, and I drove out to New York with my brother.

"I'll never forget coming through the city of Niagara Falls, which is just a typical East Coast rust-belt city. Especially if you are on the highway, you don't see much. Then I looked over the escarpment, which is an area carved out by a glacier. I looked out over this area and it was absolutely beautiful. There was little towns with little white church steeples poking up out of the trees. It's June and everything is green. I could see the Niagara River meandering down through the cut and Lake Ontario and sort of see where my station was gonna be and I drove down. There's a bunch of guys out back playing volleyball. An old white Coast Guard station that had been built in 1893. I though, if I had known this was New York, I'd been here before.

"I spent 4 years there as officer-in-charge. We had a 44-footer, but didn't have much use for it. It was slow and loud. Never really had a use for it, because our area of the lake never got into the conditions that you'd want a 44-footer. They eventually got a 41-footer. From a family point of view, I'd of stayed in Upstate New York for 20 years, if the Coast Guard had let me.

"The Ninth District [the Great Lakes region] is very different from the rest of the Coast Guard. They get less money, because I think they are viewed as a part-time job because of the ice. An absolute fallacy. There's plenty of work out there year-round. I was at a 'summer stock' station, where I had five active duty billets and we would pick up 10 or 12 reserves, put them on active duty in the summer, and send them away for the winter. You'd usually get college kids. The assumption was made that those reserves would come aboard May 15, and by Memorial Day you'd be up and running full speed. Everybody would be qualified on the boats, everybody ready to do law enforcement, as if they'd never left. Of course, a lot of the times we weren't getting the same people back, or you'd get them for 30 days. It was a real challenge keepin' everything going and doing everything everyone wanted us to do. We were really short of people in the Ninth District.

"The other thing we were short of was money. I think my operating budget was $30,000 a year to operate the station. At Cape D the operating budget is about $250,000. I spend more money on survival equipment at Cape D than Station Niagara spends to operate all year. It's a very different way of doing things. On the West Coast, if we have an engine failure, or it looks like it's going to fail, we replace it. In the Ninth District, there just wasn't the money to pay for things. You could have an engine that the mech is screamin' the engine is going to fail. The district would say run it until it breaks. Yeah, but what happens if I'm on it when it breaks?

"I guess the Cape is like a magnet to me. I wanted to remain in Upstate New York because of a better family lifestyle, but streamlining—streamlining is what they call it when they take away people but increase the number of jobs you have to do—caused Cape Disappointment to lose a Yeoman [YN, clerical position], a warrant officer and a chief petty officer. All three of these positions ended up replaced with a single E-8 to do the job of all three.

"They couldn't get an E-8 to take it, so they sent me as an E-7 to take it. I really didn't want to get into a billet that had three jobs rolled into it, but luckily I got some real good people working for me and I was able to shift my work off to them."

On one of my visits to Cape Disappointment I learned of an incident that never makes newspapers, or even Coast Guard news, but shows the skills of the people in senior positions in the small boat community. Senior Chief Doucette had the 52-footer working in the surf. The steering failed and the rudder jammed right. Then the motor lifeboat began to take 15-foot breakers on the beam. Doucette then began steering out of the breaks by maneuvering with the boat's two engines. Somehow, Senior Chief Doucette managed to get the boat out of the surf. Later, the commanding officer told me if it had been anyone else on the 52-footer, it would have rolled.

"I should mention Bill Stull, MK1 at the Cape right now. Big burly guy. Born and raised in Washington. He's on his third 52-foot MLB [motor lifeboat] station. Finest engineer I have ever run into anywhere. Talk about a guy who is serious about his job, but can have fun doing it.

"I remember doing things like survival gear inspections. Everybody would have their ready bags. You'd go through and make sure their equipment was in good shape, nothing torn up and all in working condition. Bill's bag was always about double the size of anyone else's, because he'd have extra impellers for pumps on the engines, maybe a quart of transmission fluid, a couple of extra fuel injectors. In fact, I called him one time. I said, 'Bill, what'n hell you doin' with fuel injectors in your bag? You can't change out injectors underway, you've got to have an injector-pulling tool.' He rummaged around in his bag and came up with one of those too.

"Bill is one of those guys who cannot accept a failure underway. If it was necessary to get the boat back in, he'd get out and swim, towing the boat. No one was going to tow one of his boats in. It just wasn't going to happen. We put in a lot of miles together. He is so good at what he is doing and always having fun at it too."

I observed MK1 Stull as he stood an OOD watch. During that time he learned the 52-foot MLB *Triumph* had developed a fuel leak. "Where's a toothpick when you need one?" He must have seen my quizzical look and said, "You could repair that leak with a wooden pencil and some duct tape."

In March 1997, BMCS Doucette learned no other E-8 wished to take the assignment as XPO at Cape Disappointment, so he accepted a year's extension. Then, in July 1997, he received a promotion to chief warrant officer and an assignment to Group Portland, Oregon, as Assistant Surface Operations Officer. As of December 1997, CWO2 Thomas Doucette has earned two Coast Guard Commendation Medals, with Operational Device; three Coast Guard Achievement Medals, with Operational Device; three Meritorious Unit Commendations, with Operational Device; a Meritorious Team Commendation; and other awards.

2

In 1996, Chief Warrant Officer 4 Mark Dobney was commanding the Tillamook Bay Station, Garibaldi, Oregon. He was born March 27, 1955, in Port Huron, Michigan, and grew up in Sanger, California. At 17, even though "a real good student," Mark Dobney became "bored with the school thing."

In 1972, with the draft still in effect, Dobney decided to enter the Coast Guard under the buddy system, a recruiting method of signing up with a friend and going through boot camp together. Unlike many who come into the Coast Guard, he knew something about the service, as he had "a couple of uncles" who were Coasties during the 1950s, which had helped spark his interest in the service. Dobney's friend failed to pass the examinations, but he decided to go ahead himself and enter the Coast Guard. Over 23 years later, Dobney recalled that at 17 he graduated from boot camp at Alameda, California, on a Friday in January 1973. "The next day, Katherine and I were wed in Las Vegas."

Dobney left his wife at Sanger, California, while he took off for his first duty assignment as a boot seaman apprentice. His orders read to report to Group Detroit, Michigan. "You know, at boot camp they told you if you go to a Group, you will be assigned to a small boat station, the best duty in the Coast Guard." That saying was half correct, "my first assignment was aboard the *Kaw*," a 110-foot tug homeported at Cleveland, Ohio. At the time the *Kaw* was breaking ice at Sault Ste. Marie, Michigan, and SA Dobney traveled northward to join his ship. Once the cutter returned to Cleveland, then Mark "had a chance to get an apartment and arrange for Kathy's bus trip across the country."

Despite not receiving orders to a small boat station, Dobney, in hindsight, thought the duty "a good start as a first unit." The

CWO4 Mark Dobney, commanding officer of the Tillamook Bay station at Garibaldi, Oregon, aboard the station's 44-foot motor lifeboat. SN Tara Stauffer calls out the location of nearby boats. *BM1 Martin A. Ornelas*

small tug broke ice, escorted sailboat races, and did other "odd jobs in the summer," plus the crew undertook the never-ending maintenance work of keeping a floating unit up to standards. The ship provided the "small unit exposure." The crew consisted of 18 U.S. Coast Guardsmen, commanded by a warrant boatswain. Dobney, however, still had his "eye on a small boat station."

On the *Kaw*, Dobney decided to strike for boatswain's mate. "I was interested in aviation, but I would have to wait for 2 or 3 years for school, and I couldn't afford financially to do that, and, anyways, this BM stuff was kind of fun to do aboard ship. Later, I looked around and thought: Who's in charge here? Who's giving the orders and who's taking the orders? I saw that the ship was commanded by a warrant boatswain. Most small boat stations were run by chief boatswain's mates and the boats were run by BMs. The coxswain was in charge. I had some incentive and kept going in the rate."

In 1975, Dobney, now a boatswain's mate second class, made his wishes for a small boat station known to his detailer in Coast Guard headquarters, but the young boatswain's mate heard he would be too senior for a position. Dobney also heard a refrain very familiar to anyone who has served in the Coast Guard: you are going to spend your whole enlistment in the *Kaw*, because the service did not "have the money to transfer people." There is, however, a method whereby a sailor can change duty stations without the normal official orders—a mutual exchange of stations, or, simply, a "mutual." If two sailors of the same rate and rating wish to change locations, and their commanding officers approve, they may change stations with each other, as long as they pay all costs for the transfer.

Boatswain's Mate Second Class Dobney found a Coast Guardsman of the same pay grade at Station Fort Point, California, who, for some reason, wanted to be stationed in Cleveland. Fort Point was a small boat station at the southern side of the Golden Gate, in the shadow of San Francisco's famous Golden Gate Bridge.

One of Fort Point's unusual reputations within the Coast Guard dealt with a more gruesome aspect of the Golden Gate Bridge. For reasons that perhaps a psychologist can explain, the bridge is the site many chose to leap to their deaths, and almost all take the fatal plunge from the side facing San Francisco. A Coast Guard officer, who had served at a Rescue Coordination Center (RCC), told me of a case where a woman from France flew to San Francisco, rented a car, drove through the city to the bridge, got out of her car, and leaped to her death. One of the duties of the Fort Point station was to recover the bodies of those who chose this method of suicide. Someone began to paint silhouettes on a board in the boathouse of bodies for each of the suicides the station's boats recovered, much like fighter pilots record enemy aircraft downed. Legend has it that the station recovered so many bodies that the board, with its macabre tally, stretched completely around the boathouse.

At Fort Point, BM2 Dobney "got a chance to drive a variety of boats. We had a 36-foot motor lifeboat as a backup surfboat to the 44-foot motor lifeboat, so I got a chance to qualify as a 36-footer coxswain."

The station also received the then new 41-foot utility boat. There were not "a lot of restrictions on what you could do with the boat then like there are nowadays. We learn from our experiences and then place limitations to protect each other. For example, I ran a case to tow a boat 60 miles offshore with the 41-footer, using just dead reckoning to navigate by. The weather was nice and the seas were about 10 feet in height. Nowadays we wouldn't even think about doing that with a utility boat. But at the time it worked. The 41-footer could get there fast and there wasn't a patrol boat around, so you were told 'go get that' and I went out and got it." Dobney's next comment on this unusual offshore tow with a 41-footer reflects an attitude that has been prevalent probably as long as there have been small boat stations manned by U.S. Life-Saving Service and Coast Guard people: "We didn't have loran (long range radio aids to navigation), we didn't have any luxuries, but we didn't think twice about that: just go get 'em."

Chief Warrant Officer Dobney, in 1996, recalled Fort Point "was a great start for small boat experience. Now that I look back at it, my first commanding officer was a chief warrant officer and this position shifted to a chief boatswain's mate. The chief in charge, BMC Thomas Brooks, was a District 13 surfman and I started to learn my trade with him. I don't remember the CWO being on the boats or underway at all, but Chief Brooks taught me to trust and love the 44-foot motor lifeboat and respect the 36-footer with its history."

Dobney recalled, "Although I had learned to be a coxswain before Chief Brooks got there, he really showed me what it was to be a surfman, taking my skills and moving them along. He taught through hands-on, 'let's go do it' training. Learning the tricks of the old 36-foot motor lifeboat and how the job could be done with just a tough boat, good seamanship, and some common sense. Patience helped, too. He was equally adept at using the 44-foot motor lifeboat to its extreme, getting the job done while bringing you and your crew home."

By the time Dobney left Fort Point, in 1977, he was a BM1 and had reenlisted. (The Coast Guard moved their operations to the north side of the Golden Gate Bridge and decommissioned Fort Point on 22 March 1990.) It is interesting to note that Mark Dobney had reached a senior noncommissioned rate within 4 years. Many in other branches of the armed forces, and even within much of the Coast Guard itself, will find it amazing Dobney had yet to serve with a commissioned officer. His commanding officers had been either chief warrant officers or chief petty officers. Yet this was not an unusual occurrence for those who served at small boat stations until at least the 1990s. It is also a very good example of how the small boat community in the Coast Guard has always been considered an enlisted program.

The next assignment, in 1977, took Dobney to Marina del Rey, California, near Los Angeles, aboard an 82-foot patrol boat, the *Point Bridge*. The cutter used a "blue and gold system," that is, two crews. It did this so the *Point Bridge* could be underway all the time, but not with the same people. The commanding officer, who was a lieutenant, junior grade, was in charge of one section. The other section operated under the executive officer, a chief boatswain's mate. BM1 Dobney was the senior boatswain's mate in one section.

Dobney's assignment put him in the section with the lieutenant. This "was the first time I got exposed to a commissioned officer. I thought, well, he knows what he's doing. He's an officer. Somewhere in there I caught on that maybe I was there to teach him. We both learned a lot before I left. That was a good assignment. We did lots of law enforcement and simple to complex tows for both short and long distances."

The chief petty officer of the *Point Bridge* received orders, and his replacement did not report aboard for some time after that. Because of his experience, Dobney filled the position of executive officer aboard the patrol boat and thus gained the experience of running the boat with his own crew.

In 1978, orders took Dobney from the *Point Bridge* back to the Midwest and to a small boat station at Toledo, Ohio, as executive officer. Here he worked for BMC Robert "Rocky" Roman. The Toledo station proved "very busy, with close to a thousand cases a year. Our neighboring station, Marblehead, was doing over a thousand cases a year." Most of the cases dealt with recreational boaters.

Then, about 1980, a decision by the Commandant of the Coast Guard caused a major shift in the traditional workload of the small boat stations. The largest amount of work at the stations prior to 1980 centered on the towing of disabled boats. After 1980, political and legal pressures were applied to the service in the form of a ruling that the government cannot compete with commercial enterprise. One of the main driving forces behind this decision was the rise in recreational boating, which made commercial towing a very lucrative proposition. The ruling stated that the Coast Guard could not tow a disabled craft that was not in danger, unless there were no commercial companies available. Mark Dobney feels that "because we were often overworked and undermanned, it was actually a good deal."

At the Toledo station, BM1 Dobney gained additional experience working with 30-foot, 40-foot, and 41-foot utility boats and Boston Whalers. He also gained a great deal of experience in personnel matters at a "transition period for all types of issues, from civil rights to anything else." This particular period saw many Coast Guardsmen being absent without leave (AWOL), it "was the norm, something you understood and accepted. Nowadays, you rarely see people going AWOL." I can attest to this statement. At one of the stations I visited, a second class petty officer had never heard the term AWOL, something everyone knew about when I served in the Coast Guard. This was also the post–Vietnam War period, when the Coast Guard and the other military services were trying to come to grips with a policy on drugs and alcohol. This is covered in Chapter 7.

A certain thread runs through the pattern of Chief Warrant Officer Dobney's career. As he put it: "It seems I spent no more than 2 years at a station. I kept advancing my way out of a job." True to this pattern, Dobney advanced to chief boatswain's mate while at Toledo and received orders to be officer in charge at the Port Huron, Michigan, station.

"I was 25 years old, with just under 8 years in the Coast Guard, a boot chief with only one hash mark [a red or gold diagonal stripe on the left sleeve of a dress uniform; each stripe represents 4 years of service]. I took a lot of ribbing from my peers around the Great Lakes, who were senior and master chiefs and who had lots of time and experience." Dobney's next comments reflect the views many of the enlisted men who have served as officers in charge of the small boat stations: "I loved the unit. I kept learning my trade." An additional attractive feature of the Port Huron station was the fact that the station was located in Dobney's home town.

After 3½ years, Chief Dobney received orders to Station Rio Vista, California, as executive officer, with a chief warrant officer in charge. The unit is located in the delta area of the Sacramento and San Joaquin Rivers. "I thought going from an officer in charge position to an executive officer slot was a breeze. I knew what the boss had to do, so it made it easy for me to sit back and do it."

The station proved to be different from most rescue units. Almost "everything we did involved putting boats on trailers and going to a launching site. An SAR case comes in and you have to figure out: okay, where do I launch, versus get underway and start navigatin'. I had to learn a complex area of over 1,500 miles of waterways." Following his normal career pattern, Chief Petty Officer Dobney received a promotion to senior chief, which meant he was promoted out of a job.

Senior Chief Boatswain's Mate Mark Dobney next took over the executive officer's position at Station San Francisco, on Yuerba Buena Island, in San Francisco Bay. "At least I didn't have to relocate cross country."

For Coast Guard small boat stations, this unit was large; the crew numbered 80 people. Because of its size, it was commanded by a lieutenant. The unit's primary boats were 41-footers. In addition to maintaining the boats and buildings of the station, the Group's building fell under the control of the station. "The lieutenant handled the political end, and I managed the small boats. Even though the Group operations center did the actual directing of the boats, my crews did the running."

Dobney now had over 10 years service and was contemplating which way to proceed with his career. He had taken the warrant officer tests every year since he had become eligible. But, because he competed against Coast Guardsmen who had served many more years, it was difficult to score high enough to be advanced. Part of the method then in use in determining a person's place on the list for advancement to chief warrant officer involved a formula that took into consideration test score, medals and awards, and, very importantly, time in service and grade. Dobney then considered applying for Officer Candidate School [OCS]. Years later he recalled that Station San Francisco provided experience in working with large numbers of officers of all ranks. "Once I had worked among a lot of officers at San Francisco, I said, no, OCS is not the way to go. One reason was I would have to commit over 10 years to make lieutenant commander to balance what I would make in retirement. The main thing was the officer career paths were pretty specific, and some of the stepping stones to get there were not what I wanted to do.

"I like doing my job. I like working with people. I like running the stations, but there isn't many of those for officers. The jobs like

RCC controllers did not seem too appealing. The only good jobs seemed to be the lieutenant or lieutenant, junior grade, jobs in charge of patrol boats. That would be fine, but that was only one job." The matter became a moot point when Senior Chief Dobney made chief warrant boatswain. This meant a transfer and, yet again, Dobney headed across country, this time to New York.

Chief Warrant Officer Dobney took command of Station Short Beach, later called Jones Beach, on Long Island. He spent 3 years at the unit with 44- and 41-footers and rigid hull inflatable boats. "I worked with the Coast Guard Auxiliary and joined the organization. This is much like a bus driver taking a vacation and going by bus. I enjoy teaching and I had always volunteered to work with the Auxiliary in classes, so I just took it the next step." While Dobney enjoyed the station, "the New York City metropolitan area was not exactly where I wanted to be." In 1989, Dobney made another cross-country move. This move provided a huge change from an urban area, as the orders read that he was to take charge of Station Chetco River, Brookings, Oregon, which was located in a very rural area on the rugged Oregon coast. The population of Brookings numbers roughly 4,000.

The Chetco River tour also lasted 3 years. "It took me all this time to get to District 13. It's like the old saying: 'You have to have a lot of experience to get there, but you can't get there without experience.' It was that constant catch-22, but I wasn't going to be deterred." The station had 44-foot motor lifeboats, a 30-foot SRB, and a 20-foot RHIB and ran a variety of cases. The area is not noted for high surf. It has "a nice bar, but when it breaks it gets totally nasty. It's a good place to get exposure to working in the 13th."

"Our daughter, Amy, by now had graduated from high school in a great bit of timing for my next transfer. She wanted to start college, and we had relatives nearby and thought it would be nice to stay in the area. An opportunity came to go to Group Humboldt Bay, California, as a Surface Operations Officer. So, okay, that'll work. It kept me close, plus down in Eureka, California, there's a community college and a state college. Amy went to the community college when we moved to Eureka, but I didn't exactly go to the Group first.

"They needed a CO of Station Humboldt Bay. It was a last-minute, right-away sort of thing. I said I would love to go to Station Humboldt Bay. I'm kind of experienced and been around and I'm moving to Eureka anyway. Although they placed a limit on it: we need this, but only for 1 year. I thought I could scam this and stretch it for a full tour. It didn't quite work out, but that's okay."

After the 1 year, Dobney moved into the surface operations officer position. The group that Chief Warrant Officer Dobney served in had two 110-foot patrol boats, one out of Eureka and the other out of Crescent City, California, plus the *Point Ledge*, an 82-foot patrol boat, out of Fort Bragg, California. "I worked as their direct liaison. This was my first staff tour as an officer. Otherwise I'd been out on my own for a lot of years. That was okay, but I still liked the small boat stations."

By the time Dobney served at Group Humboldt Bay, the Coast Guard had put out criteria for tours of duty aboard cutters. Dobney related, "What I'd been doing in my career is being years and years away from my afloat experience. So every time I'd asked for an afloat tour, they wouldn't give it to me. Okay, fine. I took the command tours ashore and by the time I came out of the Humboldt Bay tour, the detailer said, 'It's been over 10 years since you've been to sea, so don't plan on getting assigned to a ship.' I don't mind the sea duty, but it would keep me out of the small boat community. Then I lucked out and got the Tillamook Bay commanding officer position."

When I met CWO4 Mark Dobney at Tillamook Bay in 1996, he remarked: "I told Group Astoria when I came here just what I said to Group Humboldt Bay: I've just come from a Group, and now I'm at a station. I don't know everything, but I have just enough inside information and knowledge to hold people accountable for helping the station, so be careful. I've come up here and caused them all kinds of grief and had a good time.

"At this station, I've had a chance to run the new 47-footer, so I've gone all the way from a 36-footer to the newest boat. I'll do a 3-year tour here and see what happens next."

During my visit, Mark Dobney invited me to his quarters to continue our discussions. Near the end of our conversation, I heard a faint sound. Dobney said, "That's the SAR alarm." He excused himself and turned on a scanner he kept in his living room. I heard a car accelerating out of the area where the crew lives and where the quarters for the CO, XO, and engineering officer were located.

Tillamook Bay station has a rather unusual arrangement. The barracks area and some of the quarters are located in the old station area. The new station, built in 1982, is located over a mile away by road. All of the station's offices and boats are at this distant location. The ready boat crew has bunking facilities in the new unit.

We listened to the scanner for a few minutes. The case involved a capsized boat with people in the water. "The duty section is short-handed," said Dobney. "Want to go to the station? The XO is already down there." (The car I had heard was the XO's.) We arrived and Dobney quickly learned the status of the case. The XO was already underway in the 30-foot SRB to assist the 47-foot motor lifeboat. The watchstander informed his CO that help was needed at the docks. CWO4 Dobney sent the seaman to help, and he took over the radio and telephone watch. Eventually, the people in the water were rescued.

CWO4 Dobney mentioned that one of the outstanding lifeboatmen he has known is his XO, then BMC John Dodd. "He is equally impressive as a superior seaman and a boat driver. He is also at the other end of the spectrum from me in that he is one of the best examples of a surfman taking the newest technology out and challenging Mother Nature at her worse. Chief Dodd has shown that even with these advances and gadgets, which make the job of search and rescue easier, it still takes an experienced person at the helm to properly read the conditions and utilize what he or she has available to get the job done safely and efficiently. He is an excellent example of the fact that it's not the boat or equipment, but the crew, that really makes a mission successful."

I would add that Chief Dodd also has a good sense of humor. After the run on Tillamook's extremely long pier, and fighting with the SRB, including having the craft hit a wave and go completely airborne, Dodd came back and sat with me in the station's office. With his Mustang exposure suit half pulled down and looking exhausted, he smiled and quipped, "I still love it!" I will not go into the complicated, made-up story about how he met his wife on a South Seas Island, a story that he relayed to his son, who, in turn, relayed it to his school teacher, who then approached Dodd's unsuspecting wife with sympathy. In July 1997, BMC John Dodd received a promotion to chief warrant boatswain.

Mark Dobney related: "My family has always been the driving force or reason for working harder or advancing in the Coast Guard. They have spent many hours without me. My daughter,

Amy, has an associate of arts degree and at first thought about entering the Coast Guard, but only if she could be stationed with me. I took that as a personal threat and explained Coast Guard policy, which prohibits such assignments. She reminded me how lucky I was the Coast Guard protected me!

"Katherine has stuck with me through all sorts of times and moves."

Mark Dobney brought out something most of those who serve at the small boat rescue stations try to convey: "It is not possible to share the exhilaration of a successful rescue, the thrill-fright combination of riding a motor lifeboat across a rough bar, the confidence you get from working close with a small team like a boat crew in the face of Mother Nature's challenges, or the sense of pride when showing someone 'your' boat, which is, of course, the 'best in the fleet.' I've always felt good when someone asks, 'Are you in the Coast Guard?' which usually comes with 'We're glad you guys are there.'"

As I finished the final draft of this book, I learned that CWO4 Dobney received orders for his new station. He will be the commanding officer of the National Motor Lifeboat School, Cape Disappointment, Washington.

In 1997, CWO4 Mark Dobney's awards included three Coast Guard Commendation Medals, with Operational Device; three Coast Guard Achievement Medals, with Operational Device; one Coast Guard Unit Commendation, with Operational Device; three Coast Guard Meritorious Unit Commendations, with Operational Device; along with other medals and awards.

3

It is surprising how many people serving in the Coast Guard knew very little about the service before they decided to enlist for 4 years. I suppose I should not be amazed by this fact. Over 40 years ago I joined the Coast Guard because a recruiter spoke to the seniors at my high school. A friend said, "Let's join that, it sounds good." I do not believe I had ever read anything about the service or even seen a Coast Guard unit. A great many people at the stations I visited also joined because recruiters came to their schools. A woman from Altoona, Pennsylvania, for example, decided to come into the service because of "a recruiter at school and because her friend had always wanted to go in." Her friend, however, "dropped out in boot camp because of the stress." This is something new for one who came in many years ago; you just did not "drop out" of boot camp 40 years ago.

A seaman apprentice from Los Angeles liked the pictures of small boats rescuing people. One sailor from landlocked Wyoming said that the other services, but not the Coast Guard, came to his school's career day. A school counselor had material on the service and gave it to the student, who brought it home. He and his father looked it over and felt the Coast Guard offered more than the other services did. He is now an MK3 and is 4 months into his second enlistment.

Some younger sailors came in because they really did not know what to do with their lives. One 18-year-old told me he "wanted to see if I could make it on my own." One young sailor from Texas told me he and his mother "talked over joining the Coast Guard instead of flipping hamburgers." Yet another person told me his mother talked him into entering the service. One sailor said his father told him to either join the service or leave the house. Another Coast Guardsman informed me he entered the service because his grandfather felt everyone should do 4 years of military service. On the other hand, a petty officer told me he knew exactly what the Coast Guard was, as he "wasn't going to sign his life away for 4 years without looking into it."

One woman from El Paso said she came into the service at 28 because "of the romance of the sea." Another woman from Georgia said that having a woman recruiter helped her make her decision.

Many came into the service because of the chance for schools, training, or for the money for school through the education program offered by the military. A seaman from Palm Springs said she came in for the money for school and to obtain EMT training. "The recruiter said I could get the training, but he didn't tell me I would have to wait so long for school." One seaman from California came into the Coast Guard to learn about maintaining and handling boats. He would like to sail a 47-foot sailboat and eventually to become a fire fighter in civilian life.

A number of people came into the Coast Guard because of films or videos. Another native of El Paso, Texas, for example, said he joined because he saw "a video on a boat rolling in the surf and rescuing people. I came to a small boat station expecting to do that." A boatswain's mate from New Mexico came into the Coast Guard from college when he saw a film about the duties of the service, including law enforcement. Previously he had only observed Coast Guard Auxiliary people and thought that was the entire service. More than one person said their interest was sparked by a recruiting film made by the movie star Lou Gossett, Jr.

There are, of course, examples of those who knew something, or a great deal, about the service. One boatswain's mate said he "always knew he wanted to be in the Coast Guard." A BM1 said two of his uncles had served in the Coast Guard and "from the eighth grade he knew he wanted to be in the Coast Guard." There are examples on the East Coast of families that have sent many of their members into the Coast Guard. The Midgetts of North Carolina, for example, have a reputation of having a member in the service continuously since the 19th century. I saw one example of long family service at a West Coast unit, where a fireman apprentice (FA) said her father, grandfather, and great-grandfather had been in the Coast Guard and that all had served as enlisted men. The same FA also said she wanted to get away from home and obtain an education. A BM3 said his father was a lobster fisherman from Maine, so he knew about the service. The most memorable reason I heard was from a seaman who said he was in a boat that capsized and was rescued by the Coast Guard. When they pulled him out of the water, he thought, "This is what I want to do. Now I'm serving at the same station that rescued me." One senior petty officer told me he knew nothing about the service, but the father of his girlfriend was a warrant officer in the service. "He probably told me about the Coast Guard, hoping to get rid of me." One machinery technician with 17 years of service said he came into the Coast Guard from the U.S. Army boat service, because the Coast Guard is better, "especially in promotions." (Perhaps unknown to many, the U.S. Army operates a number of boats. My company commander in boot camp had come into the Coast Guard from the army, where he served as a tugboat skipper.) More than one sailor informed me they came into the service because they were "heading for trouble and thought coming in would square me away."

One of the more unusual reasons I heard came from a seaman, who originally had come from Hawaii. He had just finished a tour of duty on a 378-foot high-endurance cutter, and I spoke to him while he took a break from studying to become qualified as a communication watchstander.

"A group of us were going to the movies. One of my friends and I were across the street from the others. The movie theater is located in a mall, with the Coast Guard's recruiting office right next door to the mall. I was looking across the street and yelling to my friends that we were going in here. I opened the door to what I thought would take me inside the mall. I turned and saw I had entered the recruiting office. The recruiter smiled and said, 'Come on in.' So, instead of being mean and just going out, I listened to what he said and decided to enlist."

In recent years, the Coast Guard has increased their activities in law enforcement. Crews from both small boat stations and cutters now board and examine boats for drug smuggling, illegal fishing activities, and illegal immigrants. A number of people I spoke to told me they entered the service because they wanted experience in law enforcement.

One sailor at a station in North Carolina, who also came from roughly the same location as the unit, informed me he started fishing when he was very young, "as that was the only way I could have any money for myself. I fished until I came into the Coast Guard. I fished on my boot camp leave until I reported into this station." The sailor, who is 19, related, "I came into the Coast Guard to help pay back something to my community."

The chance to help others plays a large part in people's decision to come into the Coast Guard. One woman told me that she first thought about the U.S. Air Force but then decided upon the Coast Guard, because "all that the other services do is play around with bombs and train for war. We help people." A former U.S. Navy sailor came into the Coast Guard, because in the "Coast Guard it is neat drilling with equipment used to save lives."

When I served at a small boat station many years ago, the average crew size stood at eight. Most of us were on our first enlistments. Only the officer in charge, a chief boatswain's mate, and the XO, a boatswain's mate first class, had more than one enlistment. Looking back, most of us were young and most came to the unit right out of boot camp, with perhaps three having seen duty at other units. In addition to the chief and first class, there were, perhaps, two other petty officers. The rest of us were seamen (SN), or SAs, or firemen (FN)—what the service now calls nonrates.

Some unscientific statistics I gathered while living at the stations of the "new Guard" reveal a strikingly different picture.

There were 63 people aboard at a test station on the West Coast. Factoring out the CO and chief petty officers, the average age worked out to 26 years. The youngest member of the crew was 19, and the oldest was 43. There were 25 nonrated sailors aboard the unit.

Most of the reasons for the higher number of people at the stations and the rise in the average age will be shown in later chapters, but it should be remembered that many of the boat coxswains and their crews are younger than the average age of those at the test station. The higher average age is due to the service's decision to place more junior rated people at the units.

So what can be made of these unscientific statistics? First, the senior people at the small boat stations have a great deal of experience at the units. Almost all of them learned their trade from long service at rescue stations, and many also have considerable experience at sea. The crew of enlisted people at the stations came into the Coast Guard for a variety of reasons. Obtaining money for education is the reason most given, with running rescue boats, helping others, and law enforcement following close behind. Most knew nothing of the service they were entering.

If the young people are assigned to a small boat rescue station, they immediately find themselves with responsibilities far above what their contemporaries in the civilian world experience. Compare, for example, 19-year-old FA Jon DeMillo, who first handled the radio traffic during the Quillayute River incident. DeMillo was the first to respond to the sailboat's call and quickly recognized the potential danger. Later, he helped in a beach search and received injuries during this work. Many of DeMillo's age group would be just entering college or flipping hamburgers. DeMillo is not an isolated example, as the following chapters will illustrate.

What is interesting for an outside observer is to see how these young people, the majority of who have no idea of what is involved in small boat operations, gain the experience and confidence to risk their lives when they head out into heavy surf. The way they learn their trade is through the leadership of the two senior people at the station, plus the training provided by their petty officers.

chapter four

Fear Is the Text

If you wish to learn the skills needed to work in heavy seas and to be a lifeboat sailor, travel to the isolated area of Cape Disappointment, Washington, and take part in a unique Coast Guard school. At this school, students learn, in the words of writer Michael Parfit, "to work calmly while instinct shouts they are about to die. A school where heavy seas are the curriculum, fear is the text, and tests are given every day." Where part of the classroom has the name "Death Row." Cape Disappointment is the perfect school environment. Below old Fort Canby, which has never fired a shot in anger, the waves thundering on the Columbia River bar kill year after year after year. Within the classroom is Peacock Spit, named after the 10-gun sloop of the Wilkes Expedition in 1841, which survived the Antarctic but not the mouth of the Columbia River. The ribs of many other ships lie on the sandy bottom. Within 2 nautical miles between the north and south jetties, the powerful Pacific Ocean waves—not living up to the ocean's name—meet the power of the mighty Columbia River in an uneasy union that produces a maelstrom of surf at one of the world's roughest bars.

Walk out onto one of the jetties and look out onto this tempest when school is in session. Three small white boats seem to be playing like seals in the surf. They rise on the waves, roll into the troughs, and slip between walls of waves. The small boats plunge into the waves, disappear from sight, and then again ride the tops, the sides, and—amazingly—even seem to be riding the insides of

During the rigorous training, the boats sometimes seem to go inside waves. *U.S. Coast Guard*

the swells. With a pair of binoculars you can see red-clad, helmeted figures working on each boat as the combers slam again and again into the people, who seemingly are unaware of the drenching cold water. These are the students, teachers, and classroom of the U.S. Coast Guard National Motor Lifeboat School. To know why men and women *volunteer* to be pummeled by the sea aboard 44-foot motor lifeboats in the region known to sailors as the "Graveyard of the Pacific," it is necessary to understand the evolution of boats and boat crews at the small boat stations.

The U.S. Coast Guard's National Motor Lifeboat School is the result of the converging of two paths. One path concerns the type of lifeboat used by the small boat rescue stations of the service. As mentioned in Chapter 1, the prototype of the first lifeboats used in this country was a model brought to this country from England by the Treasury Department in 1873. Once the boat had been accepted by the service, however, many of the surfmen balked. The boat, weighing 2 to 4 tons, caused several surfmen to point out that the surfboats they grew up with were lighter and more maneuverable. Six men could easily handle a surfboat, while a crew of eight worked the lifeboat. Then an interesting thing happened. Reports from the Great Lakes began to filter through the service that the boat could take almost impossible seas. Skepticism changed to admiration and crews began to regard the lifeboat as "something almost supernatural," for it enabled them to provide help "when the most powerful tugs and steam-craft refused to go out of the harbor."

Constant drills helped the crewmen perfect their abilities with the lifeboat. One portion of the drill required the actual capsizing and righting of the boat. This trained the crews to react automatically if their boat was flipped during a storm. In 1912, Noel T. Methley, an authority on lifeboats, noted that constant practice enabled the lifesavers to completely right the surfboat, if it capsized within "twenty seconds." The drill was a popular show for the public, and the surfmen performed it at special events. In 1890, for example, the Marquette, Michigan, newspaper reported that the most impressive show at the 4th of July festivities was the lifeboat drill. The newspaper related the "crews capsized [the boat] eight times . . . to the repeated cheers of the crowd." How cheerful the crew felt about being dunked into the cold waters of Lake Superior is not recorded.

The next major development in lifeboats in the United States came in 1899, when the U.S. Life-Saving Service began to evaluate the results of installing a 12-horsepower gasoline engine in a 34-foot Merryman lifeboat at their station at Marquette, Michigan. By 1915, when the U.S. Life-Saving Service merged with the U.S. Revenue Cutter Service to form the Coast Guard, 80 motorized lifeboats were in service. The switch from human muscle to the internal combustion engine allowed the boats to perform at longer distances and with greater speed. Surfmen, however, tend to be very conservative and probably for good reason. New and untried boats and equipment in the surf can sometimes kill you. I recall Master Chief Tom McAdams reminiscing about an old surfman relating that he never trusted internal combustion engines crossing the Yaquina Bay bar. He still preferred to use sail and oars.

In 1918, the Coast Guard introduced a new 36-foot motor lifeboat, the Type H, and this event is another major step on the journey to Cape Disappointment. Between the two world wars, the boat underwent four major design changes and became the standard heavy-weather boat in the service. There is nothing fancy about the craft, and one can still see the basic shape of the old

English lifeboat of 1873 in the lines of the new boat. The boat continued the self-bailing and self-righting features. A lookout position is located in the bow so a crewman can stand watch. The forward portion of the boat contains an enclosed cabin for survivors, and the engine is in a compartment in the center of the boat. The crew stands in a lowered cockpit near the stern of the boat, and a rear compartment holds the towing line. A towing bit is located just aft of where the crew stands. The boat has a single screw and rudder. I remember two things most about the 36-footer. One, as Master Chief McAdams related, was that you could not stay dry or warm on wet, cold cases. You stood out in the open and took nature as it came at you. The other item was that the boat would seem to roll in a turtle's wake.

The 36-foot lifeboat was a dependable boat that was able to take an astonishing amount of punishment and bring back its crew. There were no intricate electronics aboard the craft, just a radio, although some on the coasts also had a depth finder. The boat would be lucky to make 8 knots on a calm day, but it might also make 8 knots on a very rough day. It was like the tortoise versus the hare. Many sleek pleasure boats could run circles around the 36-footer, but, when the seas began to break, the plodding lifeboat could continue the course, while the flashy boats ran for cover. Generations of Coast Guardsmen at small boat rescue stations swore by the craft. I have put out in 10-to-12-foot seas—the height of the seas seems to grow with the passing years—and, while I worried a little bit about myself, I never worried about the boat.

In 1961, the Coast Guard took the next step in the development of motor lifeboats and moved closer to the establishment of the school at Cape Disappointment. By the late 1950s, the service recognized it needed a larger motor lifeboat. One factor leading to this decision was the change that developed in the commercial fishing fleet. Most of the commercial boats were becoming too large and heavy for the 36-footer to tow. In 1961, the Coast Guard built a prototype 44-footer—a self-bailing, self-righting boat that made 15.3 knots on its trial runs with two diesel engines, each producing 185 shaft horsepower. Under general operating conditions, 14 knots was top speed. In subsequent years, age and hard use have taken their toll on the 44-footers, and in the recent past maximum speed has been closer to 12 knots.

The service delivered boat number 44300 to the West Coast

for testing in the high, powerful surf of the Pacific Ocean. Chosen to conduct the tests was Chief Boatswain's Mate Giles Vanderhoof. "We ran it down to Yaquina Bay," Vanderhoof recalls, "and then we used the heavy seas there for 5 days."

"Heavy seas" is a typical surfman's understatement. Vanderhoof and his crew pushed out into *35-foot seas*. In the new 44-footer, the coxswain now sat at a wheel in the forward part of the boat, with his head about 9 feet above the water. The mast of the boat reaches up 20½ feet above the waterline. To see the top of the seas Chief Vanderhoof was about to enter, you would have to lean forward to get an all-round view through the windshield and then look *upward*. Then, maybe you could glimpse the tops of the waves. Every day Vanderhoof and his crew dressed in wet suits and donned lifejackets. With a 52-foot motor lifeboat standing by just in case, the chief and his crew went into the surf. He ran the boat head on into the waves; he turned the stern of the boat to the waves and let the craft be hurled by the force of the seas. Vanderhoof deliberately broached, an almost fatal maneuver for boats. He put the boat sideways in the trough and waited for the inevitable crash. Then Vanderhoof brought the boat back to the engineers and welders so they could fix it. He also picked shards of glass out of his wet suit.

Every night the engineers would put stronger and stronger glass into the windshield and every night Chief Vanderhoof brought back shattered glass from the green seas. At the end of 5 days, the main cabin was crushed and holed, the aft cabin was smashed, the screws and struts had been torn loose from the hull, the engine mounts had given way, and both engines were lying askew in an engine room smeared with oil. But *the boat was still afloat.*

The strength of the 44-footer is grasped with an inevitable statistic. In 1995, 44300 was still afloat even though it had rolled over six times, it had pitchpoled (gone end-over-end) three times, and it was once rammed by a freighter. Yet, it kept its crews alive. A total of 110 44-footers were built at the U.S. Coast Guard Yard, Curtis Bay, Maryland. In 1995, 99 remained in service. It is now approaching the time for a new motor lifeboat, and in September 1990 the Coast Guard began testing a prototype 47-foot motor lifeboat, the CG-47200. After 500 operating hours and after over 200 design changes were included in the specifications, five preproduction boats were delivered to the Coast Guard by January 1994. Two years later, the National Motor Lifeboat School began evaluating the boat for training at the school.

The second major factor that would eventually lead to the establishment of the school at Cape Disappointment concerns the crews who make up the small boat rescue stations. Traditionally, those who handled the small boats of the U.S. Life-Saving Service and Coast Guard learned their skills as a coxswain at their stations, or they came into the service with a large amount of experience. There is much to be said for this type of training. The new lifeboat sailor learns one-on-one at the hands of a master, usually a chief petty officer or a senior petty officer. There is, however, another side to this type of training. If a chief is not a good instructor, or is a poor boat handler, or uses training as a means of rewarding only favorites at a station, then the program produces poor boat handlers.

In the 1960s, the Coast Guard began to require crewmen and boat coxswains to undergo and pass a task-related standardized syllabus, plus take written and oral examinations, before becoming qualified crewmen and coxswains. The highest qualification for a lifeboat sailor is surfman, which requires a more intensive and longer training period. Most surfmen are assigned to the Coast Guard's 13th District, along the rugged coastline of Washington and Oregon. Surfmen, because of their extra training and experience, can be looked upon as the elite in the small boat community. That sentence will probably bring howls of protest from some in headquarters, and strangely enough, some in the small boat community as well. Many in the service do not like to have anyone tagged as part of an elite. I have heard surfmen called prima donnas, both by officers and enlisted men. However, those who do reach the surfman level have additional responsibilities at their motor lifeboat units. By policy, in certain conditions they must be present before any Coast Guard boat can get underway. In addition, they advise the commanding officer and the officer-of-the-day on whether to send a boat. Thus, by the 1960s the Coast Guard had a strong training program in place for crews, and it had an outstanding motor lifeboat. The elements are now in place to make the final journey to Cape Disappointment.

In the late 1960s, some of the senior chief petty officers, the officers in charge of the coastal stations in the 13th District, began meeting at the Cape Disappointment station. The chiefs met and along with the inevitable sea stories came valuable shared information. To use the lexicon of the civilian world, a think tank of experts on surf came together. Someone eventually suggested sending the best surfmen in the district to train other surfmen at Cape Disappointment, which was noted for having some of the roughest surf in the United States. Some Coast Guardsmen in the district had not made the transition from the old 36-footer, and this would also help new Coasties learn the 44-foot boat and the surf from masters. One master chief boatswain's mate said that piloting a 44-footer after a 36-footer "is like going from a pickup to a sports car." By the middle 1970s, word had circulated throughout the Coast Guard that, if you really wanted to become an expert boat driver at the small boat stations, you should try to wrangle orders to the 13th District's school at "Cape D, where they roll boats over in the surf."

At first, only those stationed in the 13th District were assigned to the school. Then it opened up to other districts, with instructors assigned temporarily. The school lasted 3 weeks and sessions took place only during the winter months, when the surf is usually at its highest. Eventually, the Coast Guard decided the school should be for anyone assigned to a station with a 44-footer, and in 1982 the National Motor Lifeboat School graduated its first class.

The school now operates year-round. In 1996, Chief Warrant Officer Paul D. Bellona, with more than 17 years' experience at small boat stations, commanded the school with a staff of 38 people. To become an instructor at the school, the teacher must be a boatswain's mate first class (E-6) and a qualified surfman. There is also at least one engineering instructor in the machinery technician rating. The school attempts to obtain the best surfmen it can find for teachers by talking to people in the field. In a small speciality, the best surfmen are recognizable. Instructors are assigned to the school for 4 years.

Instructor BM1 Darrin Wallace told me that becoming an instructor at the school was "one of the hardest qualifications" he has earned in his career. It takes at least 8 months to a year to qualify. The instructor-trainee must be qualified by every instructor at the school.

CWO Bellona related that the "mission of the school is to train our coxswains to go out into weather that they must go out into. Many times our people must go into harm's way, and they don't have the experience. But the public expects them to go out in anything. If coxswains don't have that experience, chances are they might not make it to the boat that needs help and may end up hurting themselves and not making it back. If the coxswains have to go out in heavy weather or surf conditions, we want to give them enough training so they can go out and complete their mission."

The school also has the additional important mission of sending a motor lifeboat standardization team (STANTEAM) to visit all stations with lifeboats. The STANTEAM examines the conditions of the boats and the training of their crews.

Every instructor I interviewed at the school stated they felt honored to be selected for this duty. Most realized they were in a position to make a large effect on many in the service. One instructor who worked with headquarters on survival gear said he liked "making a difference at the E-6 level." This sense of an honor to be at the National Motor Lifeboat School is also recognized by the commanding officer. "This is a prestigious command," CWO Bellona said, "because of the top-notch people we have here. The best of the best come here." Bellona pointed out, "Just because a person is a highly qualified surfman does not mean they can instruct. It does take a special person to come in and do the job. We do have a lot of say who does get assigned as an instructor. It takes a little ego to be an instructor here." Some of the boatswain's mate instructors agreed that the school's teachers have to be prepared to work with people who have "a lot of ego." CWO Bellona told me the "pleasure of this command is that I get to go out and run the boats in the surf and see what my people do and what the students are learning. I do not have to stay desk bound."

The school now has three different types of "C" school (specialized) training. One is a Basic Coxswain Class, which is a place for the small boat community to have an intense course in how to handle a boat and navigate. There is also an SAR Supervisor's course for those who work in search and rescue to enable them to have a better understanding of small boats.

Then there is the Heavy Weather School, the one that attracts visiting dignitaries and media from all over the world. In three trips to the Cape Disappointment area, I observed film crews from France and from CBS and a group of safety officers from the armed forces all taking the tour of this school.

The "classroom" of the National Motor Lifeboat School's heavy weather course. *U.S. Coast Guard*

The Heavy Weather School is unique. It requires a stint in bad weather—or high seas— to enable the students to graduate. If the seas do not cooperate during the period of the school—there must be 6 to 8 feet of swell and 6 to 8 feet of surf—the students do not get a certificate for the course.

The heavy weather course is now 2 weeks in length. Students come from all over the United States and from other countries, notably Canada. Bellona said, "Potential students submit a short-term training request, and we make up a list and try to pick one or two per district so we don't stack it for just one district." To attend the heavy weather course, a Coast Guard student must be a qualified coxswain.

Any mention of the National Motor Lifeboat School at Cape Disappointment usually brings out the comment, "Oh, that's where they roll boats, isn't it?" All instructors and their commanding officer are quick to dispel this mistaken image. "When the 13th District ran the school," said CWO Bellona, "it was not uncommon for them to roll boats. The way they ran boats at that time was a little bit different than how we now run boats. We don't roll boats on purpose. Safety is paramount. When we are running the school,

Students of the heavy weather course must leap into the cold waters of the Columbia River wearing their Mustang suits and helmets to understand better the environment in which they will be working. *U.S. Coast Guard*

we always have two or three boats underway at all times during training for backup in the surf. The lookout tower at the Cape Disappointment station is manned to watch conditions as well. We suspend training when the wind speed is over 50 knots. Anything over 15-foot breaks, we'll pull the plug on it. We can't do any training if we hurt our students. We can't do it right if they're petrified, and they're not going to learn if they are holding on for dear life." The commanding officer added: "Now the only time you roll a boat is if you make a mistake. We try to teach the coxswains how to avoid breakers and how not to make mistakes. Sometimes it does happen that you go into a break and you hit it wrong and blow out a window and end up taking a roll. It does happen, but we try not to do it."

One of the first exercises in the curriculum of the heavy weather course requires the students to swim in the cold waters of Columbia River in survival suits. At one time, the school made students go out in the boats, jump into the surf, and swim to the beach. This introduced them to the coldness of the water and the power of the surf. One former instructor said once you were in the surf "you feel like a BB in a boxcar."

BM1 Wallace said, "We start by first getting the students used to the environment they will be operating in." It is difficult for the average boater or nonboater to grasp completely the concept of the classroom of the Columbia River bar. To sample some of the environment, I went out near Clatsop Spit in a 30-foot surf rescue boat from the Cape Disappointment station to watch as the 47-footer and 44-footers from the school and the 52-foot motor lifeboat from Cape D were drilling in some good-sized waves. All of the motor lifeboats had visiting officers aboard from an armed forces safety conference held at the school.

The SRB is an open boat that can make at least 30 knots and is designed to dash into the surf quickly and to pick up survivors. The SRB carries a coxswain and one to two other crewmembers. In this craft, you are going to get both wet and tossed around. Before leaving the dock, I donned a Mustang survival suit and a pyro (pyrotechnic) vest—which contains flares and other signaling devices to use if you should go into the water—and, when I boarded the boat, the crewman had me put on a helmet and goggles. Then he showed me how to use the safety belt to strap in. All this preparation before getting underway can cause you to pause and think about what is awaiting you out there.

We pulled away from the dock. The skies were gray, lowering, with intermittent rain—a typical day on the Columbia River. The rain made it so you could not taste the saltwater hitting you in the face.

Be thankful for small favors.

The coxswain, Lt. Mike White, who was the commanding officer of the Cape Disappointment station, yelled to me: "These boats are not designed for a crew." After a few minutes of being tossed around, I had to agree. I want to stress we were not operating in really rough seas on this particular day. I also would like to be on record as saying I have been in some fairly high seas on cutters—the worst in excess of 50 feet. Being on a small boat approaching the swells near the mouth of the Columbia River, however, made me wonder if perhaps I should rethink my plan of experiencing small craft so readers may better understand the training and lives of small boat sailors. I had to crane my head *upward* to see the tops of some of the swells and definitely felt a lot older than I had before leaving the dock. At one point, I watched the 52-foot motor lifeboat transiting out of the higher swells. The longest in the Coast Guard's motor lifeboat inventory, the 52-footer looked tiny. The image of that small, white boat against the large gray-green seas is forever etched in my memory. This is the classroom environment the students must face.

The class schedule for the heavy weather course is dominated by underway time. Usually, classroom time in the morning is used to discuss theory and then at least 3½ hours are devoted to underway time to put into practice what the students have learned. CWO Bellona points out that the school is "based upon performance. If a coxswain can't do the underway performance, he or she will go back to their unit without a certificate. It is impossible to teach heavy weather operations out of a book."

One of the first classroom subjects is risk assessment. This is one of the latest Coast Guard buzzwords. There is a very old saying from the days of the U.S. Life-Saving Service about small boat rescue work: "You have to go out, but you don't have to come back." For years, the Coast Guard and the few people who wrote about shore-based rescue used this phrase repeatedly. Someone in the planning areas of the "new Guard" apparently felt the small boat community did not take precautions in evaluating whether or not to send a boat out. Now there is a formula that is easy enough that even I can work it to tell whether the risk is too great to send a boat out into a storm.* The old phrase now seems to be used—not by the people at the school—to basically belittle the efforts of the old keepers and chiefs who formerly ran the stations, to make them seem to have been either irresponsible or careless with the lives of their crews. Actually, the old keepers and chiefs never willingly sent their men out into a gale knowing they would never come back. They used their years of experience and knowledge to judge whether or not to go out. They did not need a formula; it was all in their heads. To be sure, students and those who work in the SAR community should know when a boat should be sent, and more importantly, when a boat should *not* be sent.

---

*Risk management has crews assigning numerical values to six factors. The assignment is usually made when the crewmembers come on duty. The values are 0 through 10, with 10 being the highest risk. The six values are added and then the GAR (green, amber, red) Evaluation Scale is consulted. The six factors are: supervision, planning, crew selection, crew fitness, environment, and event/environmental complexity. The GAR Evaluation Scale is measured: 0–23 as green, or low risk; 23–44 as amber, or caution; and 44–60 as red, or high risk.

This can be done, however, without unconsciously demeaning the earlier lifesavers. One master chief stated: "Risk assessment is fine, but from the time they are in boot camp, Coasties basically learn that, when the alarm rings, you go. So, what do you expect when the alarm rings?"

Risk assessment or, as the even newer buzzwords now have it, team coordination training, may at first glance seem like just another bureaucratic exercise. A closer examination, however, indicates that the idea behind all of the fancy phrases is sound. If, through the use of whatever method that is devised, crews can be trained to stop and think before rushing into danger, then the small boat crews are better equipped to face their hostile environment.

The underway time on the boats during the heavy weather course has students learning to pass a pump to another boat, station keeping (being able to keep a boat in one position), and towing—with an occasional man overboard drill thrown in. BM1 Wallace related one of the basic principles in the course is to teach the student coxswains to avoid the large waves, if possible. But, they are also taught that if they cannot avoid large waves, they should meet them squarely on the bow. Another way to put this is to put the motor lifeboat perpendicular to the wave.

I mentioned that when I attended service schools there always seemed to be at least one student who thought he knew more than the instructors and at least one who paid very little attention. "In this school," replied a master chief, "many of the students have never seen waves as high as we operate in, and it is an intimidating thing." I would certainly agree with that statement. "When the students see how well the instructors operate in this environment," continued the master chief, "they realize who are the experts." BM1 Wallace seconded the master chief. "When students first see towing operations in 8-to-10-foot waves, they can be intimidated." However, BM1 Wallace said, "You have to watch some students who are more familiar with the high swells, because sometimes they become a little too cocky." Even these students, however, can be brought down a little in this watery classroom. I will attest that, once into the waves, your attention is focused very quickly. There is no false pressure put on the students. No one falls asleep in this classroom.

When it comes time to go into the outdoor classroom, students and instructors don thermal underwear, Mustangs, boots,

Trainees learn the handling characteristics of a 44-footer. *U.S. Coast Guard*

pyro vests, crash helmets, and warm gloves. They fit their safety belts around them. Each belt has two straps, with a clip at each end. The students and instructors clip into "D" rings on the boat. On a 44-foot motor lifeboat, the coxswain sits in a chair at the centerline of the boat. The engineer usually stands to his left, and his two crewmembers are slightly aft, to the left and right, and function as the lookouts. Everyone watches and constantly feeds information about the waves to the coxswain. At the school, the instructor stands to the right of the student coxswain, near the throttles. The instructors have the added responsibility of learning to control the motor lifeboat from an unusual position.

BM1 Wallace said that going out into the classroom can be "unnerving," mainly because "you have to first process the situation taking place through your mind and then transmit this to the students, who then must transfer it through their minds before reacting." Sometimes this does not leave a great deal of time, and all the time the sea is coming at you. Wallace said that, when you are in heavy seas, "you hear your engineer giving you information and you hear your crewmen shouting information at you. You hear the sound of the wave approaching. Your heart starts beating faster. You anticipate what is going to happen next. Then there is a crashing sound, as boat meets wave. If it is a 'Hawaii Five-O' type of wave, you will hit green water and hear a loud crash. The water swirls around the boat, reaching into the coxswain flat and drenching you. You are at full power, and still the force of the wave will drive the boat backward. If the wave has lost some of its energy, then you hear a rumbling sound, followed by white water hitting the windshield." Usually, the first sound after a large wave hits is the crewmen exhaling, as if someone just struck them a strong punch to the stomach.

There are very few experiences in life to compare with being in heavy weather in a 44-foot motor lifeboat and going through a large wave. One former student said, "Falling off your roof might be one." BM1 Wallace likened the experience "to surviving 30 car crashes in a row."

One instructor said, "Some guys catch on quick; some should be cooks." Instructors also feel the tension. BM1 Wallace said he has never pulled anyone out of the coxswain chair, but "I have given them the three strike routine. The first mistake you can always say, 'Anyone can make a mistake.' The second time, 'If you do that again, you're in trouble.' The third time: 'You're out of there.'"

At the end of the 2 weeks training in the heavy weather course, students will return to their units with a certificate, if the weather cooperated during the period they attended the school. The training does not make the students qualified surfmen. The coxswains I met during this project who had successfully completed the course told me they came back with more confidence in their abilities to handle cases in bad weather. During my visits to the National Motor Lifeboat School, I learned to agree with CWO Bellona: "the best of best" are here.

The training Coast Guard personnel receive at the National Motor Lifeboat School is only a very small part of what the people at the small boat rescue stations receive. Most of the training station crews receive still takes place aboard their own units.

chapter five

This Is a Drill

The standard "company line" from Coast Guard headquarters now decrees that small boat rescue stations will carry the name multimission stations. The intent of decision-makers to accurately describe what the stations do is correct, but it seems misguided: What does multimission mean to those who do not understand the service's jargon? In the end, this will make the units even more mysterious to the public. Nevertheless, the small boat rescue stations of the Coast Guard do an astonishing number of missions for units of their size. It is this large mix of duties that forces the enlisted people of the stations to undergo a wide range of training and acquire a broad knowledge. The interesting aspect of this diversity is that it begins with even the most junior person aboard a station.

The people at the Coast Guard's small boat stations must have the knowledge and skills needed to be a boat crewman. They also must know how to be a coxswain; know how to properly maintain a boat and other machinery; know how to conduct maritime searches; know first aid; be proficient with pistol, rifle, shotgun, and sometimes machine guns; know how to work in pollution control; be able to conduct search and seizures of illegal drugs; be able to conduct boardings for boating safety; know species of fish for fishery law enforcement; know federal fisheries laws to be able to board fishing vessels to check for violations; and know the procedures for boarding vessels to check for illegal immigrants. Each of the duties listed also has many subduties within it that the

A female crewmember from the Cape Hatteras, North Carolina, station fires the 9mm service pistol during pistol qualifications. After firing from this close range, she will move farther back. *Dennis L. Noble*

crews must know. To become a surfman, for example, a person must become a boat crewman, then a coxswain, and then complete all the tasks within the qualification guide for surfman, plus pass a check ride and be approved by a board made up of the senior people at a unit. The entire process may take up to 3 years.

The crews are also given training and lectures in a wide variety of other topics outside of the operational areas listed above. At one station I visited on the West Coast, for example, a senior petty officer gave a lecture on the workings of a portable stretcher, and various members of the crew worked with the device. Following this discussion and demonstration, a chief petty officer from the district Work-Life Division lectured on off-duty schooling available and the means of obtaining a college degree while still serving, using such nontraditional avenues to education as the New York State Regent's Degree Program. At another station, I listened to Rear Adm. Alan Steinman of the U.S. Public Health Service and Chief, Health and Safety at Coast Guard headquarters present a lecture on the hazards of smokeless tobacco. This proved interesting for a number of reasons. Above all, it illustrates the diversity of training lectures being given outside of operational areas—from first aid to the evils of tobacco.

When I served at a small boat station 40 years ago, I doubt seriously if an admiral would have taken the time to give us a talk and, if he had, I do not believe he would have encouraged a question-and-answer period. The talk came about because a crewman went to the Group Commander complaining about the latter's decision to curtail the sale of smokeless tobacco in the Group's exchanges. In my day, I seriously doubt if anyone would have gone to the Group Commander and asked the captain for an explanation for his decision. I find this willingness to ask questions a refreshing change, although I can imagine many a commanding officer must inwardly wince at such questions, his mind racing with thoughts of how the senior officer is going to take that one. What is he going to say to *me* after we are alone? One senior chief petty officer told me the District Commander on one visit wanted all of the crew to be present on the mess deck for a question-and-answer period. After the District Commander's presentation, a seaman raised his hand and said: "Admiral, you've talked about all the good things

At the Umpqua River, Oregon, station, SN Ruben Rivera (right) helps break in SN Sondra Neider on communications watch. *Dennis L. Noble*

about these stations. Why do we still have electronics on these boats that are as old as I am?"

The first thing a boot reporting to a unit is required to do is to become proficient in communication watchstanding. As with almost every aspect of training at the stations, there is a standardized booklet that covers each item a person must learn. A senior petty officer is required to sign off each task when the new person can show they have acquired the knowledge and skills required to perform that task. At most stations, everyone from petty officer third class and below is required to go through this training. This includes both engineers and the deck force.

The communication training is accomplished while actually standing a watch, with the trainee working alongside a qualified watchstander. Most stations now operate with radios that have many channels and with a number of telephone lines coming into the unit. Many of the units also monitor CB, which, according to one commanding officer, is against Coast Guard policy. The service would like all boaters to have VHF radio, as it is difficult to get a directional finder (DF) fix on a CB radio broadcast. This seems a reasonable goal, as safety is involved, but, in another of those policy decisions by higher echelons that makes one wonder, the word went out not to monitor the CB radios. "So, what do we do?" asked the commanding officer. "Not have the CB and risk the chance of someone drowning because all they have is a CB?" In a typical routine among the small boat community, the station overlooked a policy that seems to ignore the real world of small boats and used their own budget to provide themselves with a CB radio. At another station, the CB radio had been donated to the unit. Almost as if staged for my visit, shortly after the commanding officer's discussion about the CB radio issue, a boater lost in the fog called in on the CB and asked for assistance. The boater had no other radio. He did have GPS (Global Positioning System), which gives very accurate positions. He did have the device; it was at home in the box. Over the next 30 minutes or so, the station used old-fashioned methods to finally locate the boater. I recalled this incident when I had officers in headquarters tell me that, with all the new electronic navigation devices, it is much easier to locate people, hence there is no longer a need for so many small boat stations.

To keep track of all calls requiring assistance, each unit keeps a work sheet near the radio. When a call comes in, the watch-stander reaches for the work sheet and begins a litany of questions, beginning with "what is the nature of your distress?" followed by "are you in immediate danger?" Then the list goes on to cover other details. Perhaps some boaters or those who use scanners have overheard this series of questioning while monitoring the radio and have felt the questions rather mundane or wondered why that person is asking so many questions? As with most of the standardized items at the stations, the questions come from long experience. The questions give the responding unit, or units, as much information as possible quickly and in a standard manner. That is, two different units responding to one case will receive the same information, which will help prevent any confusion. Most importantly, when, as one watchstander put it, "a bell ringer goes off" and the adrenaline surges, with the officer-of-the-day, the boat crews, the executive officer, and the commanding officer all wanting to know what the hell's going on and the telephone is ringing and the person on the radio is still yelling, the watchstander will not forget an important fact. If I were to choose one important small change for the better in the routines of the stations since my day, I would choose the use of this work sheet. It is difficult for one who has not been in the position to know the amount of anxiety that floods into the person at the radio when a serious case occurs. I watched one watchstander deal with a case involving a sinking charter boat. While her voice at times showed the strain, she followed procedures. At one point, while the skipper of the boat debated over whether or not to abandon the boat into the cold waters of the Pacific, the watchstander, talking out loud to herself, without the radio keyed, said, "I wish I could do more for him. I feel so helpless." One of the rescued people later came to the operations room to compliment the watchstander.

To help train for the times of stress, some training petty officers will locate the break-in watchstander in one room with a portable radio and then go into another with another radio and see how well the new sailor performs. I watched one new seaman undergo this procedure. The trainer gave the new seaman her radio and said, "Got everything?" She stated she had and went into the next room. The instructor looked at me and shook his head. He picked up the radio and said, "Uh, Coast Guard I've got a problem here. I need some help." He waited. A long silence. Finally, the seaman came into the room looking a little sheepish.

"Forget something?" The seaman had forgotten the work sheet. "How can you say you're ready if you don't have that sheet nearby? Now, are you ready?"

Over the next 10 minutes the instructor at times proved obstinate, kept quiet at times when the new seaman tried to establish contact, made his voice difficult to hear and at times yelled over the radio. Then he broke off the drill and told her to come back into the room.

The trainer asked if she recognized what she was doing wrong. Then he pointed out other items she missed. Finally: "I wasn't picking on you. Everything I did during the drill I have heard on the radio during cases." The training officer then told the seaman to practice some more. Listening to tapes made during cases, you understand the truth of the petty officer's comments. In one tape I heard a hysterical woman literally screaming curse words that some sailors do not use. Between the hysterical outbursts, the

From left to right, SN Sondra Neider, SN Jeff Berner, and BM3 Don Pretlow proceed up the Umpqua River in a rigid-hull inflatable boat during Neider's area familiarization. She must learn all the aids to navigation and landmarks from the sea to eleven miles upriver. *Dennis L. Noble*

calm voice of a station's watchstander can be heard trying to get information.

At the same time the trainee is learning about handling radio traffic and the telephone switchboard, the new person must also be memorizing all of the aids to navigation in the unit's area of operations as well as locations of the possible sources for trouble. At one unit I visited, the new person must know all the aids to navigation along an 11-mile stretch of river. At this unit a BM asked me if I wanted to go along on an area fam (familiarization) trip. I donned an orange Mustang and pyro vest and climbed aboard a rigid hull inflatable boat with two BMs and the new seaman. The seaman took a chart of the area along with her. During most of the trip, one of the BMs asked such questions as: "What is the aid at mile 5?" Or, breaking out the chart, "See the little bay over there? Locate it on the chart. That's where a fishing vessel went aground once." We worked up and down the river for over an hour, with the seaman answering and asking questions.

My first time aboard an RHIB proved eye-opening. The craft is extremely fast and highly maneuverable. I said a number of times during the ride that I didn't know Coast Guard small boats went this fast. The fastest boat at my former station, a 36-foot motor lifeboat, went a whole 8 knots wide-open. The RHIB can make above 20 knots. About halfway through the fam, I remarked that this procedure of knowing everything about a river reminded me of a book I had read. The BM coxswain said, "Yeah, Mark Twain's *Life on the Mississippi*." I replied that many of my former shipmates early in my career did not read and it was nice to see young sailors reading. The new seaman added, "He's always trying to get me to read."

On top of knowing the area, running the switchboard, and handling the radio, the new person at a unit must be able to plot positions and lay out courses accurately on a nautical chart. When the watchstander feels he or she is ready, the new sailor must face a board of senior petty officers, who quiz the Coastie. Everyone must pass the board, or they remain at the telephone and radio until they do. If they take the board and do not pass it, then they cannot leave the station until they do. Communications watch is not considered the best duty aboard a unit. Remember, all of this is happening to people who have just come out of boot camp, who, most likely, are only a few months beyond having graduated from high school, and whose lives have not prepared them for what they are now facing. The commanding officers and executive officers feel that most new people will be qualified as watchstanders within 3 weeks of arriving at a unit. It continues to amaze me that this position of responsibility—the watchstander is the frontline person on any case—is given to people so junior. I recall one watchstander telling a break-in, "Don't be a hero. If you have questions, pipe [page] someone. If you screw up, you can kill someone." In almost all cases, the more astonishing fact is that the young people perform so well.

Beginning in the late 1970s, the boating public began to see a new image of the lifesavers—armed Coast Guardsmen approaching their pleasure craft. If talk radio had been alive and well in those days, the lines would have lit up. In my day, the most common remark heard on Coast Guardsmen and weapons was that "there is nothing more dangerous than a Coastie with a weapon." Yet, when opening the newest volume of *The Coast Guardsman's Manual*, the training manual and guide given to all enlisted personnel, one is struck by the amount of information on weapons training and hand-to-hand combat. The only weapons shown in older manuals were rifles in the section discussing the manual of arms. Now there even is a picture of a Coastie *with an M-60 machine gun*. Parts of the book resemble a manual you would expect to see in a police department. What happened?

Quite simply, decision-makers felt the service should become more involved in law enforcement. This decision partially came about in response to the interest of Congress and the Executive Branch as the war on drugs heated up, but many within the service eagerly accepted the role. The service traditionally has enforced maritime law as one of its functions. The U.S. Revenue Cutter Service, for example, one of the predecessors of the Coast Guard, came into being because Alexander Hamilton, the first secretary of the treasury, wanted to prevent the loss of revenue by smuggling. All of the service's officers were revenue officers. This is the reason officers and petty officers of the Coast Guard are the only people in the U.S. military who can legally board, search, and arrest U.S. civilians for violation of federal laws within the United States. The U.S. Revenue Cutter Service merged with the U.S. Life-Saving Service in 1915 to form the Coast Guard.

In the past, the personnel of small boat stations checked for violation of safety practices and assisted other law enforcement agencies, as requested. But they rarely, if ever, went aboard armed. While no one in the pleasure boat business advertises it, not everyone of the millions who put out in small craft are nice people, nor are they all engaged in family activities. Thus, the Coast Guard in many locations are now looked upon as little more than federal sea-going cops, and all too often the lifesaving duties are over-shadowed by this perception. Sometimes, Coast Guardsmen had best have a weapon handy when coming aboard a fishing vessel or a small craft. This aspect of duty at the small boat stations has been received with mixed feelings by the crews. Some Coasties fight the thought of even strapping on a weapon. If time permits, when a Coast Guard small boat gets underway, the crews are required to take law enforcement gear with them. At some sta-tions, all of those who are weapons qualified carry weapons when they get underway. Other units place the gear in briefcase-like carriers. Yet, at other locations the gear is stowed in a compart-ment and left there, only to be taken out in extreme emergencies. One senior petty officer told me his master chief wanted nothing to do with law enforcement at his station. He was a lifesaver, not a cop. "The first time I had to strap on a pistol," the petty officer related, "I couldn't get the belt to fit right, and when I got aboard a fishing vessel, it slipped off, hit the deck and the spare ammo spilled out onto the deck right in front of the fishermen." There are other stations that vigorously carry out this duty.

Crews now receive a great deal of training in law enforce-ment. Law enforcement at the stations covers a broad spectrum, including federal fishery laws. Petty officers and officers of the Coast Guard are the only ones at a station, or on a cutter, who are legally empowered to make arrests or to give out citations. The service now has courses for boarding officers at their training centers at Petaluma, California, and Yorktown, Virginia. There also are traveling teams who visit stations and give training to boat crews on law enforcement. In fact, the amount of material to learn and the duties in this field are vast. If this duty were given to another branch of the armed forces—which cannot occur, because the Posse Comitatus Act forbids the use of the military in law enforcement roles within the United States—there would be per-sonnel in just this one field. At the small boat stations of the Coast Guard, however, it is just another duty tacked onto many others.

Even with the amount of time crews must spend on other training, crews are somehow expected to keep themselves proficient in the field. How much the men and women must know is illustrated by one of my visits to the Umpqua River station.

The training petty officer at quarters in the morning announced there would be judgmental training on the rec (recreation) deck. When I asked the person next to me what that is, he replied that it dealt with law enforcement and that only certain petty officers would have to go through it. I then went to the training petty officer and inquired if I could attend, and, like every request I ever made at the small boat stations, it was greeted with a smile and "be glad to have you watch."

Judgmental training consists of a student petty officer bringing his law enforcement equipment, a belt that holds a 9mm Beretta semiautomatic pistol, holster, and other gear, such as pepper spray. The student stands in front of a television screen with an unloaded weapon drawn while a videotape is played portraying certain situations. (For security reasons, the following is a distillation of what I observed after watching many sessions. The example is *something* like the video.) For example, well into the video, after many other situations have been covered, the tape's narrator says: "You receive a message that a holdup has just occurred, with shots fired and injuries, and the perpetrators have fled in a blue and white 16-foot boat." The scene shifts to a blue and white 16-foot boat speeding by a Coast Guard 41-foot utility boat. A woman can clearly be seen pointing a pistol at the Coast Guard boat. The utility boat gives chase. The next scene shows the 16-foot boat pulling to the dock, a woman leaps out and starts to run away. By this time one can see that the petty officers are caught up in the training. When the video shows the woman running down the dock, everyone that I observed yelled, "Halt! Halt!" or "Lady! Halt! Halt!" In the video, the woman whirls and points the pistol at the camera, ready to shoot. At the point the woman's pistol starts to train on the camera, the student pulled the trigger of his unloaded Beretta. The point of this scene is to see when the petty officer would "fire" his weapon. Everyone in this training session passed. Remember, of course, that, besides these types of decisions, many of the petty officers are boat coxswains and must keep up their proficiency in that field and make difficult decisions that also can mean life or death.

While we were waiting for the next person in the judgmental training to be tested, the training petty officer said that, after the last of this training, the next thing on his agenda was to test a petty officer just returning from boarding officer school. He again allowed me to sit in on the process.

Just before the student petty officer arrived for the testing, the training petty officer remarked that this was not really a board, but basically was a debrief to see what the person learned. Thus, the person must be able to pass the school, only to face more questions in the field at Umpqua River. The quizzing surprised me for its wide-ranging coverage and the amount of knowledge the petty officer was expected to master. One question: "What can we do under the Lacy Act?" Yet another question centered on the steps needed to arrest a drunken boater and obtain a conviction. The training petty officer, however, said, "Remember, our mission is to make the water safe. Whether or not the person is convicted is not important. It is important that you removed him and made the waterway safe."

Thus far, the training petty officer's first 2 hours of the day, beginning at 8:00 in the morning for the judgmental training, had been taken up in law enforcement. Finishing up with the boarding petty officer, the next stop on the training petty officer's agenda was to see whether a new seaman could pass the qualifications to become a watchstander by herself. In the meantime, about a hundred yards away, out on the dock, a group from the engineering division was testing the pumps that are passed to vessels and boats that are taking on water. During the testing, new people were being given instructions on how to operate and maintain the devices. All of this training at the Umpqua River station came before lunch. Looking over the schedule for the day—for this week and weeks in the past—this seemed to be a normal day. In addition to the training, the crews must also keep the boats and station in proper maintenance. The training goes on at most stations 6 days a week and sometimes 7 days.

Even the petty officers who like the law enforcement aspect of duty in the Coast Guard agree that the first priority of the stations is search and rescue by small boat. Traditionally, the service has always been noted for its experts on small boat handling in rough surf. Some of the Coast Guard's officer corps, or Coasties who sail on the larger cutters, may try to dispute this, but the public and other services recognize this expertise. In World War II, for example, the U.S. Navy did not turn to the service to ask for training in ship handling. They did, however, ask the Coast Guard for help in training landing craft coxswains in surf operations, the realm of the small boat stations. This aspect of the small boat stations also requires a great deal of training.

There now are standardized training routines each person must pass before progressing to the next level of boatmanship. At the end of each level of training, the person must pass an oral board and do a check ride.

After qualifying as a communications watchstander, a new person out of boot camp, or any nonrate from a cutter or other unit, then begins boat crewman's training and receives a book to record their progress. In the deck division, a person must first become a boat crewman and then move upward to boat coxswain, progressing through each type of boat at the station. By the time a person makes coxswain, he or she is usually a petty officer. The summit for coxswains is surfman. The training record book for surfman is 28 pages long, with 18 pages devoted to instructor sign-off sheets of required tasks. Task SRF-01-10, for example, details what is required to demonstrate the ability to recover a simulated person in the water in 6-to-8-foot surf. Among other standards for this task is one stating that the "boat must proceed from a point at least 150 feet seaward from the simulated person in the water and accomplish a recovery." Recall that this is in 6-to-10-foot surf. The trainee is judged on 15 performance criteria.

During my visits to stations, I audited numerous boards dealing with boat operations. In most, the atmosphere reminded me of the oral examinations for a Ph.D., with the person being questioned as tense as a doctoral candidate.

At the Umpqua River station, I listened as a fireman apprentice in the engineering department fielded questions that, again, illustrate the amount of knowledge that even junior people must know. The board consisted of three petty officers, with the chief petty officer, who is the executive officer, coming in later to audit the proceedings. Sample questions: Can you name the controls of the 44-footer? Can you name all of the frame numbers of the compartments on the 44-footer from the bow aft? How many fire extinguishers are on the boat; where are they located; what type and weight? Then one of the petty officers said, "What type of aid to navigation is number 2, and then tell me all the aids upriver from that point?" (The FA had to know an 11-mile stretch of the river.) The questioning continued for an hour and a half, after which the nonrate left the room, while the petty officers deliberated.

The senior petty officer of the group turned to me and said, "We have three choices: we can pass him, fail him, or tell him to go back and study certain items and be tested on them again. If he fails or has to do extra studying, he does not go ashore on liberty until he passes." The three board members began to discuss the results. One petty officer said at the beginning of the discussion what eventually proved the consensus of the group: "What he knows, he knows really good. He is still weak in a number of areas." The board decided that the FA did not have to sit another board. However, he received a list of 11 subjects he needed to study. When he felt he knew the subjects, the nonrate had to return to the senior petty officer and prove to him that he knew them. He could not have liberty until he passed. During the remaining 3 days at the Umpqua River station, I would observe the FA on the rec deck and other locations, always studying. I don't know what the outcome of all the studying was, but if the amount of studying is an indication, I would say he passed.

At the Cape Disappointment station, I observed the surfman boards for two petty officers. This board consisted of a surfman—BM1 Bart Pope—the Engineering Officer, Senior Chief Machinery Technician Mike Doan, Senior Chief Boatswain's Mate Tom Doucette, the executive officer, and Commanding Officer Lt. Mike White. In short, for this examination the senior people of the station were in attendance and rightfully so, as the designation of surfman is as high as a small boat handler can go. The service specifically describes that a surfman must be present in certain weather and surf conditions, or boats cannot be operated. Further, the surfman becomes an expert adviser to the OOD and commanding officer during heavy weather operations. (Beginning in 1996, it also meant an extra $220 each month in pay.)

The questioning for the surfman's board came mainly from Senior Chief Doucette and BM1 Pope, another surfman. Very early in the questioning the nature of the queries became clear: knowledge of the equipment and conditions, plus decision-making. "What would you do if you were in the 52-foot motor lifeboat and the windows blew out?" "How would you quickly drain the water out of the compartment?" "What are the decision factors if you have a rollover?"

Many of the questions revealed the dangerous nature of duty at small boat stations. Two are very instructive. Senior Chief Doucette asked one of the petty officers: "You are in the 44-footer, 30 miles out to sea, in a 30-foot sea and howling wind. You lose the starboard engine, which makes you lose steering. What are your options?"

The petty officer responded with a number of options. After listening, Senior Chief Doucette finished by pointing out, "You could stream a drogue [put over a sea anchor] off the bow, which will keep the bow into the wind, shut everything down, and then go into the forward survivor's compartment, dog down the hatch, strap yourself in, and ride it out. The boat will take a lot of punishment."

Another: "What should you do on a rollover?" The petty officer responded with the material from the book. Doucette added: "Remember to cut back your throttle. The faster your engines are turning, the more you will flood your engine room. A rollover with screws turning can kill a crewmember if he should go back along the keel. You can survive an out-of-gear idling screw. That's what happened to a Canadian Coast Guard lifeboat coxswain. He was taught to cross the 'T' [having your boat perpendicular to the other boat] when passing a towing line. He attempted to pass the line in a 15-foot sea to a tug. The tug surfed down the swell and rammed the lifeboat. When the boat came up, the coxswain was afraid the tug would overrun him and he powered up and hit his crewman, who was back by the screws. They couldn't medevac him, and he died on the boat. Remember to cut your power. Also, don't cross the 'T' in heavy seas. Just keep your bow into the seas and don't get directly downswell of the disabled boat. Usually, you will be downwave when you come up. Once you determine all your crewmembers are accounted for, then power up and go one way or the other." Later, Doucette told me, "'The book' says a crossing-the-T approach is a heavy weather approach. This doesn't work if the disabled boat's stern is to the swell, as often happens with fishing boats. It places the motor lifeboat directly downswell, a bad thing, which allows the disabled boat to surf up and over the motor lifeboat. That is what happened in Canada."

Both petty officers received this interesting question from Senior Chief Doucette at their boards: "It is night. You are heading out. The wind is moderately high, the bar is rough, but there is no extreme danger. You are standing to the right of the coxswain, by the radar. When do you take the wheel from the coxswain?" The replies of both of the petty officers indicated they would take over immediately as a safety factor. Doucette then said, "The hardest thing to do as a surfman is let the coxswain take the wheel, with you watching and giving advice. If you don't train them, there never will be surfmen. I expect you to take the wheel in extreme danger."

About halfway through one board, Senior Chief Doucette asked one petty officer: "When do you medevac a seasick crewman who is uncomfortable?" The petty officer offered a few scenarios. Lieutenant White said, "Good question. The operative word is 'uncomfortable.' Some seasickness is dangerous. They can throw up so much they are dehydrated. Some even throw up blood, but the acute cases don't usually happen unless you've been underway for days. You are not out long enough on a motor lifeboat to reach this dangerous stage."

Senior Chief Doucette said, *"I don't want to ever hear on the radio about seasick crews.* What does the crew of a fishing vessel that's been out to sea 3 or 4 days, or more, think when they hear about a Coast Guard crewman medevaced for seasickness? *Suck it up and work!"*

One petty officer passed completely; the other passed his oral board but needed to have one more check ride in the surf with the senior chief. Earlier in the week, both of the petty officers and Doucette were combining the check-ride drill with the inevitable party of VIP officers who wanted to see what it was like in a small boat near the Columbia River bar. The petty officer told me, "I would have had my check ride completed if one of the visiting officers hadn't thrown up all over the place and caused us to come in early."

The amount of underway training and the variety needed to become expert small boat handlers and crewmen is great. The time needed must somehow be sandwiched between other required drills, operations, and routine work. A boatswain's mate at Umpqua River invited me to come aboard one of the new 47-foot motor lifeboats for towing drills with a 44-footer. This invitation came at about 8:00 on a Saturday morning. Along with most of this same boat crew, I had been out from about 10:00 at night to close to midnight the previous night on a flare-sighting case.

Well, if I wanted to depict life at a small boat station, I felt I should try to follow the routine as much as possible. So, somewhat groggy from the previous night, I gathered up my loaned SAR bag, put on my Mustang, and made my way to the 47-footer. Of course, I did not have to do anything, plus the crew allowed me to sit in the topside left-hand piloting seat whenever I wanted. The others worked. I observed.

The crew met at the dock. After firing off the boat, the senior petty officer briefed the crew on what we were to accomplish. The boat crew consisted of the senior petty officer as the trainer, a junior petty officer as coxswain, an MK3 as boat engineer, another petty officer as crewman, and a nonrate. We were to practice towing with the 44-foot motor lifeboat. The drill would encompass passing a line and towing. After a certain amount of time, we would throw off the tow and then the 44-footer would pass a line to us and we would be towed.

Both boats left the dock and proceeded seaward. In this drill, as I would find at other stations, there would be more than just towing. The senior petty officer said to me, "There's always something to learn. You may have a qualified boat crewman but have to be training another crewman. If an unqual [unqualified] is standing around doing nothing, there's something wrong." He then told the MK3 to start radar navigating the boat out to sea. Remember, this is the boat engineer, not a deck rating.

This Saturday morning we were lucky to have one of those rare, but beautiful, almost cloudless, end-of-summer days on the Oregon coast. Along the river leading to the Pacific Ocean, a number of pleasure boats were moving about, some finding fishing locations, while others lay off the mouth of the river.

The MK3 crouched by the radar set near the coxswain at the right-hand piloting station. Her job was to safely navigate the boat out to sea, using only the radar. Soon, I heard her voice calling out: "Small boat ahead, 50 yards. Turn left, 10 degrees." At one point we seemed headed into some pilings. The training petty officer took over, told the coxswain to stop, and had the MK3 stand and look where we were heading.

"See where we're heading? Do you see how this looks on the

radar screen?" He then discussed with her how important it was to give accurate commands as well as other points. We then started again with the MK3 still radar navigating.

Leaving the Umpqua River station, you proceed out to sea on the left side of the channel in certain conditions, as the right tends to build high surf when seas are running. The radar navigation stopped, and the coxswain put the throttles forward as we cleared the channel. (I have a feeling the crew on the 44-footer, armed with cameras, wanted some "action" photographs of the boat rising high and plunging in the 8-foot ocean swells as we came out of the harbor.) When the bow of the boat first plunged toward the trough, I remember thinking: "Oh, oh. You forgot about how it feels to see that bow pointed downward and then to look upward as the boat rises to meet the next one." I recalled what a senior chief said about the boat plunging downward into the trough and wondering about whether you will come up again. Talk about Disney rides!

We slowed and the boat began an easy pitching and rolling. At least compared to an old 36-footer it proved an easy ride. In addition, I had a comfortable seat to relax in, something no one ever had on the old 36-foot motor lifeboats.

The towing setup on the 47-footer needs some explanation. On the 44-foot motor lifeboat, the towing bit is just aft of the coxswain's flat and the line handlers are easy to see. On the new 47-footer, however, the coxswain sits high in the boat, much like on a flying bridge of a large pleasure craft, while the towing line, bit, and line handlers are at a lower level and some distance away. This means communications between coxswain and crewmembers working the line must be accomplished with shouts.

Again, besides just towing, the MK3 needed practice with handling the tow line, and the nonrate had no experience at all in handling the lines needed to take a vessel under tow. One of the petty officers went aft to work with the nonrate and the MK3, while the training petty officer observed from above. We would be towed first.

The MK3, the nonrate, and the petty officer donned helmets and stood by on the bow to receive the 44's heaving line. The heaving line, a light line used to pass to a vessel, is then used to bring over the heavier towing line. To give weight for heaving, one end of the line is made into a knot known as a monkey's fist. Most sailors, however, know this isn't enough heft to make the line carry, so many people wrap the monkey's fist around a piece of lead about the size of a baseball. In my day, line handlers were always warned about not getting hit by the heaving line. On one cutter I sailed in, a popular "game" centered on the executive officer's car, which would be parked on the pier when the cutter returned to home port. The deck force contributed money to a pool to see which line handler would put the heaving line through the executive officer's car window and win the money. Even though there are now other devices not as heavy to get the line over, you never know what is in the heaving line, and helmets for line handlers are an excellent precaution.

If this drill were an actual case, the coxswain would radio the boat to be towed and clearly state what he intended to do. He would also give the skipper instructions on what the towed boat should do. The 44 made the approach to our boat. The person throwing the line stood in the well deck of the boat and prepared to throw. In drills and actual cases, all crewmembers feed information to the coxswain, including their movements. For example, when a crewmember goes to the well deck to throw the heaving

BMC Steve Huffstutler, officer in charge of the Frankfort, Michigan, station, explains to FA Carolyn Jones how to operate at a towing bit during a towing drill. *Dennis L. Noble*

line, there is a shout: "Going to the well deck!" In this drill, the line handler's shout to the coxswain carried over to our boat: "Putting over the line!" The 44-footer's coxswain shouted: "Put over the line!"

The line snaked out to the bow and then tangled into a heap and fell about halfway to our motor lifeboat. Immediately from our boat came the taunts of "Girl Scouts!" and other calls. With a sheepish look on his face, the heaving line thrower pulled in the line to cries of "Faster! Faster!" Again the line handler yelled to the 44 coxswain and again the line tangled, to even louder shouts. It took three tries for the new crewman on the 44 to get the line over. To be fair, throwing a heaving line from a rolling motor lifeboat and with a bulky Mustang on is not the easiest task to complete, especially if you have never done it before. The MK3 and nonrate, under the direction of the petty officer, finally rigged the tow line and we started the tow.

As we moved through the water at the end of the tow, I looked around and saw gulls wheeling in the air, pelicans swooping low to the waves, almost a clear blue sky, and plenty of pleasure fishing boats. And here were two boat crews out on a beautiful Saturday morning working. These thoughts were interrupted when one of the petty officers said, "Dr. Noble, you used to work on lifeboats. Why don't you pass the heaving line over to the 44 on our turn? We'll make them feel really bad." Left unsaid: They will feel bad because the gray-haired guy got it over to them. The coxswain entered into it. "Come on, Dr. Noble, I'll get us close enough so you can do it." Nice of him to help an old guy.

When we broke off from being towed and set up for our towing, in their concentration on setting up the lines, they completely forgot about me and the heaving line. Later, when it was too late, they remembered. Better to keep one's mouth closed and let them think I could do it than trying and getting the same ribbing.

The MK3 did most of the work with the line at the towing bit. From my position in the left-hand piloting seat, I could hear her voice carrying over the engine and sea noise: "One and a half turns on!" Which the coxswain shouted back: "One and a half turns, aye!" Then, "Two and a half turns on!" "Two and a half turns on, aye!" Then, "Paying out nicely!" Shortly afterwards, the coxswain shouted out, "Make it off!" To which the MK3 repeated the command and started to secure the line around the towing bit. Handling a thick towing line under the strain of a heavy boat on a rolling and pitching small boat is not easy. I watched from above as the MK3 worked the line, and I could see her short arms and stature were not helping at all. I could sympathize with her, remembering the difficulties I had because of shortness.

Once we were towing nicely, the training petty officer went below to the towing area. He then began to tell the MK3 what she was doing wrong as far as technique. He stressed to her how to safely flip the line onto the bit to lessen the danger of becoming entangled in it. "This is a fairly calm day [!], but in bad weather it can be dangerous. On the *Western* case [a fishing vessel], we burned up a line in the heavy weather. You have to stay alert." The training petty officer showed the MK3 once again how to handle the line. He then went up the ladder and, after talking to the 44 on the radio, started another tow situation.

Halfway through another part of the drill, the lookout tower reported via radio a small boat coming too close to the breakers on the right-hand side of the channel leading out to sea. At the coxswain's command, the MK3 threw off the tow line and, in a turn more like a speedboat, we heeled sharply over and the coxswain shoved the throttles all the way forward. The 47-footer wheeled around and came up to speed quickly. We sped to the location, spotted the boat, and told it to move to the other side of the channel and heave to.

We then came alongside the approximately 16-foot aluminum outboard. There were five people aboard—one adult and four children, none over the age of 16. The senior petty officer went to the bow of the 47-footer and called over to the boat owner. He told him to remain on this side of the channel and then asked him if he had lifejackets aboard. The owner had to rummage around to locate them. Meanwhile, the young people all were sitting with smirks on their faces.

We left, and, as the petty officer made his way up from the bow, the coxswain said, "We warn this group constantly and they continue to take risks. All for sport fishing." The other petty officer shook his head and said that he probably should have cited the operator for not having his lifejackets in an accessible location.

We then went over to near the entrance of the channel and started to do more work. This area proved how much the 47-footer could pitch and roll as the Pacific swells came into the channel. What followed next I pieced together on the way back into the station from various crewmen on the boat.

The nonrate began to become queasy from the motion of the boat. He then made the mistake of saying, apparently in the wrong tone, "Let's go in. I'm feeling bad." The senior petty officer then ordered the man to go to the lower steering area, which is completely enclosed, to learn the electronics of that station. While I am not exactly accusing the senior petty officer of doing something, there is nothing worse, I think, when feeling the first gut-wrenching pangs of seasickness than being in an enclosed compartment. Not long afterwards, the inevitable happened in the compartment and shortly thereafter the nonrate came topside and made a pale-faced quick movement to the stern, but not quite making it to the rail. Shortly thereafter the senior petty officer, after looking at the towing area in the stern, took over the coxswain position and began to back down into higher swells, using the seas to wash off some of the stern area. As I said, I am not accusing the senior petty officer of anything, but I did hear a snatch of conversation that sounded suspiciously like: "Maybe that will teach him to keep his mouth shut."

We eventually began the trip back to the station, with the MK3 back to radar navigation. The senior petty officer then went aft and told the nonrate to get up topside and watch and start to learn what radar navigation entails. Nearing the end of the drill, the senior petty officer broke the MK3 off her duties and again explained the importance of the radar navigator by beginning with the statement: "A short sea story." After the senior petty officer finished, the coxswain of the boat then reenforced that importance by beginning another short sea story about a navigator on the cutter he served in.

We finally backed into the slip at the station. The senior petty officer then mustered the crew on the stern of the 47-footer and gave them a debrief, pointing out things that needed to be corrected. He then turned to the nonrate and said, "I know you were sick and didn't feel like working, but you've either got to get some medicine for the seasickness or learn to work while you're sick." The crew then turned to scrubbing and washing down the boat, with the nonrate having to clean up the inside piloting station by himself. All total, we were underway approximately 3½ hours.

Remember, for most of the crew this training was on top of working their normal 8-hour day on Friday and then being out in the boat to close to midnight on a case. I should mention riding motor lifeboats is hard on the back and knees. Most lifeboat sailors who have served for a long time at the stations tend to have bad backs and knees. I know for many days after this drill I could feel my age.

The towing drill is only one among many the station crews must constantly practice. Two others include the man overboard drill and the survival swim in surf. At one station I rode a boat while the crew practiced the man overboard drill. Depending on

The Coast Guard's lifeboat sailors work closely with the "airdales," their aviator brethren. Here an HH-60 Jayhawk moves a rescue basket closer to a 47-foot motor lifeboat during a drill. *U.S. Coast Guard*

the type of boat, to help the coxswain in his maneuvering, the crewmen will shout out the location of the person in the water. For example, "At the first vent! At the first stanchion!" Thus, the crewman is not only there to pull the person out of the water, but also is another set of eyes for the coxswain.

One aspect of the drills must be emphasized. The nature of sea rescue work is inherently dangerous, therefore even drilling can be hazardous. Nowhere is this more graphically illustrated than in a drill that is constantly run between the small boats and the helicopters of the service's air stations, known as helo ops (operations).

Helo ops are run day and night, in calm weather and in seas of some size. Most civilians only see this operation in good weather, during demonstrations for the public. It is too bad there are no photographs showing this operation in rough seas, bad weather, or at night, when the potential dangers are easier to grasp. Picture being in a small boat, pitching and rolling, and there above you is a large, noisy machine slowly settling downward, closer and closer to you. As it descends, the wind from its main rotor begins to whip up the water, and you can see the spray rise as the machine moves toward you. The wind increases until it approaches hurricane force. Then the noise. Donning helmet and goggles, and usually wearing a bulky Mustang, you must work below the machine, or very close to under it. A boat crewman told me she hated the "way the spray kicked up from the rotor wash stung when it hit your face."

The helicopter approaches the small boat, and the pilot begins transmitting, via radio, to the boat a standardized procedures checkoff list used by the aviators for all at-sea hoists from small boats. In the only times I ever heard deviations from the litany, some pilots would say, "Okay, Boats" instead of "sir" or "captain" in an actual case.

The helo ops cover a number of things, including hoisting and lowering a rescue stretcher from the boat or lowering and hoisting a rescue swimmer from the helo. Some drills have the rescue swimmer jump into the sea, swim to the boat, and then be hoisted back aboard the machine. Most of the drills are routine, but the danger to both the helicopter and small boat crews is always present.

The status board on March 28, 1984, of the Grays Harbor

station indicated night helo ops with Coast Guard Air Station Astoria, Oregon. The 44-foot motor lifeboat arrived on location, about a quarter of a mile from the station, to begin working with the HH-3, helicopter number 1482. The schedule called for using a litter (a metal stretcher with sides) with a trail line, the line that crews on a boat use to guide the litter to the boat.

The pilot made his normal prehoist radio transmission, outlining what operations would take place. The boat crew put the litter on the front edge of the turtleback (the top of the back compartment). The 1482 came to a hover aft of the 44-footer. The boat crew hooked the wire hoist line dangling from the helo to the litter, and the hoist operator on 1482 engaged the hoist. The litter cleared the boat and moved up to the door of the machine. All perfectly routine. It is done on many nights when air stations and small boats drill together.

On the ninth hoist, the boat crew placed the litter on the forward part of the turtleback. With the trail line still coiled in the well deck, the litter slipped and fell into the well deck. The boat crew grabbed the litter and again placed it in the pickup location but had not properly stowed the trail line in the litter. The hoist operator, who guides the helicopter pilot by intercom radio over the people or objects for pickup, thought the boat crew was now ready for pickup.

The hoist operator conned the pilot over the litter and gave the hold command to the pilot. Once the 1482 came to hover, the operator engaged the hoist to take the slack out of the cable. Just then, the stern of the 44-footer dropped suddenly off a swell. The 1482's practice rescue gear became tangled on the 44-footer, and, when the motor lifeboat dipped, it started to drag the helicopter downward by its right side. The cable parted. The tension-released wire struck the main blades and again parted. At the same instant, the cable struck the right pitot static probe (gives air speed) and damaged the pilot's windshield. Another crewman assisting the hoist operator called immediately for the cable to be sheared and reported via the helicopter's intercom system a blade strike. The copilot activated his shear switch with no results and called out to the pilot for an immediate landing in the water. All of this happened quicker than it took to write this passage. Remember, of course, that this machine is hovering near the stern, probably about 15 feet above, of the 44-foot motor lifeboat.

The pilot somehow managed to make a no-hover landing in the water with the wheels down near the motor lifeboat, but with his blade still turning at 55 percent torque to stabilize the helicopter in the water. The HH-3 is an amphibious craft, but the seas were too rough for the machine to float, and there was a chance of the blades striking the swells. The pilot then made the decision that to shut down completely and have his crew try to make it into the sea was too dangerous. He chose to raise the 1482, and after a quick check, hover-taxied his aircraft to the helo pad at Grays Harbor. Upon shutdown, the pilot learned his hoist operator suffered a fractured arm from the cable parting. The hoist cable actually cut through portions of the main rotor. The 1482 suffered over $93,000 worth of damage, but, due to fine airmanship and luck, no one was killed.

The amount of training required by the crews of the small boat stations is almost overwhelming. If the primary mission of the small boat stations is search and rescue, then one can recognize the complaint by many boat crewmen that much of their time is taken up in "routine matters," such as preparing for an admiral's inspection, instead of working with their boats. One junior petty officer put it this way: "I think there are a lot of nonrates and petty officers who are disgusted and wasted because they don't get to practice what they know. We should at least be able to get underway and train more instead of doing just routine work." I can also sympathize with those who command the small boat stations. There are only 24 hours in the day. How do you get the underway time required to keep up proficiency in boatmanship when you also must train in law enforcement and pollution control? In addition, you must keep up boat maintenance, prepare for inspections, keep up the buildings, and have lectures on other subjects, such as career development, civil rights, and a host of other required topics. (Interestingly, I saw no evidence of any lectures on the history of the Coast Guard.) Even with a drill schedule of 6 days a week, it seems an almost impossible task, given that regulations state that you can drill in only certain weather conditions and given that this will always cut into the training schedule. Furthermore, headquarters decrees that you should only work crews a certain amount of time every week. The lack of time available is also graphically demonstrated in the daily routine aboard small boat stations.

chapter six

We Somehow Get the Job Done

1

A boatswain's mate second class receives a call from the local police department about a boat in the surf with a person aboard who refuses to come off the craft. "Boats" picks a nonrate to assist him, gives him the portable radio, and then departs in the station truck to survey the situation. The boatswain's mate is wearing his law enforcement equipment belt, which contains, among other items, a 9mm Beretta automatic and a telescoping metal baton.

The two Coast Guardsmen drive to the scene in the station's pickup. From the beach they see a sailboat with its mast cut off and with a small outboard engine. The boat is aground and is flopping back and forth in the surf. There are plenty of onlookers lining the beach, including local police officers.

The two Coast Guardsmen start to wade out into the surf. As the water begins to get deeper, the nonrate with the radio suddenly decides he does not really want to go in any farther and makes the excuse that he had better stay in shallow water to keep the radio from getting ruined by seawater.

The boatswain's mate, who is over 6 feet tall, continues to fight his way through the surf, the water well above his knees. He finally reaches the boat, extends his telescoping baton, and raps it on the hull. "U.S. Coast Guard!" he shouts. "You're going to have to come off the boat!"

Nothing happens.

Then, someone rushes out of the boat's cabin and leaps into the water, feet first, close to Boats. Boats is now staring at a man with an unkempt beard; his face is smeared with peanut butter and tuna fish.

In his hand is a large kitchen knife.

Boats tries to back up rapidly, stumbles and looses his baton. He tries to get the club so he does not have to depend only on his Beretta. As he tries to retrieve the baton, the man talks like there is someone else around.

"Why don't they just leave me alone?" says the strange person.

Finally, Boats retrieves his baton. He tells the man he will have to come with him to the beach. Boats is starting to worry he might have to use force on the man.

"The hand of God put me here," says the man, "and the hand of God will put me back to sea." With that, he climbs back onto the boat and goes into the cabin. Boats is not very enthusiastic about trying by himself to get what certainly appears to be a demented person out of a cabin against his will.

He wades back to the beach.

Boats asks for help from the police officers standing and watching on the shore. The police officers respond, "He's in the water. It's not our jurisdiction, so it's your case."

Worried, Boats starts back toward the boat. Of course, the tide is now coming in.

He reaches the boat and the water is now at his chest. Then he remembers training from another time that said to talk to people in their own language.

The man is again out of the cabin and shouting about the hand of God.

Boats remembers he has seen the man at a shopping center carrying a sandwich board with biblical quotes upon it. Boats then says to the man, "I'm a Christian like you. You know, God has put everyone here for a purpose. He put you here to let everyone know about the Bible."

"That's right."

"God put me here," continues Boats, "to take you off this boat, so that you can live and tell people about the Bible."

The man looks at Boats. Then he puts the knife on the deck, clambers over the side, and wades to shore with Boats. Boats tells the police officers, "Here he is, you can have him now." They again say no. So Boats borrows a cell telephone from an officer and calls a mission about a half hour's drive away. The mission will take the man, if someone can drive him to the location.

The local police, apparently not wanting additional paperwork, once again refuse to help.

A bystander by the name of Donald says he will take the man to the mission. Boats goes over to talk to the man.

By now the disturbed man is Boats's friend. Boats takes him over to the bystander and says, "Donald is put here to take you to the mission." The man goes without trouble. Later, the mission hires him as a part-time janitor and Bible teacher.

After relating this story to me, Boats admitted, "If I had known more about federal law enforcement then, I'd have ordered the local police to take the man." A pause. "Or, really pissed them off by commandeering their car."

2

"We received this call," a chief machinery technician told me, "that a boat was in trouble on the other side of the bay. We got underway in the 44-footer." This incident took place some time before the MK made chief petty officer. "You gotta bear in mind that, when most of what I tell you took place, the Group Commander had come down to a dock and could see everything happening."

This case soon became one of those no one at small boat stations appreciates—everything that can go wrong seems to go wrong.

"We started out across the bay. The wind and tide were workin' against us. We were in for a long run. A sheriff's department marine patrol decides to give us a hand. They are closer. Great. We may be able to bag this one.

"Then we get a call the sheriff's boat is in trouble.

"Next, some helicopters from, I think, the army are going to give us a hand. Guess what? One crashes. Ever get a feeling things may not be going to go so good?

"We are still plodding along, trying to get there. Then we get the word a Coast Guard 95-foot patrol boat is going to help us, as the boat who started all this is now nearing the surf line. The lieutenant jg who is in command of the patrol boat apparently thinks he is God's gift to boat handlers. Can you imagine? He decides to try to take the patrol boat *into the surf*!

"We arrive just as he's going in. I later talked to a guy who was on the bridge of the patrol boat. The surf was high and the water shallow. The guy on the bridge swore he could see bottom in the trough. The jg is backing down hard. I mean *hard*!

"Somehow the jg gets out of it.

"I don't remember now how, but we got the towing line in our screws and are being set into the beach. The jg is now gonna save us. Remember, the Group CO is watching everything.

"Apparently, the jg thought he would approach us on the crest of a swell and then somehow surf down the wave and come close enough to just casually hand the tow line over.

"Yeah, showing off.

"Well, he miscalculated. I looked up and all I could see was the black boot topping from the bottom of that 95-footer as it came down on us *from above*. I remember thinking: 'I'm gonna die. I'm gonna die.' The patrol boat hit the towing bit right behind the coxswain flat and drove us down into the water. It didn't hole the patrol boat.

"When everyone got things finally straightened out and our hearts started beating normally again, we eventually got back to the unit. The 95-footer tied up near us. When the jg got his boat secured, there was a message for him to report to the Group Commander. He was back in less than a half hour, packed his bags, and left. He was relieved that quick."

3

At another small boat station in the northern states, the radio watchstander hears a frantic call: "Coast Guard! You gotta come to the marina. There's a sea monster on my boat. Help me!" The boatswain's mate third class thinks, "I've got a live one here." A call is a call, so he drives in the station's vehicle over to the nearby marina. In the darkening evening, Boats sees a small crowd gathered near a sailboat. He walks up and asks who made the call.

The boat owner says, "I don't know what it was, but it looked scaly and had red eyes. It went down in my forward compartment. You have to get it out of there."

The owner doesn't look drunk, so Boats begins to wonder just what is down there. Everyone is watching him.

Boats takes a flashlight and starts into the compartment. To reach it he has to do a little crawling. He is moving *very* slowly through the dark and then he hears a rustling sound ahead of him. Boats stops, takes a deep breath, and switches on his flashlight.

A pair of red eyes shine out at him, followed by what can only be described as the rustling of scales.

There is some dispute as to who moved first or fastest. In any case, Boats emerges from the yacht's compartment breathing rapidly. People crowd around him. Boats uses his portable radio to call the station. He wants more Coast Guard people at the marina, and this time everyone had better have law enforcement gear. He is not sure what is aboard the boat.

By the time the backup from the station arrives, the media and state police have arrived. There is now a large crowd of people, some with cameras, on the dock. The senior petty officer now on the scene is trying to decide what to do next.

Suddenly, a man is running down the dock shouting, "Don't kill it! Don't kill it!"

"Kill what?" says the petty officer.

The man, without hesitation, leaps aboard the boat and comes out with an armadillo. He had sailed from Texas with the animal as a pet. It had gotten off the sailboat and looked for some place warm to hide.

4

The three incidents described above illustrate the diversity of what can happen almost on a daily basis at a small boat station. I recall the words of one petty officer who had the OOD: "The most consistent thing about this duty is its inconsistency." With all the duties and training at a small boat station, perhaps a diverse routine should not come as a surprise. In addition, the stations represent a part of the community and many times are treated much like a friendly, helpful neighbor you do not hesitate to ask for favors, knowing he will oblige you. This is an aspect of the small boat stations I do not believe officers in Coast Guard headquarters quite grasp. Despite all of the training and happenings at a unit, routine work, such as painting and cleaning, must be accomplished. One senior chief said, "Somehow we manage to get the job done."

At many units, the routine workday begins as it did 40 years ago, when I served at a station: reveille, followed by morning cleanup. Some of the units do their boat checks before breakfast, and the early morning silence is broken by the sounds of engines revving up and horns and sirens being tested, as the boat crews run through their standardized checkoff lists.

Breakfast and all other meals still remind me of the Old Guard, with a few exceptions. There is still the same bantering at the table. As one petty officer put it: "The main conversation at meals seems to center on sex, food, and body functions. And no one cuts the cook any slack." Most units I visited subscribed to at least one newspaper, and the crews, like many Americans, read the newspaper during breakfast. I thought most people at the units would, as in my day, turn to the sports page. Indeed, a great many did just that and many talked about hunting or fishing. At more than one unit, however, some petty officers turned to the financial pages and a few nonrates could talk about investments quite knowledgeably. I do not believe the nonrates had the wherewithal to invest but were biding their time until they reached the petty officer level and earned more money. One BM1 gave me a very good briefing on why to invest in futures. I know I never heard talk like that around the table in the old Guard.

Before proceeding with describing the daily routine, I have two observations to make concerning the units. At no station did I see any evidence of a library for the crew. There were large-screen television sets, pool tables—I have never seen a Coast Guard small boat station without a pool table—and video games, but no evidence of a library. Some units had a few paperback books on a shelf, and one unit had a dated encyclopedia set. Very few stations even had a good collection of books on the history of the Coast Guard. The few stations that did usually kept the volumes in the commanding officer's office. (The COs would loan out the books to anyone who wanted to read them.) At many of the stations I visited, crewmembers would ask if I could recommend books on the service.

Forty years ago there were a total of two items on the walls of the two main buildings that made up my station: a framed chart of Lake Michigan and a framed copy of the Uniform Code of

Military Justice (UCMJ). When, as a young boot, I asked why the UCMJ was on the wall, the chief replied, "So you know what they can hang you for." Those two items were the only decorations in the entire station. The walls were painted in accordance with the *Paint and Color Manual*. One of the more pleasant surprises I found in the new Guard is the decor of the units. Framed historic photographs, photographs of the boats assigned to the unit, charts, prints, and other items line the walls. The stations are also painted in a friendlier color scheme. In other words, sometime between 1960, when I left small boat stations, and 1996, when I began this project, someone decided there were actually people living in the stations and perhaps it might be a good idea to provide them with a more pleasing environment.

The next event after breakfast is usually morning muster and colors. At my former unit, we would finish breakfast, cleanup and sit around talking until 8:00 A.M., and then wander into the dayroom. Remember, there were perhaps eight of us. In the dayroom, the BMI or chief would tell us what he wanted us to do for that day, unless we were working on a long-term project, such as a large painting job. Every so often, we would stand on the porch and salute for morning colors. I never understood why we performed the salute when we did, other than that perhaps the chief wanted to break the normal routine.

At most of the units I visited, muster would be held before morning colors. Some of the units had a semiformal type of muster. That is, everyone in the deck department would stand in one location, and the engineers would stand in another location. At the Yaquina Bay station, Amber, the unit's German shepherd mascot, would walk up to everyone at muster and sniff them. This took place at every muster. I wonder if this is a better system than calling names. Other units were formal, with the station complement arranged in divisions and at attention and with the senior people saluting and reporting on their divisions—a far cry from my days. Yet other units were relaxed and everyone sat in chairs on the mess deck.

In all cases, the musters are used to pass information. At some stations, the times of high and low tides and ebbs are given, along with forecasted weather and weather warnings. I found it interesting to note that, in almost every case, the commanding officer or executive officer asked if there were any questions. I do

Most small boat stations do their own boat maintenance. At a Florida station, a 41-foot utility boat is hauled out for work. *U.S. Coast Guard/PA3 Scott Carr*

not believe we were ever asked if we had any questions on any-thing at my former unit. After colors, it is time for the station to "turn to."

The daily routine includes training, as detailed in Chapter 5. The work required to maintain the boats and the station must somehow be squeezed in between training. Because of the number of duties to cover, many units contract out some work, such as cutting the grass. But others do not have the budget to do so. In my time, I can recall many times going to the garage, where we stored much of our paint, watching the senior seaman mix up what we needed for the day, grabbing a bucket and brush, and starting in to paint. Sailors are always battling rust, hence the constant need for painting. Today, crewmembers at some units usually put on a respirator before even opening up a can of paint. Many units use disposable paint brushes to stop the former practices of cleaning brushes. In my day, when we were finished painting, we would go back to the garage, get rid of our excess paint, and then clean our brushes by hand in a bucket of diesel fuel. Once they were clean, we would then shake the brushes out on the ground until they were dry. When the brushes were too old to use, we would throw them into the trash. I do not remember what we did with the old diesel fuel, but I suspect someone dumped it on the ground.

At one of the first stations I visited, I watched a crew working on one of their motor lifeboats, preparing it for painting. In my day, you would receive some sandpaper and handscraping tools and go to it. There would be a rush to grab the only radio at the unit. The first one to get it determined the type of music you would listen to as you worked. The engineers usually listened to country music, which the deckies could not stand. Whoever won the grab, the rest of the group would constantly harp on "who wants to listen to that

All sailors know how to paint. *U.S. Coast Guard/PA3 Scott Carr*

crap?" One of my sources at a station told me engineering still likes country music, at least at his unit.

In today's Coast Guard, I watched people get into long coveralls, secured tightly by the neck, arms, and legs, before sanding boats. They will then get something to cover their hair, then don a respirator and goggles, then cover any other skin that might be exposed. (We worked in our dungarees, with our sleeves rolled up, if it was warm enough.) The crews today then obtain power sanders and wire brushes and go to work. They must be careful that no paint or dust gets into the water. (We would brush our dust and chips off into the water, if it was convenient.) Radios or CD players still put out music in the work spaces. It is strange sounding music to my old ears, however.

At some stations on the West Coast, crewmen are up at first light to check the bar. On the first day of this project, I heard the bar patrol awakened at 4:30 in the morning and then the OOD told them they were being diverted to a tow job. I heard mumbling through the thin walls, and apparently someone asked what the name of the boat was. "*What*? We just towed him in last week." This proved to be a very long tow and by 8:30 in the evening the boat still had not returned to the station.

At times during this project, I wondered how any work could be finished at a station. For example, at one unit every boat was out on cases by 2:30 in the afternoon, and then a petty officer departed the station by truck to help nearby park rangers with an unconscious woman in a campground.

The petty officer helping park rangers illustrates how many civilians view the role of the small boat rescue stations. One East Coast MK3 told me he was at work one morning in the engine room of the motor lifeboat when a shipmate yelled that they had piped him to the office on the double. The MK3 is a qualified EMT. When he arrived, he found a woman and her daughter in the office, with the older woman showing all the signs of a heart attack. The EMT managed to stabilize her and get an ambulance and civilian EMTs to the station. The MK3 then returned to his work in the engine room. What is interesting is the daughter saw the sign to the Coast Guard station and turned in there for help with her mother.

At a West Coast unit I watched an elderly woman from the local historical society come to the OOD and ask if he could find some volunteers to help an older member of the society move from her house to an apartment, apparently because she could not afford movers and had no family in the area. I watched three real volunteers, not ones assigned, help the woman. Each had their electronic beepers in case the station needed them. What this indicates is that the stations continue the tradition set in the old U.S. Life-Saving Service days. In those days, and in many cases today, the stations were looked upon as *our* stations, not some far-off entity in Washington, D.C.

It would present a false picture if I gave the impression there was no friction between the small boat stations and the civilian community. At one unit, for example, a couple moored their sailboat near the haul-out for the station, where all the major work is done on the unit's boats. The couple complained long and loudly that the commercial radio the crew played was disturbing them, so there was no more music for the troops. At another unit, a civilian watched with a spotting scope to make sure no dust or paint chips got into the water. One commanding officer put it this way: "How people feel about this station depends on which hat I am wearing. If I have on my lifesaver and community leader hat, everyone loves us. If I put on my law enforcement hat, especially when dealing with fisheries, then it is a different story." In other words, people love the stations when they help out in the community and save lives, but it is a different story when the Coast Guard is perceived as a police officer on the water. A petty officer at another unit summed it up nicely: "Sometimes the station gets a chief petty officer who wants nothing to do with the locals. Perhaps he stresses law enforcement overly much. The community sort of shrugs and says, 'This too will pass,' and waits for the next officer-in-charge who will want to be a part of the community." In the long run, however, the stations do represent a closer tie to the local community than almost any other federal government entity. Yet, when one commanding officer tried to explain to headquarters the amount of time he spent on community projects, he was told, "Just tell them no." The commanding officer said to me, "Doesn't headquarters realize we are a part of the community?"

The duty sections are changed at some point in the daily routine. Duty rotation varies. At one unit, the oncoming section worked 2 days and then had 2 days off, with an entire weekend every other week. Some units have everyone aboard on a certain day to accommodate training for the entire station.

The daily routine continues, with training and work somehow squeezed into the mix. This is really no different than it was during my few years at a small boat station.

No matter how much work there is to do at a unit, calls always come first. BM1 Richard Belisle, then stationed at Tillamook Bay station, told me of a case he remembers as a boot seaman apprentice at Seattle, Washington. This entails one of the more gruesome aspects of duty on a small boat station, one recruiters do not advertise. The station received a call from a woman reporting a dead body floating under a pier. Many of the piers in Seattle run a long distance out over the water. The station's utility boat, with SA Belise and three others, got underway and proceeded to the location.

"By the time we arrived, the tide had come in and there was no room for the boat to go under the pier," recalled Belise. "Someone would have to swim under the pier, tie a line to the body, and tow it out. The coxswain turns to us and said, 'Rate check!'

"This was a new term for me. I soon found out what it meant.

"The coxswain was a BM2. The engineer was an MK3 and the other crewmember was an SN. With me being only an SA, guess who went under the pier?"

While cases have priority over daily work, just getting to the boats can sometimes be an adventure. Retired BMC Glen Butler, former executive officer at the Yaquina Bay station, told me how things used to be at the unit. The barracks and administration offices of the station sit atop a bluff at least a hundred feet above the boat docks. Previously, to reach the boathouse you ran down a very steep stairway. Chief Butler said when the alarm rang, "you would run down the stairs as fast as possible, holding onto the rail. You didn't hold onto the rail to steady yourself. It was for bailing out. You'd be going down the stairs and hear an 'Oh, shit!' and someone behind you would stumble and fall. You'd grab the rail, roll over it, and watch the guy rolling down the stairs, then roll back over the rail and continue on down, jump on the boat, and, when underway, call the watchstander and tell him there was someone lying at the bottom of the stairs."

Since that time, a gradual set of steps has been cut diagonally across the bluff. But it still takes concentration to run down the stairs, as I observed one day at the unit while I walked down to the boats. The SAR alarm rang and I scurried up onto some rocks, knowing people were not going to be polite when reacting to the alarm. I heard the thump of boots and soon saw the crew hurrying down the stairs, their eyes downward, concentrating on the steps as they went.

At the station at Ocean City, Maryland, Barney—for Barnacle—the large Labrador mascot of the station, in his younger days proved interesting for those running to the dock. When the alarm rang, Barney would nip at the last person in the line running to the boat. One crewman told me he happened to be last one time and "Barney was nipping me in the ass all the way. I kept yelling, 'Barney, I'm going as fast as I can!'"

Barney only goes as far as the ramp leading to the dock. Interestingly, Barney does not like boats. One crewman told me: "The last thing you see when you pull out on a case with an alarm is Barney standing by the ramp. And the first thing you see when you come in is Barney waiting for you."

Perhaps this is the time for a few words about Barney, who became a legend in his own time. In his younger days, Barney did not like anything flying onto his station. He would stalk seagulls, creeping much like a cat, and would pounce at them when close enough. His greatest defense from invaders from the air, however, came when the watchstander received a call from a Coast Guard helicopter trying to land at the station. "Would you come out and get your dog? He won't let us land," came the pilot's voice over the radio. Every time the machine approached, Barney would be under it, barking.

Before Barney made a special trip to the vet, he managed to get the mayor's dog pregnant. This caused the official to become angry. The mayor told the commanding officer to get rid of the dog. At muster, the crew learned of the mayor's demand. The commanding officer said, "We'll get rid of Barney. From now on call him Fred until the mayor gets over this."

When a new commanding officer's wife visited the station for the first time, in full view of the crew, Barney walked up to her and stuck his head up her skirt. Barney goes into a barking routine when he sees anyone in uniform with shoulder boards—denoting an officer's rank—come aboard the unit. When I visited Ocean City, Barney had reached old age and, like others who reach the twilight of their career, wanted to rest a great deal. He would go out for a run, but only when one woman stationed at the unit appeared in civilian clothes. Then he would get his leash and carry it in his mouth to the woman. She and Barney went for a short run, with the woman carrying the leash. The city has a leash law that applies to all dogs, except Barney. Everyone knows him in the local area. I noticed Barney would not go to his bed at night unless everyone at the station had turned in for the night. One observer noted that, if you are accepted by Barney, the crew will accept you. In fact, some of the crew of Ocean City seemed more excited about Barney appearing in a book than seeing themselves in print.

It would be inaccurate if I portrayed stations as constantly busy, with nothing but work and cases and no rest. Most stations have a busy season and a slower one. In some areas, such as in Florida, it is constantly busy, and there are as many cases of law enforcement as there are of rescues. In fact, sometimes more.

It is instructive to listen to the crew during busy and slow periods. When it is busy, there tends to be less griping. The slower the times, the more information you can "dig" out of crewmembers.

There are always inspections. One commanding officer informed me he had undergone five in 6 months. Preparing for inspections, as any veteran will tell you, takes up time. I visited one station just after the new district commander's first visit, so I heard a great deal of grousing about the event. One woman said, "They called us in off liberty so we could paint everything." Her shipmate said, "We even painted over rust, just so we had fresh paint on it." At another station, the crew had to polish the station's rain gutters for an admiral's visit.

One of the complaints I heard most often during the working routine by petty officers second class and above was: "What are they teaching them in boot camp these days?" One BM1 said, "They should start teaching more seamanship in boot camp. These boots get here and hear a fisherman on the radio saying they have a line in their wheel [propeller], and they think he is talking about a wheel on a car.

"Guess what? On their practical factors, they do not have to know how to do an eye splice in a line, but they must know how to handle stress. And they certainly know their rights."

Many of the complaints are probably the normal ones received from experienced people looking at people who have no experience, forgetting that at one time someone probably said the same thing about them. I will admit that people going to basic training appear to be treated entirely different than they were in my day. As mentioned before, you now are allowed to "drop out" of boot camp. At the time of the writing of this book, however, the Coast Guard seemed to be reacting to complaints from the field about boot camp in the way of all bureaucracies—they are thinking of forming a group to look into the matter.

A constant sarcastic refrain from everyone at the stations except the newest people from boot camp, is: "This is a kinder, gentler Coast Guard." One petty officer told me: "In your day you could tell some guy who has screwed up to go clean heads [toilets] after duty. Nowadays, you have so much paperwork when you deal with people that many petty officers do not want to go through the hassle. These new people may not know much about seamanship, but they certainly know their rights."

I found an interesting convergence of the new Guard and superstition at more than one small boat station. A BM3 at one unit, for example, told me she ran into problems with the old superstitious fishermen whenever she drew boarding duty. Most of the old-time fishermen in her area think a woman on a vessel is bad luck. The boatswain's mate said that once she had just started stepping off the rigid hull inflatable boat and onto a fishing vessel when the skipper put the engine ahead and the motion threw her back into the RHIB. The fisherman did not want a woman on his boat.

The case of the woman boatswain's mate reflects one of the major changes from my days at small boat stations over 40 years ago. In my time, most stations were crewed by white males. In today's Coast Guard, there is diversity. In over 20 years of active duty, I met very few Latinos. At almost every station I visited in researching this book, there were Latinos, African-Americans, Hawaiians, and other ethnic groups. Forty years ago no women served at a small boat station. When I asked one male commanding officer how women were working out at stations, he indignantly responded: "Women are now at the stations and working as a part of the crew. Why talk about it?" This is a commendable attitude but dodges the issue. My observations, in fact, indicate that women are well integrated into the crews. I saw no real effort to treat them any differently than men. There is, however, a subtle undercurrent at many stations. One male commanding officer stated that women "didn't have the upper body strength to do the job." When I asked a female BM3 about women not being able to, say, throw the heaving line the pre-scribed distance, her response was that "if a woman cannot com-plete the boat crewman qualifications, then she should not be on the boat, just like a man failing the quals." However, a captain in headquarters said that, if the qualifications are too difficult, perhaps they should be lowered.

Returning to the working day, sometime around 4:00 P.M. the crew stops the normal working day routine. If there is a great deal of work left after evening chow at 5:00 P.M., the duty crew goes back to work. At one unit, the station had been busy preparing a motor lifeboat for painting and had also been handling assistance cases during routine working hours, so the duty crew kept working until midnight. They were still required to awaken again at reveille at 6:30 and work their normal hours the next day. If there had been a case in the night, the ready boat crew, who were among the workers, would have been out on the case.

What I observed at a semi-isolated station will be instructive. A seaman took over the communications watch at 7:30 in the morning. He had a short relief for lunch at 12:00 and then went back on watch until 4:00 in the afternoon. After supper at 5:00, he donned work clothes and worked until 10:00 at night to prepare the motor lifeboat for painting. Again, if there had been an SAR case, he would have had to stop his work and respond, or, if it had occurred after 10:00, he would have had to get out of bed and go on the boat.

To limit crew fatigue, headquarters has set a time limit crews can be underway. Commanding officers are to use a formula that takes into account boat type and weather. For example, maximum underway hours a crew on a motor lifeboat can be expected to work in seas greater than 4 feet is 8 hours, and then the crewmem-ber must be given 10 hours rest-recovery time upon completion of the mission. One chief said he remembered when, as a BM3, he was so tired he would just about go to sleep at the wheel. I heard a BM2, after he returned at 9:00 in the morning from a case that began around 10:00 the previous night and that entailed crossing a rough bar, say, "This is the first time I've been so tired I had to turn the wheel over to someone else for a short time." I recalled how tired his voice sounded at 5:00 in the morning when he radioed his position report.

A 1991 study of the stations brought attention to the large number of hours station people worked. Since then, headquarters has initiated programs to reduce hours. This is discussed in more detail in Chapter 9. Suffice it to say, the majority of people at the stations still remark how tired they are when they go off duty. One woman said, "The district says they want to stress family. I am so tired when I come off duty that I must sleep most of my first day. Then they go and recall us for painting and getting ready for an admiral's inspection."

If there is no pressing work to be done at stations with enough people in the duty section and the weather allows it, the standby boat crew is allowed to go home, subject to immediate recall. The electronic age of beepers and cell telephones have allowed such an arrangement. At a number of stations I visited, the standby crews were recalled because of cases in progress—once the ready crew is underway, the standby crew is recalled.

Evening hours on duty are somewhat the same as in my day, but with some very large differences. The first difference I noticed at some stations is families coming to the station for the evening meal. One unit kept a child's highchair on the mess deck.

Another feature of most evening routines is the physical workouts of the crewmembers. Every unit had at least a weight room and some had very good exercise machines, such as treadmills and stair steppers. Many played basketball or other sports in the evening and at lunch time.

In my time, recreational resources were limited. With no more than six people in a duty section, it was difficult to have any type of team sports. The entire recreational gear at my station consisted of one tired basketball, one pool table, and one television set. The television set was located in the room where the pool table sat and, because of the lack of room, it proved difficult to watch television and play pool at the same time, so we did one or the other. Every station I visited still had a pool table. (Warning: never play pool with anyone who has spent a few years at a small boat station.) Little attention was paid to exercise.

The focus of the Coast Guard's physical fitness effort today is weight loss. "The quickest way to get out of the Coast Guard," said a chief, "is to be overweight. We had a guy who we were trying to get out on a psychological discharge. We had to spend months documenting, documenting, and documenting. At the same time, we had another guy who wanted out and he got 5 pounds over-weight and refused to loose it. He was out immediately. There was another man here who wanted to stay in, was a good worker, liked the Coast Guard, but he just could not control his weight. He was not allowed to reenlist. Sure seems wrong sometimes."

At almost every station I visited, a large-screen television set and comfortable chairs and couches sat either in a recreation deck or in a television room. What amazed me was that, for the most part, the sets were rarely used. Many times the crew had their own sets in their rooms, so they preferred to retreat to a private place. However, during special sporting events, such as the Super Bowl, the television rooms are crowded. In many of my visits, the rooms remained unused because the crew had to work late into the night. The large-screen television is used mostly for training videos.

Another aspect of duty days remains constant: studying. In order to be promoted, enlisted people must take correspondence courses in their field and pass the end-of-course examinations. Other enlisted people take college-level correspondence courses for credit toward a degree. At one station that I visited four times, I noted a machinery technician who, when not working, always had a book in front of him. On my last visit, the man informed me he had just passed the college-level proficiency test (CLEP) for sociology. At another station, a woman and her shipmate were helping each other in a homework assignment for a physics class at a nearby community college.

One interesting aspect of duty at small boat stations is the diversity of some extracurricular tasks placed upon the units. At two stations I visited, for example, one conducted a school for boating safety and another helped transport archaelogists to a dig. Included in the variety of extra duties are the number and range of questions the people at the small boat stations receive. At one unit, within 1 hour the communications watchstander received the fol-lowing questions by radio, telephone, or in person: What are the fishing limits in Alaska? When do the birds begin to flock at a nearby point? Is it against the law to shine a fishing vessel's halogen lights into the windows of a person's house? Can I have a tour of the station and nearby lighthouse? The number and variety

The crews of the small boat stations are called upon to do a variety of duties. Here, BM3 Chris Tinley (right) of the Marathon, Florida, station assists a Florida wildlife rescue worker move a 10-foot pygmy sperm whale stranded in shallow water. *U.S. Coast Guard/*Lt(jg) *Rich Condit*

of questions fielded reminded me of a reference desk at a public library.

Not all of the incidents small boat stations respond to are life-threatening. Take, for example, two cases at Cape Disappointment. A coxswain told me that, while returning from a patrol to the dangerous Columbia River bar, he looked out, did a double take, and then called the lookout tower. "Do you see what I see?" Making his way out of the Columbia River was a fisherman in a float-casting outfit—an inner tube with waders attached—and with a small outboard engine attached, ready to do battle with the fish.

Another boatswain's mate said they spotted a pontoon boat, basically built for lakes, sheltered waters, and rivers, with a barbecue smoking, and a small outboard engine, making its way toward the bar. Aboard were a man and a woman. The BM pulled alongside the craft and tried to explain to the man the dangers of proceeding out to sea in such a craft. Boats recognized he was getting nowhere with the man, but the woman seemed nervous.

Finally, the BM said loud enough for the woman to hear, "I can't stop you, but in about 2 hours the tide is going to be coming in so fast your engine won't be able to handle it. The waves will be kicking up so much you will have to stand on top of the barbecue to keep dry. If we have to tow you, you'll have to come off the craft and the thing will be damaged. But, hey, do what you want and have a nice day."

The woman's eyes grew larger and larger as Boats did his talk.

The Coast Guard boat pulled away. Boats watched as he moved toward the bar. The pontoon boat turned and the woman was going at the man, with her finger wagging in his face.

There is nothing that focuses the attention of the people aboard a small boat station more than a radio call that begins "Mayday"—the international signal for distress. Very shortly after a Mayday call the alarm will sound and the crew will race toward the ready boat. At another station, a boatswain's mate told me of a pleasure boater who, the first time he used the radio, called the Coast Guard beginning with "Mayday," which brought about the inevitable reaction from the station's crew. Using the questions found on the standard work sheets for radio watchstanders, the Coast Guardsman on watch determined the boater thought "Mayday" was how you began any call to the Coast Guard.

At night at some stations, the communications watch is secured at 10:00 P.M. and the Group handles the radio traffic. The person on watch at this time usually sleeps either in the radio room or next to a telephone. The watchstander is expected to answer any telephone calls. If someone calls the station by radio, the Group will respond. If the station needs to be alerted, the Group radio watchstander will call the station by telephone. The people who stand this watch—usually called the "sleeper"—do not sleep deeply. One woman called it dozing. The radio is kept on, and, because they are not in deep sleep, most watchstanders told me they usually hear their station being called even though the Group responds. In the incident at Quillayute River that opened this book, the call from the sailboat in distress, the *Gale Runner*, occurred during a "sleeper" watch. Tape recordings of the radio conversations show that the watchstander, FA Jon DeMillo, awoke when the boat called and had information for the Group's radio watchstander when she called. The live watch begins again at various times in the early morning hours. In my time, mainly because of the technology then available, a live watch was maintained 24 hours a day, even when the channel was clogged with ice and the lifeboat could not be launched.

Even with the radio watch secured, sometimes there still is a special need to keep someone awake at night. At some units I visited, a member of the crew had to stay awake at night either at the station or in the tower to watch for suspected drug-smuggling vessels entering and leaving a harbor at night. Enlisted Coasties are known to make up unusual titles for their operations. This one was called a "secret squirrel watch."

I believe there is a subtle undercurrent circulating within the service that has made its way to the civilian community to make people believe the small boat stations are unimportant. Whether deliberate or unintentional, the current is there. One of the problems with this undercurrent is that it has been in place so long that even the people at the stations now believe it. This is too bad, because there have always been amazing stories about the units, if one is willing to believe enlisted people have stories to tell and are willing to ask questions and to listen.

For example, there is the story of the mascot of the Yaquina Bay station at Newport, Oregon. While visiting the station, I asked who had named the dog? There were at least three Coasties sitting in the communications room when I asked the question. "Oh, she was found on the beach after the loss of the *Amber Dawn*."

"Yeah, I remember that case," said BM3 Gary Clark. According to official records, in the evening hours of December 6, 1994, the fishing vessel *Amber Dawn II* attempted to make the harbor at Newport, Oregon, during a fierce winter storm. When the Yaquina Bay Coast Guard station learned of the master's decision to try crossing a rough bar, the station posted lookouts in the tower and at an observation point to monitor the vessel's inbound transit. (The Coast Guard in the 13th District can close the bar to recreational craft but not to commercial vessels.) During the attempt to cross the bar, the *Amber Dawn II* capsized, and the four fishermen aboard were lost. This is how Petty Officer Clark remembers the incident:

"We didn't actually see him go over. The visibility was really bad. The wind was blowing really hard—60 to 70 knots, hailing, rain—you could just see the mast lights of the vessel. You couldn't see the breaks on the bar very much.

"We were watching the *Amber Dawn* come in from about the whistle buoy. BM1 Jake N. Albinio, the surfman, and I were on the north side of the parking lot. [The parking lot is a 2-minute drive from the station.]

"Then you could see the first breaker come and swallow him up. You could see his halogen lights on his mast swallowed up. After that, all you heard was him screaming on the radio, 'Help me! Help me! I've lost a crewman over the side!' We saw him turn around. We don't know if he was turning to get out of the breaks or to get his buddy who got swept over the side. That was the last thing he ever said on the radio.

"We went flying back to the station.

"The three of us in the beach rig were on first boat and we went runnin' down to the dock and jumped on the *Victory*, the 52-foot motor lifeboat, and got out to the tips of the jetty. Once we got out there, you could see the helo out by south reef tellin' us we had to get in there, these guys were in a lot of trouble.

"We had to wait for 10 or 15 minutes for a second boat to get out there. There was no way we were going to cross by ourselves. [The second boat provides a backup in case of trouble.]

"It was easily breaking 20 to 25 feet. Just solid all the way. Just lines of them. Usually in the winter time, we'll get a good storm and you'll get rows of breakers across the bar three or four deep, that's about it. About three or four rows of breaks outside the tips of the jetty and then big peaked swells. That night it was just solid breaks all the way out to the whistle buoy, which is well over a mile from the tips. Just solid. Just a solid pipeline. Then, from our whistle buoy to Alsea Bay, about 10 miles, it was huge rollers. It kept on hailing.

"The second boat showed up, and we went across the bar. We got out to about where number 1 buoy sits. We stopped for a little while. Jake said he didn't think he had steering. We tested the steering. Everybody was gettin' nervous as hell. What happened, something down below had shifted and hit our automatic pilot and turned our rudders off, and the automatic pilot was trying to drive the boat. So we rectified that real quick.

"We shot off some parachute flares, because once we got out around the whistle buoy, we couldn't see anything. We didn't want to go into the reef, because, I think, if we had gotten in there, we wouldn't have gotten out. If it was breaking 25 feet in good water,

"It was outrageous inside the reef." *CWO F. Scott Clendenin*

it was just outrageous inside the reef. There was debris and crabpots everywhere. This guy was pretty well loaded down with his gear when coming across. We didn't know how many people were on board or what we were lookin' for.

"We did a surf line search. We ran parallel to the beach outside the surf line. This put us broadside to the surf.

"Everybody on the boat, except Jake and me, was seasick. Jake just strapped a couple of the guys into the deck. He sent the engineer below in the foul weather flat to strap himself in. I climbed up on top of the coxswain flat and strapped myself into the mast base. I grabbed two spotlights and sat up there for hours. Lookin' for crabpots. Lookin' for anything with the spotlights.

"It got kinda spooky near the end. You couldn't see the breaks comin', but you could hear 'em and they'd break just inside of you, like 50 to 60 feet from you, maybe a couple hundred yards. After awhile, you'd start wonderin' if the next one was goin' to hit you. Take you out and you'd be inside the reef floatin' around with these guys.

"We searched, I think, for a few hours. I don't remember what time we came back across the bar. The inbound approach was

The *Amber Dawn II* Case

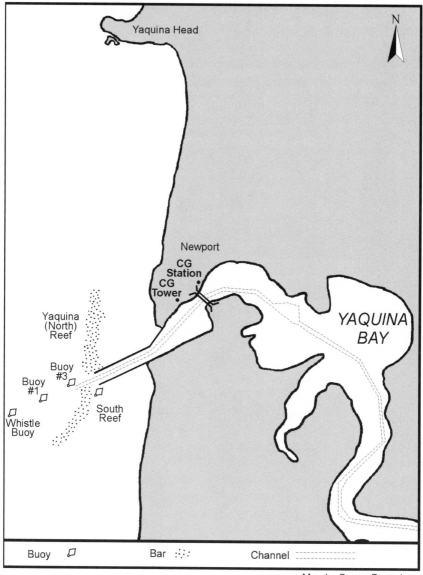

Map by Susan Browning

really scary. We started comin' in. Couldn't see the series. Couldn't really tell where you were at, but you could see the jetty tips. We had the helo flyin' around and they were tryin' to light up everything for us. Even with them and that big searchlight, we still couldn't get a real good time on the series. By the time they could get it lit up, it was too late. It was already on top of you.

"We got down between buoy 3 and the tips. We timed it wrong. We were right in the middle of the series. I remember sitting so low in the trough one time I couldn't even see the helo anymore. There was nothin' but green water comin' up over the stern.

"So, Jake powered around and came around to port, and it hit just as we were gettin' around beam to. It hit us so hard it spun us around 180 degrees and we surfed in. On the 52, it doesn't tend to roll like the 44s do. It's so heavy and designed to take the surf and white water. We surfed in straight in across the tips. We called the 44-footer, who was in center channel, to get the hell out of the way we're comin' in and we're not stoppin'. [Officially, at 0047 the 52-footer made it safely across the bar and at 0106 the motor lifeboat moored at the station.]

"We got inside and Jake pretty much just collapsed. The whole crew was shot. We were all just drained emotionally and physically. Just wasted.

"It was really a bad case. Everything you're trained to do. Everything we thought we're so proficient at, you couldn't do anything in the situation no matter if we'd been sittin' on that bar. Later, a lot of people around town questioned, 'Why weren't you guys out there when it came across?' It was so bad, I could've been 6 feet from that boat and not be able to do a thing.

"We got in and slept for about 2 hours and went back out again at first light, and it was the same thing. Absolute chaos. Breaks. I mean for 10 miles down the coast. We searched for about another 6 hours and didn't find anything. During the night, a couple of bodies had washed up on the beach that the beach crew found.

"We came back in and got relieved. I think they continued to search throughout the next night. When I came back on duty, it was like a changed area. It was glass. It was flat, so we went inside the reef and found where the diesel oil was all bubbling up just about where number 4 buoy sits. Two days later the whole boat washed up on the beach.

"Strange case, because this guy had been fishin' this bar for

35 to 40 years and this time did not make it. Everybody in town knew him. He had a real big family. His second mate was well liked, so it was pretty tough. That was the last fishin' boat we've lost on this bar. It was rather quick. It's amazing how fast it happened.

"It was tough on a lot of the guys in our crew. We were so pumped up. We hadn't lost anybody in a long time. Saved all these people and then, bam! All you've trained for and all the equipment and you can't do a damned thing. Just sat there.

"Lookin' back on it now, it was real excitin'. At the time, you were so scared, pumped up, you just reacted to everything you're trained to do. You didn't even think, you just did it. Probably the worse case I've ever been on, as far as conditions.

"I was extremely happy I was on the 52 and not the 44. I think it would have chewed up the 44 and spit it out, it was that bad. If we'd been hit by that break comin' in with the 44, we'd've easily rolled three times.

"It made me realize we weren't invincible. Not always the good guys. We can't save everyone. It tore a lot of people at the station up. Beach crews had a real hard time with it, because the families were there when they retrieved the bodies. Half the town was there. There was maybe a thousand people on the beach. Took me a while to get over it.

"It did give me more confidence in the *Victory*. She's a good old girl. She brought me home that night and never complained. Took it out 2 hours later and pushed it for another 6 hours. Hopefully they won't get rid of them before I leave the stations."

After the loss of the *Amber Dawn II*, Coast Guard beach patrols found an abandoned German shepherd puppy. They took it back to the station and named it Amber after the fishing vessel they had tried to help. Amber now has the run of the station and holds muster in her own style. For those who believe there are no stories worth telling from the small boat stations, I would tell them that even the mascot of a station is the beginning of a story.

chapter seven

Hit the Beach

Part of the story of the small boat rescue stations takes place away from the units. To most sailors, the time "ashore" or away from the station, known as liberty, is as important, if not more so, than the time on duty. Forty years ago my shipmates and I, when we "hit the beach," spent a great deal of our time drinking and, for those of us who were single, looking for female companionship. The few married men at the station usually went home and did whatever married people did; they were out of our loop. When I began work on this book, I must admit I looked forward to researching how sailors at small boat stations now spend their liberty hours.

The location of a station is the single most important factor in how sailors spend their off-duty hours. The Coasties stationed at Ocean City, Maryland, for example, are close to an amusement park and a long ocean boardwalk, where hundreds of thousands stroll in the summer. The opportunities for doing things and meeting people are much greater than they are for the person stationed at the Quillayute River station, which is located on an Indian reservation and about a half hour's drive to the nearest town, which only has a population of around 1,000.

At one location along Washington's rugged coastline, I asked a young crewman what he did on liberty. His reply: "Nothing that has anything with women involved." He went on to explain that all of the women in the small town near the station leave to attend college when they graduate high school. The ones that returned were dropouts and usually came home as single mothers. "The only thing they are interested in now is sitting around in bars on the weekend. I'm not old enough to drink, and I really don't care about being with people who think sitting in a bar all night is fun." This Coast Guardsman said he has learned it is fun to go camping and do a little fishing.

Other crewmen said they enjoyed hunting. I visited some units just before hunting season, and most of the talk around the mess deck table centered on locations where the hunters felt the best chance of getting an elk. One commanding officer told me he takes off at a certain time every year to go hunting with his family. I found fishing, however, to be the single most common off-duty pursuit at the units. When not on watch or working, many people will throw a line into the water off the station's dock. One petty officer told me that he and his wife had just returned from a week's trip up a river camping, fishing, and hunting. "We got our limit of fish, and my wife got a deer."

A single, nonrated woman told me that she tries to go shopping with another woman in her section in the nearest city, about

SN Tanya Beck in her own room at the Cape Disappointment, Washington, station. Individual rooms are one of the major changes in stations today. *Brett Powers*

an hour's drive from the station. She also said that being under the legal drinking age limited the things to do in the area. "I sit in my room and think a lot," she said. A few women said they also enjoy camping and fishing.

One of the major changes in modern stations from 40 years ago is the privacy the sailors can now have when they live aboard a unit. At my former unit, we lived in a squad bay, a large room with no partitions. Today, especially at the newer stations, many of the single enlisted sailors have rooms of their own or share a room with someone else. They are able to buy their own telephones and television sets and install them in their rooms. Thus, they do not have to leave the privacy of their quarters to call friends or to watch television, as they would have had to do in the past.

The greatest change in off-duty pursuits that I could see from my day is the attitude toward drinking. Back then, I believe an unwritten code existed for enlisted sailors: you went out and drank as much as possible and staggered back to the unit. No one much cared, and I believe officers expected enlisted men to behave in this manner. There were only two rules: you had to be able to get up the next morning to work and you could not do anything to disgrace the command. An interesting aspect of this is that most of the young people I met at the stations seemed to think everyone in the old Guard remained drunk 24 hours a day, on and off-duty. Part of the reason they think this way is the strong emphasis today's Coast Guard places upon drug and alcohol abuse prevention. To show how bad alcohol and drugs are, instructors either describe some fairly bad scenes about the old Guard or their sea stories tend to concentrate on drunk sailors. There is no question drugs and alcohol were used to excess in years past, but, as seems to happen in most organizations, to make a point there is a tendency to overstate the case. I hate to disillusion the new Guard, but in the past many stations had commanding officers who made sure no one drank aboard their units.

The policy on alcohol, in brief, says that, if you have an "alcohol incident"—you get into trouble due to drinking—and are E-2 (SA or FA) and have more than 2 years in the Coast Guard, you will usually be discharged for unsuitability. There are exceptions, but, if the person is not discharged, then another incident will result in a discharge. All other ranks are given one chance and, if charged with a second incident, they are discharged. Again, there are exceptions, but if the exceptions are granted, another incident brings about discharge.

The Coast Guard uses random drug sampling. If you are caught using illegal substances, you are out.

The alcohol policy leads some officers to believe drinking has now been curtailed. When I mentioned to a watchstander that I had been told no one drank anymore, he smiled. Let me relate an incident.

At 4:00 P.M., a crewmember asked if I would like to go on liberty to a local pub to sample some microbrew beers. In the interest of research for this book, I accepted.

It turned out there were five of us, with all the Coasties in civilian clothing. Smith (I am using fictitious names), new to the station, did not drink at all, while Jones drank moderately. Johnson drank rapidly, one after another, without showing any effects of the brew, while Anderson tried to keep up, without too much success. Anderson's level of intoxication rose rapidly. This arrangement took me back to the old Guard: for some unknown reason almost any group had this type of makeup. I will not comment upon the observer/historian's capabilities.

After a few rounds, we shifted from the bar to an attached pool room, where a somewhat loose game of eight ball commenced, while someone brought in more beer. (Remember: Never play pool with anyone who has ever spent any time on a small boat station.) Between pints of beer and belches, Johnson informed me that police work would be the next stop after leaving the Coast Guard. I replied that Johnson seemed to have a good start on some of the basic qualifications.

Time passed. Beer flowed.

Someone suggested moving to another bar to continue drinking and to dance. Anderson staggered all over the sidewalk. I suggested that Anderson return with me to the station, as I had sufficient notes for the evening. As with many Coasties before, Anderson insisted that nothing seemed amiss and weaved on to the next establishment.

Anderson commenced drinking at the new location but shortly fell on the table, and everything, including Anderson, landed on the deck. Thereupon, someone finally decided they had to get Anderson back to the unit. But how? Using the time-honored ingenuity native to all Coast Guard personnel, a passing fisherman, who no doubt appreciated the service's rescues, draped Anderson across his shoulders. Anderson ended up dumped upon the lawn of the station, while a shipmate went to summon assistance. Exhibiting extreme determination, Anderson managed to crawl across the lawn, halfway down a passageway, losing in the process most of the evening's samplings, which the station dog helped clean up, and then, in a remarkable spurt of extra effort, crawled upstairs to bed.

The next morning, at 6:00, I found Anderson on the rec deck, apparently comatose on a couch except for the odd moan. (Anderson happened to be the mess cook and had to be up at least by 4:30.) In the interest of educating younger active duty Coasties, I tried to impart some historical anecdote on liberty parties to Anderson, which drew a dark look and some additional awful sounds that I believe passed for speech. A few hours later, while standing at quarters, Anderson suddenly, with very wide eyes, expressed an urgent need to leave formation, to the accompaniment of many grins and snickers. As in the old Guard, Anderson's foray became the talk of the station for the rest of my visit. Even on a revisit, that infamous liberty night came up in conversation. The last I talked to her, Anderson swore "never again." Did I mention all four of the Coasties in the liberty party were women?

Then we have the Coast Guardsman who came in drunk, passed out in his shower, which blocked the drain, which in turn caused flooding and leakage to the deck below. To say the service's drinking policy has curtailed drinking in the Coast Guard is to not know what is happening. It is better, I think, to say it is not usual, as in my day, to have liberty parties coming back to the unit drunk. What the policy has done is make people go to a friend's house, or their own apartment, instead of a station.

Contrary to what most people may think about sailors, not all of them drink. Even in my day there were many who did not care to spend their time in bars. Some people at the units I visited worked on cars. BM2 W. Brent Cookingham, of the Quillayute River station, paints; another Coastie did woodwork; and yet another sailor made remote control model cars and aircraft. In short, many off-duty Coast Guardsmen can be found pursuing the same sorts of hobbies and crafts that anyone else in their age and educational groupings might pursue.

Many stations also promote off-duty station activities. Golf is one of the more popular of these enterprises. I witnessed at least three tournaments with other stations within a Group. The sport is usually followed by a station cookout for everyone, including families.

Shore duty is more conducive to off-duty part-time jobs to supplement regular pay. Those wishing to add to their income must find employers who are willing to work around duty schedules, but I found people working as waitresses, clothing salesmen, tow truck operators, and mechanics. One off-duty Coast Guardsman held a most unusual position—mortician.

Family life continues to exert a strong influence on the small boat stations. There appears, at least in some districts, to be a major effort to consider all aspects of a Coastie's life, even the off-duty hours. The concern for families has always been an important aspect of life at a small boat station. Recall the comments of CW04 Mark Dobney in Chapter 3. During my years on active duty, I observed many Coast Guardsmen who, even without much money, had a happy family. On the other extreme, I observed men who thought very little of their families. Not surprisingly, on this project I observed active duty men and women who also had happy families as well as those who faced marital difficulties.

The life of a wife or husband of an active duty person in the Coast Guard is never an easy one. For one thing, they must move every few years. In the case of those accompanying husbands or wives to small boat units, many of the locations are far from mainstream urban American life. This can be a difficult transition for many. One nonrate and his wife, both natives of Florida, found themselves on the Oregon coast, which is cool year round. The seaman's wife, pregnant with their first child, seemed to be having particular difficulty with the weather. I recall when the seaman came aboard from liberty and said to one of the petty officers: "You were right, it worked." The petty officer, it turned out, suggested bringing her flowers every week. "But not the same kind every week. Give a variety."

When I asked some wives what they thought about their husbands being stationed at small boat stations, more than one said, "I am proud of what my husband does and I wish people knew more about what they do at the stations." One woman said it made her feel good when someone stops her "in the store and says, 'Oh, your husband was one that helped those people last night.'"

At some of the more isolated units, the wives help each other. But, as one wife remarked, "While we help each other, sometimes we live too close together." All of the wives felt their husbands worked too many hours, and, even when housing units were on station property, they commented about the amount of time their spouses were at the unit.

One new change for me in the new Coast Guard is the husbands of active duty women. One woman at a station said her husband joined the wives club and was accepted. Another woman said her husband could not find a job in the area and had to stay home to take care of their baby.

One wife said the constant moving is the hardest part of being the wife of a Coast Guardsman. She mentioned that it is not too hard for the children when they are younger—they seem to take it in stride—but once they reach high school age it becomes very difficult for them to make the change. The transfers, she pointed out, can also be interesting. You can meet many new people and form a variety of friendships.

Another aspect of being the spouse of someone at a small boat station is, interestingly enough, the telephone. Stations must be able to reach crew members by telephone. The more senior people must keep a line open at all times. Anyone with teenage children will immediately recognize the conflict. Call waiting has helped this somewhat.

At some units, the spouses join a wives club. Besides the social aspect, many of the clubs do community work. A very good example of what a Coast Guard wives club can accomplish is what takes place every Memorial Day at the isolated station of Neah Bay, Washington.

In 1909, Surfmen John Jacobsen and John Sunstrom, of the U.S. Life-Saving Service, drowned while on duty at Waddah Island, a former location of the Neah Bay station. Normally, the men would simply have been added to the statistics of the service and forgotten, as the area was very isolated. Even today, located on the Makah Indian Reservation, at the very northwestern tip of the contiguous United States, the Neah Bay station is remote.

Every Memorial Day the Neah Bay wives club journeys to Waddah Island to clear away brush on the trail to the graves of Surfmen Jacobsen and Sunstrom and to keep the site in good repair. This is not as simple as it sounds. The Neah Bay region is in a rain forest, which means there is a rapid and very dense growth of brush. Maintaining a trail on the island is not unlike hacking your way through a jungle. The efforts of the Neah Bay wives club help preserve a part of Coast Guard history.

A failing of many books that try to show the lives of people is that authors tend to have the people portrayed as saints. To badly paraphrase Rudyard Kipling, life at a Coast Guard small boat station among sailors does not make saints. Every year there are usually a number of incidents causing people to run afoul of civilian law or Coast Guard policy. Most of the problems involve episodes during off-duty hours. One unit had two cases concerning alcohol and minors with the same person involved. The person received punishment and reduction in rate and eventually dismissal from the service. At another unit, a sailor overdosed on drugs. The small boat stations of the Coast Guard today, as well as in the past, are made up of human beings, some you would like your mother to meet and some you would not want anywhere near your hometown.

While working on this project, I heard a proposal made at a training lecture from the leadership of the Coast Guard that indicates the changes that have been taking place since I served at a small boat station. In my day, it seemed almost a "duty" for a sailor to get a tattoo. The saltier the sailor, the more tattoos. I have seen some strange creations and located on even stranger parts of the anatomy. Many in the new Guard continue this tradition. The leadership, however, is apparently concerned that the sight of some Coastie with tattooed arms might be "offensive" to their "customers" (boaters). At the training session, a senior chief petty officer explained there would be an instruction coming out that, if you had tattoos on your arms, you would have to wear long-sleeved shirts while performing boarding duties, no matter how hot the day.

Coast Guard personnel seem to be lifesavers even when off duty. Early on the Sunday afternoon of November 26, 1995 11-year-old Clyde J. ("CJ") Hubbs, from Chinook, Washington; his 13-year-old brother, Ed; and three neighborhood girls were looking for something to do. They decided to play under the Astoria-Megler Bridge, the long span that crosses the Columbia River from Washington to Astoria, Oregon. The boys remembered they had a rope used to secure some belongings to a concrete bridge support pier located out in the river. CJ and Ed left the girls on the riverbank and raced under the bridge and out over the water along a narrow steel girder 15 feet above the river that led to the pier. "We were showing off for the girls," Ed later related. They had been over this girder many times.

Then, CJ slipped and plunged the 15 feet into the water.

"I know how to swim real good. I'm not scared of the water," CJ later told interviewers. "But I had on a heavy sweatshirt, which was taking me down. I kept going down and bobbing up. I thought, 'I know I'm not going to get out of this.'"

"I saw him hit the water," Ed said, "and ran to get the rope. But I couldn't get the knot untied. Then he was too far out. I yelled to the girls to flag down cars and get Dad." Ed ran back to the shoreline and began running along the bank helplessly and yelling after his brother.

The Columbia River that the 11-year-old plunged into was under the influence of the incoming tide, which caused a swift current to sweep CJ upstream. Washington State Patrol officers later reported "currents in this particular area are among some of the strongest on the entire river. There are often large whirlpools just off the rocky riverbank." The river temperature did not top 51 degrees.

The girls managed to stop motorists, and approximately 50 people or more were standing around trying to figure out what to do as CJ bobbed up and down in the rapid current. At just this time, Subsistence Specialist (cook) Third Class Michael E. Early, off duty from the Coast Guard Cape Disappointment station, approached the bridge on his way to Portland, Oregon, with a friend and her son. Petty Officer Early thought there must be a wreck and decided to stop to see if he could help. Once out of his car, he heard children yelling that their friend was in the water. He turned and there, at least 75 yards offshore, bobbed CJ. Petty Officer Early yelled for someone to call the Coast Guard and the sheriff's department as he ran to the shoreline.

Petty Officer Early threw off his coat and ran upriver trying to judge where he could best intercept the floundering boy. Just before entering the water, someone tied a rope to Early's waist. He plunged into the numbing water. "I was scared beyond all belief," he later admitted. During the 4 minutes of grueling swimming, Early kept calling out to CJ, attempting to reassure him and get him to swim toward his rescuer.

Ten minutes had passed since CJ had plunged into the cold torrent. The boy had gone under a number of times. "You think that when you drown that it's going to hurt and you'll freak out," said CJ later. "It wasn't like that. It was like being in a nice, comfortable bed, looking around where it's all quiet. As I bobbed up and down, I saw bubbles coming out of my mouth each time I went under and started seeing stars with red. It was real quiet. Then I came up again and saw someone swimming out to me."

As Petty Officer Early approached CJ, he felt "the lifeline to which he was secured dragging him under, yet he feared to untie it, because he was unsure he would be able to make it ashore on his own." Early kept the thrashing boy at arms' length while trying to calm him down and preventing him from climbing on top of him. Once Early had CJ securely in his grasp, onlookers ashore pulled them to safety.

The Washington State Patrol and an aid car arrived and CJ was quickly transported to the hospital for hypothermia treatment. Washington State Patrol Trooper Scott Johnson later reported that "undeniably" had not Early acted "without hesitation and without regard for his personal safety, CJ would have perished." Trooper Johnson noted that "Early quietly left the scene without taking any credit for his actions." Trooper Johnson felt Petty Officer Early "deserves recognition for his heroism."

On July 29, 1996, Rear Adm. J. David Spade, Commander, Coast Guard District 13, awarded Petty Officer Michael E. Early the Gold Life Saving Medal, the second highest award for heroism in peacetime an enlisted person at a small boat station can receive. In over 20 years of active service, I never saw the medal awarded. Early also received a letter from Washington State Senator Sid Snyder and a Certificate of Commendation from Washington State Governor Mike Lowry.

The written report made by Petty Officer Michael E. Early's commanding officer, Lt. Mike White, describes what is best about the crews of the Coast Guard's small boat stations: "[Petty Officer] Early's effort was a selfless act that displayed the qualities the community has always valued in our Coast Guard men and women: a willingness to act, even at extreme risk, and a sense of duty, particularly when lives are at stake. His dedication, professional- ism, and humanitarian service are commendable and represent the fact that on or off duty, members of our service are always ready."

Approximately 6 months later, and many miles to the south, BM3 Seth D. Freeman, on his way home from a Coquille River, Oregon, patrol, saw a car run off the road, plummet over a 20-foot rock embankment, and splash into the water. Petty Officer Freeman stopped his car, leaped out, and climbed down the embankment. Without hesitation, Freeman went into the 50-degree water and made his way to the passenger side of the car, but was unable to open the door. As the car sank, the passenger moved to the back seat to take advantage of a small air pocket. Seeing the passenger pleading for help, Freeman then swam to the rear of the car. Taking out his survival knife, he swung and in a single blow shattered the rear window of the car. As the water rushed in, Petty Officer Freeman reached through the window, grabbed the passenger, and forcefully dragged him out. Freeman helped the passenger toward the shore, where onlookers awaited. For his rescue, BM3 Seth D. Freeman received the Coast Guard Commendation Medal.

If the stations of the Coast Guard's small boat rescue units are little known, then the off-duty lives of the crews are a complete enigma to most civilians. What little that is known to outside observers is usually the stereotyped image of a rowdy sailor ashore. This, in some cases, is an accurate image. In most cases, however, the men and women of the stations on their off-duty times do whatever other Americans of the same educational level pursue. Those who have children take them on sightseeing forays, worry about their education and future, and, just as their contemporaries in civilian life, try to make ends meet. What really sets these people apart from most of the civilian world is the dangerous nature of their work and their willingness to risk their lives for others.

chapter eight

Through Surf and Howling Gale

In his night orders, BMCS R. L. Bennington, Officer-in-Charge of the Ocean City, Maryland, station wrote: "SA Doxsey spent his first full day as a qualified crewman on Saturday as the watchstander. That morning he responded to and helped coordinate the rescue of a raft off the beach with people in the water. Later that same day he was deployed as a rescue swimmer from the boat to help in the rescue of three kids trapped under the Ocean City fishing pier! I wonder what he has planned for today!"

The small boat rescue stations of the Coast Guard have routinely carried out days as described by Senior Chief Bennington. The stations have received so little publicity, however, that very few of their dramatic rescues are known to the nation. This chapter is a small effort to rectify this injustice to many brave men and women. The focus is on rescues that took place from 1980 to 1996. There were many rescues during this 16-year span, but I knew I could not include all. I therefore selected cases from throughout the United States that illustrate a diversity of rescues.

Not every assistance case that the small boat stations perform is dramatic. I sat in a government pickup with BM1 Jon Placido and SA Benjamin Wingo (the survivor of the crew from CG-44363) of the Quillayute River station, as Placido worked via radio with two pleasure craft trying to cross the tricky bar at Quillayute River in fairly rough seas. One of the two 44-foot motor lifeboats, with Master Chief LaForge aboard, which had been recalled from drills, escorted a sailboat to near the entrance of the bar, while Placido talked to the skipper by radio. The other 44-footer stood by near the bar. Both motor lifeboats then stood by the bar while the second boat made the transit. Neither incident would make the newspapers or even be mentioned in the Coast Guard's magazine, but the two skippers were grateful for the assistance and for the knowledge that two lifeboats were standing by. This is a good example of what the people at the stations call "preventive SAR."

Most crews would rather be involved in a case where lives are dramatically saved, but routine tows—called "triple A" cases—are just as important to the boater who suddenly experiences a sinking feeling in his stomach when the engine sputters to a stop far from shore. The cases in this chapter will show the efforts and courage of the crews of the small boat stations and their struggles should be known. The reality of their work is that at any time they are subject to what happened at the Quillayute River station on February 12, 1997.

Although all of the stations I visited wanted to take me with them on the "routine" cases—newspaper people do just this sort of thing—as an over-the-hill retiree without modern boat training, I felt I would be adding just another burden to the coxswain's already large responsibilities. I did, however, go out twice in situations that reflect what the Coast Guard small boat stations accomplish without ever being acknowledged. At the Umpqua River, Oregon, station I rode a prototype 47-foot motor lifeboat in a cool, fall night, which was searching a shoreline for a reported flare sighting.

I carried my loaned SAR bag to the boat, climbed into my Mustang, and stowed the bag. I then went topside to the exposed coxswain area. Soon, a member of the boat crew yelled to the coxswain, "Bow line off!" and then the other lines were thrown off and we proceeded upriver. Just a few yards upriver, however, the coxswain put the boat at slow ahead, gathered the crew together, and briefed them on what the case entailed and what he expected. I was allowed to sit in the left-hand seat. The other crewmembers took their stations around the boat and began to scan the area. This case caused me to dredge up from my memory my last case at a small boat station in November 1959 on Lake Michigan in a 36-foot motor lifeboat. We were also searching then because of a reported flare sighting.

Through Surf and Howling Gale

The differences in flare-sighting cases were enormous. In 1959, the crew consisted of me, at the time a seaman, and an EN2 as coxswain. No briefings, just, "We've gotta go out and run a search pattern looking to see if there's somebody in trouble." In the modern Coast Guard, however, the crew of the 47-footer consisted of four people. Both cases happened at night. Even though too many years have passed, I can still recall how cold we were, for as Master Chief McAdams pointed out earlier, there is no place to get warm on a 36-footer. On the 47-footer in 1996, I could sit for long periods of time in a warm exposure suit. If really cold, part of the crew could seek shelter in an enclosed cabin.

Night flare sighting cases consist of long stretches of examining the darkness, seeking to spot a boat in trouble. In 1996, the crew had use of MK-127A flares, which, shot high in the air, flutter down on parachutes and produce an eerie illumination to permit better area searches. This type of case is usually long and very boring, and there seldom are any results. Later, the Group decided that the person reporting the flares had seen meteorites. The boat-crew, just as in training, continually called out information to the coxswain. We did not settle in at the station until close to midnight. The next morning most of the same crewmembers were out at 8:30 for 3½ hours of towing drills.

At the Ocean City, Maryland, station I went out with a BM and an MK in a rigid hull inflatable boat to the scene of a boat aground. The Ocean City area has a commercial towing service. Since the grounded boat seemed to be in no danger, the commercial company had the case. Where there are commercial towing companies, the Coast Guard does not tow craft, unless there is imminent danger. The station, however, set up a radio schedule with the boat until the towing service could arrive. At some point the station learned that the owner of the boat had a heart problem, and the OOD felt it would be better to have an RHIB standing by the scene, just in case. The BM asked if I wanted to come along and I told her I would.

We proceeded at the usual fast clip of an RHIB, bouncing across some wakes. We stood by for about a half an hour to an hour. Just before the towing company finally arrived, another boat called that it too had hit bottom. We went to the location and stood by until the towing service could arrive. Then we returned to the station.

By no stretch of the imagination can either case be called

interesting. Just routine, everyday work. It is important to realize that most cases are just that: routine, boring work. What people at the stations never know is when the routine will become frightening. There is an old saying at the small boat stations that applies: hours and hours of boredom, followed by minutes of terror.

1. "There I Was, Crawling Across the Ice"

One of the interesting aspects of the small boat stations is the initiative of the people at the units and how it can make a difference. Take the case of BM1 Jeffery Kihlmire, now stationed at Cape Disappointment, Washington. While a BM2 at the station at Charlevoix, Michigan, Petty Officer Kihlmire attended a weekend seminar on ice rescue sponsored by Dive Rescue International. "They'd broken it down into more of a line rescue, rather than a boat rescue system," Kihlmire told me. "At the time, the old training methods had you dragging the boat [an ice skiff] and trying to do everything from the boat. When I got back from the seminar, my chief let me run with the ball, so to speak. I set up qualification standards for the station on ice rescue, something like the boat crews have to go through on boats. We got it approved up through the district. I also set up a training program. When the ice came in, we'd be out there crawling around drilling every Monday, Wednesday, and Friday. We also did a lot of training with the fire department and had a real close relationship with the local fire department as far as ice rescue."

Many people feel the sailors of the Ninth Coast Guard District—the Great Lakes—basically go into hibernation during the winter months. The actions on the night of February 10, 1996, defy this notion.

The day started bright and sunny, but then the skies began to cloud over. Then freezing rain began to fall, and by dark an almost blinding snowstorm struck with 30-mile-an-hour winds—not unusual winter weather for this northern Lake Michigan town.

"At approximately 8:05 P.M.," said Petty Officer Kihlmire, "the watchstander got a call from one of the residents who lived down the street from the station that they could hear someone out on the ice hollering for help. At the time myself and two other crewmen were on the station. The watchstander piped us to go out to the berm, which is right across the street from the station. When we reached the berm, we could hear hollering. We could just barely see something on the ice." What the crew of the Charlevoix station could dimly observe proved to be a snowmobiler in the water.

Kihlmire then related, "Myself and another crewman, FN Garret Powell, ran out into the garage and got into our dry suits and we grabbed our shore ice rescue equipment. The watchstander ran back into the comcenter and started making phone calls to get more people down to the location and to get the fire department. My wife, Pam, was visiting me at the station at the time. She had 6 years in the Coast Guard before we got married. Even though she was out of the service, her training probably helped when she went in and assisted in making telephone calls. They called the fire department and the rest of our crew. The call came in at 8:05, and by 8:08 myself and my crewman were on our way out to get to them with our line pack and ice slide."

The snowmobiler struggled approximately 200 yards offshore, right in an area where the ice is always thin. The earlier freezing rain added to the danger. Petty Officer Kihlmire described the ice as "porous, like a sponge" and anywhere "from ¼ to 3 inches thick." The rotted ice made it almost impossible for anyone to walk across it.

In this type of case, according to Kihlmire, "you wear a dry suit and a Type 3 life jacket, which is like a fishing vest and looks almost like a down vest. You also wear wet suit gloves, and whoever goes out for the rescue is at the end of a tethered line in a harness. You carry a boat hook to tap the ice. When you get into thin ice, you can hear a distinct thud rather than a crisp sound. When you're crawling, the boat hook also helps to distribute your weight so you can go onto thinner ice, while someone without the boat hook would have real trouble crossing. Plus, you can reach out with it if they're conscious."

When Kihlmire and Powell arrived, they saw one person on the ice. BM2 Kihlmire and FN Powell started out over the thicker portions of the ice and then they reached the area of thin ice. Interestingly, Fireman Powell earlier that morning had just started learning how to do ice rescue. The practice was the first time he had been on the ice. Now, on his second time on the ice, he found himself in a life-and-death situation.

"Going out, the visibility was poor," said Kihlmire, "with the snow coming down sideways and dark. So there I was, crawling on my belly across the ice, with a flashlight in my mouth to see where I was going, in the dark and in a snowstorm. Every few feet my elbows would break through the ice as I crawled. I went a good 25 yards that way. The man was somewhat conscious when I got to him. First thing I asked him: What happened? Was he on a snowmobile? If he had been driving and smashed through the ice, you could be dealing with internal injuries and have to be careful of how you move him around. I also asked him if there was anybody with him. His level of consciousness was so low that he said no.

"I started to work him out. My line tender, FN Powell, would pull us a little bit and we'd break through. I would get him back up on the ice and we'd break through again. Both my weight and his weight were just too much. After what seemed like forever, but it was only a matter of a few minutes, we got two more of our crew out there on the ice with us. One of the other fellows came out with a sled—a plastic ski tote with flotation tubes on each side—and we got the person in the sled and even that kept breaking through. So, it was real slow, arduous work before we finally got him to thicker ice and finally off the ice. As we timed it later, we actually had him off the ice in about 10 to 15 minutes."

The man was placed in an ambulance and started toward the emergency room. "When they got him in the ambulance and removing all his wet clothes they tried to get his arms down and he was so froze up they couldn't get his arms down. Of the paramedics that arrived on scene, the one that was cutting off the clothes from his lower extremities later found it was her son-in-law. She didn't recognize him, he was so blue and distorted from being in the cold. His body core temperature when he got to the hospital was 86, I think, so he was very near death."

The story is not yet complete. Once the man started to come to in the hospital, the rescuers learned the man's brother was on another snowmobile right behind him.

"So we turned right around and went right back out again," said Petty Officer Kihlmire. "Half of our station had been recalled. This time we launched the ice skiff and broke ice in there as far as we could looking, but his brother had gone under the ice some time before. The nearest they could figure, before we were notified, he was out there for approximately 25 minutes to a half-hour. We searched for a long time, and so did other agencies, but his brother has not been found as of early 1997."

Later, it was learned that the two brothers, each on his own machine, had started out across the ice, had become disoriented in the weather, and had stopped. Once they stopped, their machines broke through the thin ice.

At his new station at Cape Disappointment, halfway across country, BM1 Kihlmire told me, "In 11 years in the Coast Guard, the ice rescue is probably the craziest thing I ever did. When I enlisted in the Coast Guard it's the last thing I ever thought I would be doing, crawling across the ice on my stomach in a whiteout in the middle of Lake Charlevoix in Michigan. It's something I would do again if I had to, but it's not something I would want to do all the time. Funny part is that the flashlight made it back after I got to him. I put it inside the life jacket. That's one of the things I didn't loose."

For the actions on this cold, stormy February night in Michigan, BM1 Jeffery Kihlmire won the Coast Guard Commendation Medal. FN Garret Powell, the line tender, received the Coast Guard Achievement Medal, and the two sled tenders and another seaman won letters of commendation. Everyone at the station that had something to do with the rescue, including the fire department personnel who reported into the unit to help, received the Team Award. Pam Kihlmire also received the Team Award. "She may now have more medals than me," said her husband.

2. "I Could See the Terror in the Eyes of the Crew"

On a bright, sunny day in June 1980, Ron Valquette, a retired naval officer, set out on his 58-foot trawler-yacht, the *Fantasy Isle*, from the Channel Islands Marina, Oxnard, California, bound northward to the San Juan Islands. The islands, a popular summer cruising location, lie between Washington State and British Columbia, Canada. Leonard McDaniel, an ex-merchant sailor, served as engineer and three inexperienced young people also "came along for the ride." The boat made a steady 9½ knots with nothing uneventful taking place until, on July 3, near the central Oregon coastal town of Newport, it ran into an unforecasted, recently developed tropical depression. Sixty-knot winds and heavy seas battered the craft. Valquette decided to seek shelter in Tillamook Bay.

The skipper of the *Fantasy Isle* radioed the U.S. Guard Station Tillamook Bay for a bar advisory and an escort at approximately 4:38 in the afternoon. Tillamook Bay is a small coastal estuary. At the northern end, the only navigable portion of the bay, is the small town of Garibaldi, the location of the Coast Guard small boat rescue station. The mile-long entrance to the bay is between two stone jetties less than 400 yards apart and running almost east to west. The bottom shoals up rapidly just outside the jetties, often causing large swells and seas to peak up and break. When large waves are generated during a storm, the bar becomes treacherous, with breaking seas covering the entire bar, at times reaching more than a mile offshore. Breaking seas are more dangerous to ships and small craft than those that have not broken. At the time, Tillamook Bay Coast Guard station routinely escorted small craft across the bar, dubbing it "preventive search and rescue."

Valquette received the news that the bar could be crossed but that he should call again when closer and receive an update. Almost 2 hours later, the skipper arrived off Tillamook Bay and called for another report. Master Chief Boatswain's Mate Richard

What crews of small boat rescue stations can face when putting out to help those in distress. *U.S. Coast Guard*

Harshfield, the commanding officer, having realized the conditions were worsening, ordered his two 44-foot motor lifeboats to cross the bar and rendezvous with the *Fantasy Isle*. Master Chief Harshfield then went to the lookout tower, located about a thousand feet in from the tip of the north jetty, to observe the crossing.

The two motor lifeboats, one under the command of BM1 Richard Dixon and the other under BM2 George Langlois, stopped just before crossing the bar to make sure their boats were ready for the pounding they would receive. After checking hatches and survival gear, the coxswains made sure their three crewmen were strapped in and then put their throttles forward. The two coxswains plowed into a confused breaking sea of 20 to 30 feet. The seas were so high that Master Chief Harshfield would loose sight of the boats. Winds howled close to 70 knots. Tops of waves were knocked off by the gale, turning the sea into a white froth. The two motor lifeboats were constantly being inundated completely by the breaking seas. Finally, the motor lifeboats arrived near the *Fantasy Isle*. BM1 Dixon then radioed the surf and wind conditions to Harshfield back in the station's lookout tower.

Taking into account the conditions reported by BM1 Dixon and his own observations, Master Chief Harshfield considered the bar impassable to the *Fantasy Isle*. Harshfield recommended that the yacht remain outside until the seas laid down. Valquette by now skippered a boat with an exhausted and seasick crew, and the *Fantasy Isle* only sluggishly responded to her rudder. Valquette radioed Master Chief Harshfield that he felt the boat could no longer make it outside and, in a "do or die attempt," he must try to cross the bar. In the blunt way of many master chief boatswain's mates, Harshfield radioed the skipper's chances were "nil to none." Later, in a letter of thanks, Valquette would write to the commandant of the Coast Guard, "I could see the terror in the eyes of my crew as I informed the Coast Guard officer in charge and he informed me of our chances."

There is no way, of course, the Coast Guard could physically prevent the skipper of the *Fantasy Isle* from crossing the bar. Valquette, knowing the condition of his crew and craft, decided to go against Master Chief Harshfield's advice and cross. The crew of the *Fantasy Isle* donned their lifejackets and stood in the hatchway, ready to leap overboard if the yacht capsized. Master Chief Harshfield continued to keep a lookout from the tower. He would direct the *Fantasy Isle's* skipper through the best course across the bar. One motor lifeboat took station on the port quarter and two waves behind the yacht, the other on the starboard quarter and four waves behind. Once all three boats were lined up, Master Chief Harshfield, again gauging everything, gave the command to start across.

BM1 Dixon and BM2 Langlois in their motor lifeboats knew the dangers awaiting the *Fantasy Isle*. Fortunately, the Tillamook Bay station had practiced for just such an event. The two motor lifeboats would use a technique to provide a "window" for the yacht by taking most of the energy of the wave on themselves. Just the description of the method should make the palms of anyone who has ever been in rough weather sweat a little. The method entails the coxswain of the motor lifeboat placing his stern to the wave that is beginning to break. Then the coxswain puts his wheel hard left and pushes his throttles full power. The stern of the motor lifeboat begins to swing to the right and the boat is now almost parallel to the breaking sea. The throttles are backed off and the wheel eased to steady the boat up 70 to 80 degrees off the original course, the coxswain tries to avoid becoming completely broadside to the wave. The boat should roll slightly to starboard. Just before the wave breaks on the bottom of the motor lifeboat, the coxswain puts the helm hard right and again goes ahead full throttle and recovers from the breaker. In this last movement, the boat is likely to be on beams end and engulfed in white water. It takes 12-foot waves to roll a 44-foot motor lifeboat, and the breakers BM1 Dixon and BM2 Langlois were working in measured at least 20 feet in height, with some approaching 30 feet. They were deliberately putting their boats in a position to roll if they made a mistake.

With a flat stern and not enough speed to outrun a wave, the *Fantasy Isle* faced one of the more dangerous adversaries a sailor will encounter—a high breaking bar. Skipper Valquette also ran the possibility of a wave breaking on his stern, a sure invitation to capsizing. Valquette later would write: "At this point, the lives of my crew and myself were in the hands of God, two Coast Guard rescue boats, and the master chief in the tower." The three boats began their transit of the bar.

Off the starboard quarter of the *Fantasy Isle*, BM1 Dixon maneuvered to take the first wave in sea conditions, which substantially exceeded the design limits of a motor lifeboat. He put the wheel over hard to port and pushed the throttles forward. The stern swung to the right. The boat took the force of the wave, knocking it on beam's end. The coxswain turned to the right. When Dixon regained a straight-ahead course, he ended up on the yacht's port quarter. The maneuver created at least a 35-foot window for the *Fantasy Isle*. BM2 Langlois then began his run from the port quarter and knocked down another wave and ended up on the yacht's starboard quarter. The coxswains of the two 44-foot motor lifeboats ran a figure-eight pattern to provide windows for the *Fantasy Isle*. Master Chief Harshfield continued to direct all three boats from the tower. Forty minutes later, the *Fantasy Isle* and the two motor lifeboats reached the safety of the harbor.

There is no doubt that the skill of the two coxswains saved the lives of the crew of the *Fantasy Isle*. On July 3, 1980, BM1 Richard D. Dixon and BM2 George R. Langlois received the Coast Guard Medal, the highest award a Coast Guardsman can receive for heroism in peacetime. In a postscript, the Tillamook Bay station experienced extremely busy days on July 4 and again on September 20. In an awards ceremony, on April 7, 1981, the crew of this single station earned 11 Coast Guard Medals—the largest group to receive the medal in over a decade—seven Commendation Medals, one letter of commendation, and four letters of appreciation. Among the awards were two Coast Guard Medals to Master Chief Richard A. Harshfield and Boatswain's Mate First Class Richard D. Dixon.

3. "She Did What Was Necessary"

On the afternoon of February 9, 1992, SA Cathy P. Zogopoulas, 22 years old and just 4 months out of boot camp, received an assignment from a supervisor at her station of Islamorada, Florida. The station had received word from the Florida Marine Patrol of two 55-gallon drums of hazardous material washing up on the Cormorant Drive boat ramp in Key Largo near some mobile homes.

SA Zogopoulas drew the assignment of taking a camera and photographing the drums for evidence. While photographing, she heard Florida Marine Patrol Officer Robert J. Dube calling for help.

"I heard someone yelling 'Fire! Fire!' next to a trailer home," Zogopoulas later recalled. "Officer Dube was getting a fire extinguisher out of his car, and he told me he hadn't checked for people inside. I started banging on the door. . . ." The fire caused the door to be very hot to the touch, but Seaman Apprentice Zogopoulas continued to work at the entrance and finally forced the door open.

She entered the mobile home, now completely filled with thick smoke. Zogopoulas retreated back outside for air and then entered again. "I called out, 'Is anyone in here?' and I heard an elderly woman answer, 'I'm here.' I found her on the kitchen floor." Zogopoulas also related, "Flames were shooting up from the wall where the heater was.

"Once outside, I asked her if she was okay and she said yes, but that her husband was still inside, where he was taking a nap." Seaman Apprentice Zogopoulas then helped the woman outside and, in the words of the official report of the incident, despite "the rapid progress of the fire and the obvious danger to herself," went into the mobile home to locate the man. The walls of the home were now ablaze. Despite the fire and thick smoke, she found the man, managed to get him awake and, in her matter-of-fact way of reporting on her heroism, said, "I helped him out."

She and Officer Dube began first aid on the elderly man and woman. Then Seaman Apprentice Zogopoulas once again entered the inferno, this time to secure the circuit breakers to cut off the electricity. She then went outside and helped Officer Dube rig a garden hose to fight the fire until the fire department arrived.

Once the fire department arrived, Seaman Apprentice Zogopoulas returned to her duties of photographing the barrels. She returned to the station and, according to later reports, felt hesitant "about telling her story." In a later interview, she said, "Anybody else would have done the same thing. I didn't think about it, I just did what needed to be done." Her commanding officer wrote, "She did what was necessary."

For just doing "what needed to be done," Seaman Apprentice Cathy P. Zogopoulas received the Coast Guard Medal.

4. Into the Inferno

On the night of August 31, 1991, a crew of five from the Coast Guard station at Southwest Harbor, Maine, pulled the not disagreeable duty of taking their 41-foot utility boat and providing a safety zone around a barge used as a platform for a large fireworks display at Northwest Harbor, Maine. The good duty would soon turn to something far different.

The night sky lit up from the fireworks, accompanied by claps and voices of exclamation and appreciation at the display. Suddenly, sparks from the display ignited stockpiled pyrotechnics on the deck of the barge. The explosion caused a huge fireball to shoot into the sky. Three people from the barge leaped into the water, another person lay unconscious and on fire, and a fifth person hid behind a 55-gallon drum.

Quickly and skillfully, BM2 Paul J. Dupuis, the coxswain of CG-41439, maneuvered the 41-footer alongside the barge so his crew could begin applying water to the numerous fires and could help the people from the barge. As Petty Officer Dupuis brought the utility boat closer to the barge, boat engineer MK3 Bruce E. Sherwood activated the boat's fire pump and then grabbed a heaving line to throw to the men in the water. When the 41-footer drew closer to the barge, Sherwood noticed a man lying face down on the burning barge. Without thinking of his own safety, Petty Officer Sherwood, who also served as an emergency medical technician, grabbed the EMT kit and leaped aboard the barge. He managed to get the man to his feet and aboard CG-41439, where he started first aid on the man.

At approximately the same time that Petty Officer Sherwood leaped to the barge, SA Carol A. James threw a life ring overboard toward one of the men in the water. She then grabbed another heaving line and threw it to another survivor and then helped pull the men safely aboard. Then James helped another crewmember move the stokes litter (a metal stretcher with sides) and other medical equipment from the lower cabin to the main deck. Without thinking of her own safety, SA James then leaped to the barge to help others.

Another crew member, SN Robert A Bowen, manned the fire monitor on the 41-footer's bow after Petty Officer Sherwood turned on the boat's fire valve in preparation for fighting the fire. As BM2 Dupuis maneuvered the boat closer to the barge, Seaman Bowen began to apply water on both the burning man and the deck fire. Once the flames had been knocked down, he helped SA James with the medical equipment from the lower cabin. Then Seaman Bowen leaped to the barge.

The other member of the crew, Port Securityman Third Class

(PS3) Brian P. Baker, a reservist on active duty, immediately grabbed a heaving line and threw it to a person in the water. Petty Officer Baker then pulled a victim from the water. When BM2 Dupuis had maneuvered CG-41439 alongside the barge, Baker, without hesitation, leaped aboard the burning inferno and rescued two people. PS3 Baker then went to the bow of the Coast Guard 41-footer and manned the fire monitor.

With all survivors aboard, Dupuis began backing the CG-41439 away from the barge. Then a second, more powerful explosion occurred, scattering burning debris and shrapnel in all directions. When the explosion rocked the small boat, Sherwood used his body to shelter his patients on deck. Baker, who was at the fire monitor, took the full force of the second explosion, which hurled him backward into the boat's superstructure. He received burns and wounds on his face and legs, a cut on his hand, and bruises on his body. James rushed to Baker and assisted him back to the well deck with the other patients.

The second explosion had disabled the boat's radar and cabin lights, dislodged the radio and clock from their mounting brackets, and filled the cabin's interior with smoke. A newspaper photograph of the second explosion shows a large fireball. Viewing it, you wonder how anyone aboard the Coast Guard boat survived. Somehow, Dupuis managed to navigate his boat to Northwest Harbor, and all survivors were transported to a hospital.

For their successful rescue in the face of grave danger, BM2 Paul J. Dupuis, MK3 Bruce E. Sherwood, PS3 Brian P. Baker, SN Robert A. Bowen, and SA Carol A. James received the Coast Guard Medal.

5. "It's My Job"

In the dark, predawn hours of December 29, 1996, the Grays Harbor, Washington, station responded to a call from the 58-foot wooden-hulled crabber *Lee Rose*. Her skipper radioed that he was 12 miles northwest of Grays Harbor, in 8-foot seas and a 50-knot wind, along with rain and hail showers, and that he was taking on water.

Chief Warrant Officer Randy Lewis, the commanding officer, recalled, "It had been stormy the night of the 28th before I went to bed, near 10:00. We had about 3 inches of snow, and my kids were

Left to right: BM2 Steve Schuch, BMCS Thomas Doucette, and MK3 Brian Richey, of the Cape Disappointment station return from training in the 30-foot surf rescue boat. Most of the equipment and clothing small boat crews wear on their boats in colder waters is shown. Near BMCS Doucette's hand are the three surf belts that strap in the crew in rough water. Doucette's helmet is attached to a belt; the other helmets are stowed out of sight. Each of the sailors is wearing a Mustang survival suit with reflective tape. Over the upper part of the suit they all wear a "pyro vest," which contains survival signaling gear. *Brett Powers*

going crazy. They were going to have a lot of fun the next day playing in the snow.

"The station called about 3:00 in the morning and said they had this guy taking on water, so I drove in, and, as I got into the station, the snow had pretty much changed to rain. I got in and started to figure out who, what, and where. There was a helo on the way from Astoria, Oregon, to the south, but they were really fighting the weather. The wind was coming out of the northwest and was really screaming. During the whole case it was probably 40 to 50 knots, with gusts upwards to 70 to 75. We decided to go with the *Invincible*, the 52-foot motor lifeboat, and the 44-footer. I would be the coxswain on the *Invincible* and BM1 Daniel L. Smock would be the coxswain on the other boat. We were still on our holiday routine and working with fewer people in the duty sections, so the 44-footer had a crew of three and I had four."

The *Lee Rose* proceeded toward Grays Harbor bar. The fishing vessel *Jamie Marie* escorted the crabber until they rendezvoused with the two Coast Guard boats 2 to 3 miles north of the entrance.

Petty Officer Smock recalled, "It was a pretty decent ride out with about 3 to 4 feet of wind chop coming out of the east. About 15 minutes after we got on scene, the temperature went from about 30 degrees, with a 30-knot east wind, to 55 degrees, and about a 40-knot southwest wind. Even the weather buoy reports changed. The seas went from a 3- to 4-foot chop to a southwest 14- to 20-foot swell at about a 5-second interval. It was close, choppy and blowing hard. The windshield on the 44-footer fogged up, and I couldn't see until the windshield warmed enough. The warm front was like a curtain rolling right over us."

"The weather was so bad," said Chief Warrant Officer Lewis, "that the helicopter went right over us and couldn't see our lights. We actually got on scene before the helo did. They had to almost get right down on the deck before they could see anything. On the way out, I kept looking at the range marks for reference. I looked back once and said, 'Crap! The fog's moved in.' One of the crewmen turned around and said, 'No, the lights went out.' The whole town lost power. Comms were bad and we were basically on our own. Group Astoria called the helo and said they had no lights at the airport at all. The helo called me and asked if I wanted him to stay around. I said, 'You're not going to put a rescue swimmer in this stuff, especially with the boats around. You'd better work your way home.' I talked to one of the pilots later, and he said they put the helicopter at 400 feet to miss anything on their route and started toward Astoria, along the coast. The weather was so bad they figured they were only making 10 to 20 knots speed over the ground."

The four boats started for the shelter of Westport, Washington. The *Jamie Marie* went first, then the two Coast Guard boats, and then the *Lee Rose.*

The *Lee Rose* "had pumps running and all he could tell us was that water was coming into his engine room from somewhere and he was just keeping ahead of it," said CWO Lewis. "As we got nearer the entrance, there's an area called 'The Triangle,' which ends up being an ugly area for waves. The channel heads to the

A 44-foot motor lifeboat approaches a wave at the Grays Harbor, Washington, bar.
CWO Thomas Doucette

southwest and there's a green line [the line that represents the left-hand side of a channel coming in from the sea] that goes to the north and west, and the area between the two ends up ugly. He was going into that area. He started to take some good swells. I had just turned to a crewman and said, 'Man, if he has troubles down here, we're not going to be able to help him.' About 5 minutes later, he took a series of three, about 25-footers that just stood the boat on its stern.

"He called and said his crewman had just come up and said the pumps weren't keeping up and the water was coming in fast. He said he could either run offshore or keep trying to run inshore.

"So I told him you got basically two choices. Offshore it's just going to get bigger and it would take at least a half hour's running heading in before you get into good enough water where we can get alongside to pass a pump. His decks were awash and a pump would flood out.

"He said, 'I am going to put a crewman on the wheel and look for myself.' He came back and said, 'Nope, the steering pump is going under at any time. I am amazed that I still have steering.'

"I really thought it was time for him to get off it. I'd had some of those old, crusty skippers who will start to argue with you. Somehow, someway he was going to do it. But the skipper was a younger guy and he decided to leave the boat.

"I called the helo and told them they'd better come back and stand by just in case. They turned and, now with the wind on their

The *Lee Rose* Case

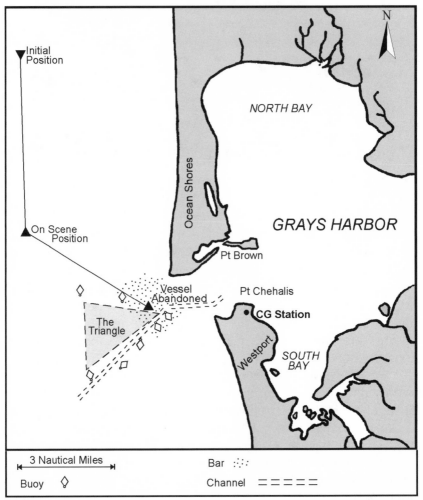

Map by Susan Browning

tail, they came back at a speed later calculated to be over 200 miles per hour."

The *Jamie Marie* heard the radio traffic, and, in the best tradition of the sea, returned to the scene from seeking safe moorage and used their strong sodium lights to illuminate the area.

CWO Lewis was maneuvering a 52-foot motor lifeboat, a craft that is noted for its rolling when rough—one crewman called it like a weeble-wobble toy; keeping track of the 44-foot motor lifeboat

178

and a crabber in serious trouble; and coordinating a helicopter and the *Jamie Marie*. All of this is more than enough to juggle in a dry office, but imagine it on a windy, wet deck.

Lewis suggested that the fishing crew, now in their exposure suits, jump from the stern one at a time and that a motor lifeboat would pick up each person. "I talked it over on the radio with the CO," said BM1 Smock, "and decided to take the first pickup. The skipper of the *Lee Rose* would keep steering right into the swells at a slow bell [slow speed] and have a crewman walk to the stern and I'd be sitting right behind him. I'd peel off and pick him up, and the 52 was sitting right behind me. He'd pull up into position and then I'd stand off."

"On the first pickup," said SN Daniel C. Butenschoen, a crewman aboard the 44-foot motor lifeboat, "we were in our surf belts, clipped to the boat, and we worked ourselves down to the well deck, the lowest point in the middle of the boat, where it is easiest to grab a person in the water. I didn't even see him jump off the boat until all of a sudden I see something floating in the water. Is that him? Oh, crap!

"Petty Officer Smock did a great job in getting us alongside the person in the water. For some reason we couldn't get the boat's lifelines unsnapped. Our hands were really cold. We're trying to pick him up with the lifelines in place. I'm trying to bring this guy, who's all crinkled up from the cold, over the lines, while Mike's [MK3 Mike Fratusco] trying to bring him under. So, finally, we just picked him up over the lines, checked him out, got him up to the coxswain's flat, and put him into one of the extra surf belts. Then we backed off and let the *Invinc'* go in to pick up the second person."

"Fortunately, all of the people in the water were conscious when we pulled them out, which helps a lot," CWO Lewis said. "It takes a lot of courage on the 52-footer to get someone out of the water in rough seas because of the high freeboard. There's at least one guy who has to belt himself in at the base of the two stanchions of the lifelines, lay on his belly, and the other two guys either hold onto his feet or sit on top of them as he reaches out over the side. So you're hanging over the side of the boat, and, when the boat rolls one way, you go down to about your chest in the water and then when you roll the other way, you can easily hear the props breaking suction. The exhaust is right there and you're getting that in the face. Actually, it is probably better to do it at nighttime, because you can't see the seas coming. In the daytime, you look down the hull and see all those breakers coming at you. Makes you want to do it a lot quicker."

"We were clipped into the lifeline, so we could slide up and down the boat," said MK3 Randy Merritt, a crewman on the 52-footer. "I was clipped on the bottom lifeline. I grabbed him and then the other two crewmen grabbed him. I then clipped onto the top lifeline and helped them bring him aboard. Petty Officer Merritt had done this before, but it was the first time for the rest of the crewmen. So it came down to a test. Whether we were going to be able to do what we trained for. Our adrenaline was so honked, we did it so fast, we were all proud of ourselves.

"We asked the *Lee Rose* crewman if he was all right and he said he was fine. We put him in a surf belt and took him up to where the commanding officer was at on the wheel. The CO then backed out, and the 44-footer went in for the third person."

"After the third guy went off," said CWO Lewis, "I talked to the skipper of the *Lee Rose* and asked if he felt safe pulling the boat out of gear so it wouldn't just steam ahead offshore and collide with somebody. He said, yeah, he'd do it.

"You learn a lot in hindsight. I didn't tell him which way to jump, so he jumped off the downslope quarter of the boat like his crewmen."

"The skipper jumped off the leeward side of the stern, and the boat was drifting in on him," said Petty Officer Smock.

"He paddled like mad and was able to get 50 to 70 feet away from the stern," said CWO Lewis.

"There was no room for the 52 to go in and make the pickup. We were just standing by watching," said Smock. "Oh, shit! This is gonna get ugly. At just that time there must have been a 16-to-18-foot break hit the *Lee Rose* broadside and came over the top of the wheelhouse. All we saw was white water completely over the top of the wheelhouse, the boat heeled over, and then the swell let go of it. The white water that came over the top hit the skipper in the water and washed him about 20 yards away from the boat, which was far enough for the *Invinc'* to pick him up."

Both Smock and Lewis remarked how much the sodium lights of the *Jamie Marie* had helped in spotting people in the water on a dark, stormy night, with crab pots also floating in the area. The

44-foot and 52-foot motor lifeboats then started in over the bar. The sea still had a few punches left, however.

"I let the 44-footer go in first," said CWO Lewis.

"On the transit in," said Petty Officer Smock, "we had the opportunity to surf a nice 14-footer. It was just a big, sluffing sea break. I got slapped broadside and we heeled over 70 to 80 degrees. It was an easy transit, except that during nighttime, when the wind is blowing, the visibility is low, and there is about 16 feet of white water. The pucker factor on that one . . . I know the *Invincible* got slapped hard."

"Coming in," said CWO Lewis, "we were being set toward the north jetty so we had to run in the trough. At night it's hard getting the proper depth perception. At one point we skirted around a swell, and the next thing I saw was a wall of water coming at us. I thought about turning into it, but, nope, I wouldn't have time. So, I yelled for everyone to hold on. We rolled far enough to dump fuel out of the vents. I wouldn't want to do that in a 44-footer."

"A wall of water hit us on the way in," related BM3 Brian Gaunt. "If I wasn't clipped in, I'd probably gone over the side. Took a couple more swells and drank about 200 gallons of water.

"Pretty scary ride, not being able to see the waves at night. That's when you get scared. People who say they aren't scared, there's something wrong with them. It's all right to be scared. At the time you're doing it you're not scared. . . ."

At this point, Seaman Butenschoen interrupted with: "Uh-uh, at the time *I was scared!*"

The two motor lifeboats with the four rescued fishermen finally made the safety of the harbor. The *Lee Rose* drifted at least 20 miles, to Point Grenville, before breaking up. For their work in the early morning hours of December 29, 1996, Chief Warrant Officer Randy D. Lewis and BM1 Daniel L. Smock received the Coast Guard Commendation Medal. FN George L. Paradis, SN Daniel C. Butenschoen, MK3 Mike Fratusco, MK3 Randy Merritt, and BM3 Brian Gaunt all received Coast Guard Achievement Medals.

Later, when asked if he would do it again, BM3 Brian Gaunt replied: "Yeah. It's my job."

Many of the dramatic rescues performed by the crews of the small boat stations are the type that should be the lead stories on national television network news. Some do receive recognition, but usually only in local papers. It is safe to say their successes are accompanied by loud applause, but their very few mistakes, or where there are no rescues and people are lost, are accompanied by whispered innuendoes that are deafening.

Strange as it may seem, one of the problems in writing about the rescues of the crews of the small boat stations is a reluctance on the part of the men and women to relate their experiences. However, most will tell you their accounts, if you press them. The crews say they prefer the feeling they receive from helping someone in distress. (Another large problem is obtaining information from some district public affairs offices.) BM2 John Yeager, who left the service and then returned, told me he wished "he had a camera" when he was attached to Station Islamorada, Florida, and had taken 41-footers out to pick up Cuban refugees. "The looks on their faces when you pulled them aboard. They would kiss your hand, your feet.

"I remember one 8-year-old boy," said Yeager. "We received a call about a Cuban family overdue somewhere in the northern area of our responsibility. At the time I was a break-in coxswain. We searched well into the night and then were told to return to the station to rest and then get back underway at first light to search with the help of an HH-65A Dolphin helicopter. I always carried a candy bar with me on the searches. We were halfway to the search area, when the helo called us and informed us they found them anchored in some mangroves. They had been disabled all night without food or water.

"When we located the family and took them aboard the boat, the little 8-year-old looked up at me. I had to give him my candy bar. I still remember that look the boy gave me; it was like he knew what he had to do for his family. The kid took it and broke it into pieces and gave one to each member of his family before he would eat his piece. I will never forget that 8-year-old."

In June 1997, the watchstander at a West Coast unit received a call of the possibility of a capsized boat in the surf and people in the water. The SAR alarm sounded and the SRB began its dash to the location. Meanwhile, the commanding officer, just returned from yet another meeting, set out in his Jeep to evaluate the report. Because the SRB needed to traverse a circuitous route, the CO arrived on scene first. After speaking to the person who had called the station, the officer obtained the approximate location of the capsizing and began to work out the drift of the survivors. The CO relayed the information to the station. The commanding officer then stood on top of his Jeep and began to scan the area. He spotted two people struggling in the surf and called the boat with the information. When he realized one of the victims might not make it, the CO, in his dress uniform, plunged into the numbing breakers, as an HH-60 helicopter arrived on scene. One of the survivors could just make it out of the water, while the second collapsed. The CO helped the victim to the beach and started treatment for shock and hypothermia.

Later, the rescue swimmer from the HH-60 told the commanding officer that he "did a good job" and he would gladly let the CO "preserve his uniforms in the future if he would quit scoring him out of rescues." The commanding officer told me after the rescue, "I'll take that over hardware [medals] any day. It was a feel-good day." He did not want his name used in describing this rescue.

chapter nine

"Small Boats, Small Problems"

Many of the comments made to me by small boat personnel reveal a frustration, one that is directed toward the decision-makers at command levels. In addition to all of the training exercises and many mission burdens put on the units, this feeling of frustration is an important factor of life in the small boat stations. Most civilians do not see it. But, to reveal life at a small boat station, the tension between officers, especially those at headquarters, and the enlisted people at the units must be shown.

In general, there is a very strong perception among the people at the stations that they are at the bottom of everything in the Coast Guard. As some put it: "We are bottom feeders." I am sure the Commandant of the Coast Guard would say this is not true, but the people at every station I visited felt this way. While the frustration is strongest in the senior people, it can be seen at the lower ranks as well. The story of the stations, in short, is not only one concerning the feats of courage and routine work, but it is also one that shows a clash about how one group of experienced people thinks the important work of small boat rescue should be carried out, versus how, in their own argot, "the bean counters" see the mission. This is a far-reaching struggle for, in fact, the future of the small boat stations rests upon its outcome.

The best illustration of the background to an aspect of the gap between decision-makers and those at the stations came from a master chief boatswain's mate. His observations are based upon units on the West Coast but can be applied to almost any location.

"Traditionally, the small boat stations always had chiefs in charge. In the 1960s and 1970s, as the sport salmon fishing grew, so did the number of search and rescue cases. People bought boats and put them into the water without the slightest idea of how to operate them, another reason for the large number of SAR cases. We called it the 'Armada of Madness.' It was not unusual for crews to work 100 to 200 hours a week, and some stations reached caseloads of up to 800 a year. The chiefs managed to cope with small crews.

"Then came the end of the Vietnam War.

"Now there were fewer people coming into the Coast Guard and less people willing to put up with such stressful conditions. Officers from the district and headquarters began to tell the chiefs: 'You can't work these people this way. You have to slack off.' The chiefs said, if they slacked off any, people were going to die and the chiefs weren't going to slack off. They knew what was going on and the officers did not. The officers would then reply: 'Your responses are a cultural thing. You've always done the work at the small boat stations this way, but this does not mean it has to be that way.' The chiefs, however, would not budge. Officers brought more pressure to bear, but the chiefs still said no. Finally, the chiefs said, if you want us to slack off the hours the crews must work and give the crews a 'better quality of life,' then you give us the additional resources, mainly men.

"Stations now started to have crews of 25, 40, or more. Now, officers said the crews were too big for enlisted men to command, and officers needed to be stationed at the units. Once officers began to be assigned to a small boat unit, they needed a staff. They needed a yeoman and a storekeeper for office work and ordering supplies, people a chief never had. A chief would be up until midnight trying to get his paperwork finished, but an officer couldn't be expected to do that. Grays Harbor station, for example, was built with the idea of a lieutenant and his staff, a station with maybe 70 to 80 people.

"Then the salmon fishery went dead.

"Now there were fewer and fewer cases and crew sizes were reduced, but the officer billet was not removed. When there were chiefs in charge of a station, they would say no to changes they felt were not in the best interests of safety, but now with officers in charge, people who had to worry about fitness reports, districts, and headquarters had people who would do what they were told. That's how they broke our culture."

Those who have never served in the Coast Guard should know a little bit about it and about its officer corps. The Coast Guard is the smallest of all the U.S. armed forces. For such a small organization, it has a large number of missions. The number of duties the small boat stations cover are perfect examples of the myriad tasks placed upon the organization. The present Commandant of the Coast Guard, however, continues to stress that the service is a lifesaving organization. Indeed, the Coast Guard for years has told Congress that the value of the lives and property it saves is larger than its operating budget, which is correct. It is important to keep these two statements in mind.

The Coast Guard is also an organization that is controlled by the Coast Guard Academy officer corps. Very few nonacademy officers reach the rank of admiral. A basic unwritten tenant of the service is: If the academy officer corps does not have a career path through a field, then the field is looked upon as little more than worthless. *There is no career path through the small boat stations for the academy officer corps.* In fact, very few academy officers have served at the units. One can also say that very few officers at all—even officers who have served as enlisted men or who came into the service from college—have served at small boat stations. Those few who have served at the stations rarely, if ever, make it to the higher levels of command.

Most decision-makers argue that the new 47-foot motor lifeboat coming slowly onto line and the use of helicopters have lessened the need for small boat stations. The use of helicopters has helped in SAR, and many aviators have performed amazing feats of rescue. There is no question the machines can sometimes reach a sinking boat faster than a motor lifeboat can. There should also be no question that helicopters have limitations. They cannot always fly in bad weather, and bad weather is when many cases take place. Some of the service's helicopters have a small load capability. The HH-65A Dolphin, for example, usually carries a crew of four and can only pick up three to six survivors, depending on weather, fuel capacity, and other factors. Then, what happens if the hoist cable parts? This has happened more than once. As one salt put it: "There are more helicopters at the bottom of the sea than lifeboats in the air." There never seems to be a statement from many who should know better that a combination of helicopters *and* small boats makes a good SAR team capable of helping those on the waters. Furthermore, no one in command seems to acknowledge the fact that, according to the Coast Guard's own published statistics, small boat stations accomplish *53.8* percent of all SAR operations undertaken by the service, Groups performed 19.1 percent, while air stations ranked third, with *10.3* percent. These are amazing statistics. Yet, a captain in headquarters said "small boat stations were *only a small part* of the SAR effort." When I quoted the above figures to him, his response was: "I don't know the exact figures."

Perhaps it is not fair to single out the captain. In his latest budget, Adm. Robert E. Kramek, Commandant of the Coast Guard, assigns only 12 percent of the funds to search and rescue, which must be spread over all aspects of SAR, not just to the stations. Furthermore, when asked months in advance for an interview to discuss the stations that accomplish 53.8 percent of all the SAR in his service, neither he nor his staff bothered to reply.

When issues between the small boat stations and decision-makers become very heated—and, interestingly enough, most of the issues deal with the safe operations of the small boat stations—many of the officers in the Coast Guard seem to bring their arguments down to the personal level instead of trying to discuss them. A number of senior enlisted people told me of officers calling them "Neanderthals," or much worse, when they tried to point out policies that seemed to go against established practices of safe small boat operations. Favorite phrases included "Your culture makes you say these things, but that doesn't mean they are correct." Many enlisted men have received threats. After listening to similar statements from almost everyone I interviewed, I began to wonder if all the situations described could possibly be true, or was it simply the age-old officer versus enlisted man story? On February 3, 1997, I had my eyes opened to some of the problems.

I met with the assistant branch chief, Office of Search and Rescue (OSR), of a Coast Guard district. The senior officer I spoke to noted at one point that people in the field "do not have the big picture." He quickly became enamored with the idea that all people speaking to me at the stations, especially the chief petty officers, were dissidents and were giving me erroneous ideas as to what was really taking place in the field. While staring directly at me, he noted that he equated dissent with "disloyalty." This sudden statement certainly caught me by surprise. It seemed strange that a senior officer would, without asking me to explain how I obtained information, suddenly call his most experienced petty officers disloyal and, by implication, hint that there might even be a streak of disloyalty in me. This officer convinced me by his actions that I should guard the names of the people I had interviewed. It also indicated to me that the name-calling and the lack of respect given to senior enlisted people that I kept hearing about was true. (Of course, the people at the stations are, in turn, very quick to lash out at people in headquarters with names that are much earthier than "Neanderthals.")

This refusal to listen to senior enlisted personnel seems strange in an organization that touts, almost reverently, the princi-

Lt. Michael F. White, Jr., one of the few commissioned officers to command a small boat station. At the Cape Disappointment station, Lieutenant White has a crew of 48 men and women, a tenant command of the National Motor Lifeboat School attached, and a total station size of 200 acres. The station is one of the largest of the Coast Guard's small boat stations. *Brett Powers*

ples of TQM (total quality management). Some have gone so far as to hint that TQM is one of the driving factors of today's Coast Guard. One of the principles of TQM, as I understand it, is to listen to your workforce.

The nature of officer leadership is one of the issues that stood out during this project. I am amazed at the low esteem the enlisted force of the small boat stations hold for their officers. During my early years in the Coast Guard, most of the rankers said very little about the gold stripers. Only old crusty chiefs held forth with their salty views. I found it enlightening, and Admiral Kramek should find it uneasy, when people at the nonrate levels say: "I wouldn't want an officer in charge at the station level. An officer would be so worried about his OER [Officer Evaluation Report] that he might not make the hard decision and might get someone killed." Some hint that officers' OERs are one of the three driving factors of the Coast Guard, the others being TQM and money.

Although I found that enlisted personnel at the stations respected those officers who they believed would not be afraid to put their careers on the line for them, most felt very few fell into that category. The nonrates do recognize those officers who are good leaders and show some concern for their subordinates. A crewmember at Cape Disappointment informed me: "We had been working a tough SAR case into the early morning hours. We were all tired and worn out. Then, over the radio, we heard the Group Commander [Capt. David W. Kunkel] say, 'Well done! Semper Paratus!' [Always ready, the Coast Guard's motto.] It was a nice feeling knowing the captain had stayed up along with us on the case and had thought enough to tell us we had done a good job." A number of the crew of Cape Disappointment told me they liked serving with their commanding officer, Lt. Michael F. White, Jr., because "he is willing to put his career on the line for us."

As mentioned earlier, some have stated how money seems to be one of the driving factors in the Coast Guard. Most taxpayers would probably agree that a government organization should watch spending. In the light of shrinking budgets, I do not envy the decisions the Commandant must make. To help reduce the budget, a number of changes in how the Coast Guard handles personnel and how they staff the stations have been adopted, which have led to some serious problems.

The academy officer corps has always prided itself that the

service is a sea-going outfit. The only way to become a leader, in their view, is through sea duty. Command at sea is a coveted assignment and is the goal of most academy officers. Therefore, officers and as many enlisted personnel as possible should, as the academy leadership sees it, rotate to sea duty. As some enlisted people have pointed out, however, "if sea duty is so great, why do officers threaten to send us to sea if we mess up?" Because of this requirement, boatswain's mates, the rating in charge of many of the small boat stations, shoulder some additional requirements that are not required of most other rates in the service. As with many other rates, they are required to have 12 months of sea duty as a petty officer to be promoted to chief petty officer. Then, to advance to senior and master chief petty officer, boatswain's mates must be certified as officer-in-charge afloat and ashore. The certification for afloat requires the individual to become qualified as a deck watch officer, which is accomplished by sea duty (a policy that is in the process of being reevaluated as a result of the Quillayute River incident). To obtain the certification as an officer-in-charge of a small boat station, boatswain's mates must pass a review board made up of officers and a senior enlisted member. Interestingly enough, in most cases none of the officers on the board have ever served at a small boat station.

When the service felt the pinch of reduced budgets and received an order to reduce the size of the military, decision-makers began what became known as "streamlining." At the stations it also went by the name "right sizing." What this means is the reduction of the size of the enlisted force in the service. "Reduction" does not really convey what decision-makers did to the Coast Guard's enlisted force. At nearly the same time, headquarters also took over the control of transferring the nonrates.

Again, the average taxpayer may say this is not an altogether bad thing. Perhaps the original intent was good, but, as seems to happen all too often in the case of the small boat stations, plans seem to go awry. In 1991, the Coast Guard undertook a station staffing study. Nearly all of the senior enlisted people I spoke to said the study finally brought all of the grievances of the stations out into the open. One of the problems identified was the hours crews put on duty. Over *100 hours a week* was revealed to be the normal. A number of solutions were offered and a goal of reducing the hours to *only* 67 was set. To reduce the number of hours crews worked, the study recommended assigning additional people to the units. Somewhere in all of this headquarters decided that, to attain a better quality of life, all transfers would come in the summer months. Either no one in headquarters realized this is the busiest time of the year for SAR, or they chose to ignore that fact. Then came the reduction of the enlisted force. One chief told me that, because the Coast Guard was now reducing the number of people in the service, this made the study "a dead issue." The hours the people at the stations work, of course, continue to be high.

Adding to the above is the method the Coast Guard uses to retain its enlisted force. Most civilians may think that once a person is in the military and decides to make a career of the service, they stay in, are promoted, and, eventually, serve their 20 or 30 years and retire. In my time, this was true; today's Coast Guard is far different. There are two concepts items known as "high year tenure" and "CFTRR."

High year tenure is defined by Coast Guard headquarters as limiting "the amount of time an active duty enlisted member can remain in each paygrade. It is designed to increase personnel flow and to compel members to advance in their rating. This allows for more consistent training and advancement opportunities for the enlisted workforce. With more balanced and consistent opportunities, the Coast Guard can retain the most highly motivated personnel. In turn, these members will gain experience, and ensure the Coast Guard retains its leadership and professional continuity." In short, upward mobility or you are out, abbreviated by most service personnel as "up or out." This policy began on July 1, 1995.

Centralized first-term reenlistment review (CFTRR) is defined by headquarters as a process that "takes into account the latest workforce trends (loss of rates, billet additions/deletions, etc.) as it clears qualified personnel to enter the Coast Guard's career force. CFTRR also limits reenlistments in rating projected to have a surplus of career personnel." In other words, if you are in a field that has a large number of people in it, you are out of the Coast Guard, even if you are otherwise qualified to reenlist. On the other hand, if you are in a field that is projected to have very few people, known as a "critical rate," then you have a better chance of remaining. If the people who forecast "workforce trends" miss their predictions, then there will be either too many people in a field, or, conversely, a large deficit. This policy began on July 1, 1994. Both of these specific policies are only for enlisted personnel, although there are similar management programs for officers.

These good intentions and a changing personnel policy have brought unfortunate results. Nonrates who are now assigned to a station out of boot camp, if they are not striking—that is, learning about a field on the job—for boatswain's mate or another rate on the station, will be transferred in 2 years. As soon as strikers make petty officer, they are transferred. To fulfill the "up or out" policy, enlisted people must either strike, as already mentioned, or go to a service school to learn the skills needed to make petty officer in a particular field. This causes many of the nonrates to receive orders for school in fewer than 5 or 6 months after arriving at their unit. Thus, the stations lose people who are just getting some experience in being boat crew qualified. At the petty officer level—the people who will be in charge of operating the boats at a station—the same type of problem exists. Most petty officers in the boatswain's mate rating arrive at the small boat station without qualifications as coxswains. Using the 13th District as an example, if these petty officers move with average learning abilities, they may reach the level of surfman in 3 years. These petty officers are now the most experienced junior boat handlers at the station (the officer in charge and executive officer being the most senior) and should logically spend at least the next 3 to 4 years passing on their training to others. Yet, what invariably happens is that, if the petty officer wishes to advance, the high year tenure system will force him or her either to go to sea or to be denied promotion and thus be forced to leave the service.

I saw this clearly illustrated at one of the stations I visited. A petty officer second class made surfman and a few weeks later made petty officer first class. Within a month, he received orders for a patrol boat out of Guam. For many years, the senior enlisted people of the stations in the 13th District requested a policy of back-to-back tours for surfmen. That is, a newly qualified surfman should have a waiver of sea duty without hurting his or her chances of promotion and be able to spend another tour at a station so that his or her knowledge can be passed on. In this case this suggestion fell on deaf ears. Again, because of the Quillayute River incident, this policy is being reevaluated.

These policies and the reduction of enlisted personnel can account for a shortage of people in the BM and MK ratings, the primary rates at a small boat station. The ratings currently are so short that, as I worked on the final drafts of this book, the Coast Guard sent out requests for volunteers in the reserve to come onto extended active duty to help fill billets.

When some senior enlisted people at the stations pointed out to headquarters staff that they needed more people to gain the required experience levels at the units, they were told that the high costs of transfers prevented the adoption of this idea. Furthermore, some at headquarters felt this could create a group of "inbreds," which means, I think, that they were worried people would not be going to sea and might become too specialized on small boats. For some strange reason this seems an abhorrent idea to many in headquarters. Yet, as another chief pointed out, "When was the last time an air station or large cutter went without enough pilots or deck watch officers to get underway?"

Many in the enlisted force question the equal reduction in the size of the Coast Guard's personnel force. To test whether there may be a reason behind the questioning, I checked the number of people serving on active duty over time:

Year	Officers[2]	Enlisted	Total[3]	Ratio of officers to enlisted
1945	12,902	158,290	171,192	1:12
1955	4,053	24,554	28,607	1:6
1965	4,825	26,832	31,700	1:6
1975	6,807	29,981	36,788	1:4
1985	7,508	31,087	38,595	1:4
1995	8,330	28,401	36,731	1:3
1996	7,908	27,129	35,037[4]	1:3

Notice the ratio of officers to men. In 1995, about the time of streamlining, the cutbacks caused the makeup of the Coast Guard's personnel force to equal one officer for every three enlisted persons. Also in 1995, the year the enlisted force plummeted, the number of officers actually increased. In 1996, the U.S. Navy's ratio

[2]Includes cadets at the Coast Guard Academy.
[3]*World Almanac*, 1970, p 160; and for the year 1997, p 179.
[4]Coast Guard, Office of Personnel

was one officer for every six enlisted persons, while the Coast Guard's remains one in three.[5] Is the Coast Guard's enlisted force so bad that it really needs this many officers to supervise them?

Furthermore, the number and ratio of admirals to other personnel in the service are revealing:

Year	Number of Admirals[6]	Ratio of Admirals/ Other Officers	Ratio Admirals/ Enlisted
1945	16	1:806	1:9,893
1955	15	1:270	1:1,637
1965	22	1:219	1:1,220
1975	27	1:252	1:1,110
1985	28	1:268	1:1,110
1997	30	1:265	1:892

With an increase in the number of admirals, there is an increase in staffs. This costs money. If the idea is to save money, all of the above statistics seem strange. Yet, one of many reasons given to small boat rescue stations for the lack of experienced personnel is that there is not enough money to transfer enlisted men to the units. Perhaps what should be said is that officers are more important to the service than experienced enlisted people at small boat stations. One BM3 commented: "I stayed an SNBM [E-3] for 18 months because those appointed above me were trying to reduce numbers. Now we are short of personnel in the BM rating. Of course, those appointed above me were not affected." Another enlisted man said to me: "We are eating our young."

What all of the personnel policy translates to is that, at the time of the deaths of the three Coast Guardsmen at Quillayute River, "82 to 86 percent" of the crew of the station had changed in 10 months. Such a turnover places a tremendous training burden on the officer-in-charge and on the crew to develop qualified boat coxswains and crew members. At the same time, the crew must be receiving training in law enforcement and pollution response, plus a myriad of

---

[5]The U.S. Navy reported it had 60,013 officers and 376,595 enlisted personnel on duty in 1996.
[6]Numbers are from the Coast Guard's Register of Officers.

other subjects. Further, people are both transferring out and trying to train during the busiest time of the year. Commanding officers are sometimes put into a bind about who they will qualify. Because there are so few qualified people to chose from, they may allow a marginal person to become a coxswain so they can fill out their boat crews. As one commanding officer put it: "You have to work with what you've got. You may qualify a marginal person, but try to make sure that person is never put into a bad situation." Thus, the stations must operate at the edges of having enough qualified people to survive in a hostile environment. Commanding officers are also forced to keep people simply because there are no replacements because of a flawed personnel policy. If there were no problems, why have some changes in policy begun since the deaths at Quillayute River?

A contributing factor to the continuation of the small boat station's problems is what I call a "suck it up and do it no matter what" attitude. When discussing the issues of the stations, someone would eventually say, "Oh, well, we've always had these problems. The Coast Guard has always been this way." In short, take it in stride and get on with the job. The attitude is a commendable one, and one that is traditional in the small boat community, but unfortunately it does not solve the problems. Lt. Comdr. Bob Steiner, in a service publication for stations with 41-footers, wrote about the need for the senior boatswain's mates to spend time training personnel. "Pleading a paperwork overload is beating a dead horse. Everyone who has been around long enough to recall the Station Staffing Study . . . knows what the net result has been. . . .The station administrative load obviously has not, and will not decrease. If you want to be an OIC [officer-in-charge], suck it up and stay late to get your administrative work done." While Lieutenant Commander Steiner is correct about senior people needing to be on the boats training their personnel, does this solve the problem of the officer-in-charge receiving a poor inspection report, or the wrath of his Group Commander, if the paperwork is not done? Once again, the officer-in-charge is placed in an untenable position.

Consistently throughout this project I heard that the bottom line is money. Government agencies should be conscious of where their money comes from. But in the case of the Coast Guard's small boat rescue stations, the bottom line is not money. The bottom line is the young men and women who risk their lives when they put out to sea. When I mentioned to a captain in headquarters that the small boat stations were complaining about too few people to do the work, his comment was: "People in the field must realize that headquarters also took a 15 percent cut." Apparently, the captain equates the danger of being swamped by headquarters paperwork with being swamped by a 30-foot wave. All too often planners far from the high surf get caught up in their numbers and graphs and seem to forget that the real bottom line at the small boat stations is what happened at Quillayute River.

In the almost desperate search for ways to cut the budget but still perform the same jobs, the Coast Guard has tried a number of experiments. "Streamlining" and "right sizing" are but two examples. At about the time I began writing this book, headquarters decided that rigid hull inflatable boats might be a way to provide boats for lower cost. RHIBs are fast, require small crews, and, of course, they do not cost as much as lifeboats. Planners point out that the boats are used extensively by the Canadian Coast Guard and by the Royal National Lifeboat Institute (RNLI), Great Britain's largely volunteer maritime lifesaving force.

Most people at the small boat stations believe the RHIBs are excellent for sheltered waters and can be used in some seas, but they hesitate at the suggestion the craft should be used in surf. The largest concern of the senior people at the stations centers on what happens if you are rolled over. Headquarters planners, who have no experience at the stations, say float bags will be put on the boats, then all that has to be done is to inflate the bag and climb into the boat if the RHIB capsizes. The experienced people at the stations point out that this assumes too much. It presumes that you will come up beside the boat following a rollover. Further, it surmises that you will not be disoriented or injured and can quickly find the lanyard to inflate the boat. There is even some question as to whether the boat will then right itself. Most importantly, it also assumes you can even get into the boat from the water, all of which is extremely doubtful at best. While it is true the RNLI uses the RHIB, it is also true the organization has motor lifeboats, some of which are larger than those the Coast Guard operates. Plans are underway to conduct experiments with the RHIB in the surf.

At about the time I began work on this book, the service's magazine began to run more and more articles about the Coast Guard Auxiliary, a sure sign that something was in the wind. The

Auxiliary is made up of boaters who voluntarily perform boat safety checks for the Coast Guard, among other things. For this work, they wear a uniform similar to the one worn by Coast Guardsmen—their officers wear silver instead of gold—and their fuel and food is paid for by the Coast Guard when they are working with the Coast Guard. In general, the people in the Auxiliary flotillas tend to be made up mainly of civilian retirees.

Proposals have been put forward to have the Auxiliary take over a number of the search and rescue duties performed by the Coast Guard. When I asked the Office of Auxiliary Operations Division in Coast Guard headquarters about the role of the Auxiliary at the small boat stations, the officer who replied stated that there were many missions in which Auxiliarists can benefit the Coast Guard in various capacities, "thus providing Coast Guard units valuable force-multiplying support. By maximizing the employment of the Auxiliarists and providing them with appropriate tools, execution and success of Coast Guard missions will be advanced." At many of the stations I visited, I saw Auxiliarists helping out in the communications room. The plan to use Auxiliarists in some of the work of the stations is commendable.

Plans also call for Auxiliarists to use some Coast Guard equipment to perform SAR. One proposal is to have the volunteers use a 7-meter RHIB—capable of doing in excess of 30 knots—and work in sheltered waters performing routine SAR. (I do not think there is anything that can be called "routine" SAR. A simple tow can sometimes turn into disaster.) There is also the notion circulating from decision-makers that Auxiliarists can be used as coxswains and crew on Coast Guard boats.

No one at the stations objects too much at having the Auxiliary do work in sheltered waters. All of the senior people at the stations agree it could take a burden off the units. In fact, it is so logical it should have been implemented years ago. (Why it probably remained in the background will be made clear later.) Some of the senior people at the small boat stations disagree with using a 7-meter RHIB, or, as I gather, any RHIB as now configured, for the Auxiliary. The main concern is speed. Operating an RHIB takes coordination and very good reflexes. I can attest to how the boat seems to fly across the water and will bounce with the slightest wave. How is a senior citizen going to react? I know my reflexes are much too slow to handle the boat at high speed. One chief indicated that the only way to prevent accidents is to put governors on the boats used by the Auxiliary.

Where most senior people at the stations have grave misgivings is the use of Auxiliary in the surf, one of the most dangerous areas of operations. Most of the concerns center on two aspects of the Auxiliary that cannot be brushed off: the nature of the organization and the age of its members.

The greatest obstacle to overcome, and I see no way around this in the immediate future, is the age of people who make up the Auxiliary. As one who has more years behind him than ahead of him, I know I can no longer do what I did as a seaman apprentice on a boat. Headquarters states that the "majority of Auxiliarists are age 50 and above; and over half (55 percent) of Auxiliarists are still employed." This, of course, does not state the age of the people who are employed. In my visits to stations, I must have been unlucky enough to see the minority, for, of all the Auxiliarists I observed, only three were still employed and, of these three, two were well over 50 years old. One Auxiliarist told me he knows he can no longer lift as much as before, so they take three people on his boat in case someone needs to be pulled aboard. What would happen if an Auxiliary boat, crewed by two people, a man and a woman, who were 65 and 68, had a boat in tow that suddenly capsized? If you were in the water, would you have a lot of confidence they could pull you out? The scenario just proposed is not outlandish. "The recommended minimum for normal operating conditions," headquarters states, "is one coxswain and one crewman."

Some in headquarters (although not in the Office of Auxiliary Operations) believe that, if the Auxiliary is given more "exciting" things to do, it may attract younger people to its ranks. Perhaps, but this will take time. Meanwhile, can senior citizens do the "exciting" work? To me, "exciting" work is the type most likely to get Coast Guardsmen and civilians killed.

This leads to another aspect of the concerns. It takes months and years to get regular Coast Guard personnel qualified as boat crewmen and coxswains. Will the Auxiliarists be held to the same standards as regular service personnel? The current standards are: run a minimum 1.5 mile in under 15 minutes, lift a 180-pound man from the water assisted by one other person, 20 pushups, 40 situps, and jumping your height in a standing broad jump. If the same standards will be maintained, this is a step in the right direction. Headquarters states: "As the needs of the Coast Guard dictate, any Auxiliarist may be authorized to train on Coast Guard units and replace or augment Coast Guard crews provided the Auxiliarist has completed the Auxiliary's New Member Indoctrination and Entry Training Program and meets certain Auxiliary qualifications and all necessary Coast Guard requirements. Specifically, Auxiliarists may be qualified and certified per current Coast Guard standards (that is, the Coast Guard's boat crew training and qualification program) for any position on a Coast Guard boat or cutter and may be assigned to any crew position except coxswain. . . ." The idea to use Auxiliarists as coxswains, however, is now in circulation and, as will be shown, headquarters knows about the idea despite the previous statement. Can a 65-year-old meet the demands of the standards for younger people? If so, he or she deserves to be called a boat crewman. I think, however, that it will be very difficult to have volunteers of the age of many of the Auxiliarists put in the kind of work and have the physical prowess needed to pass the requirements. There have been a few who have done just this, but they are in the minority.

As I began to work on the final draft of this book, I received a letter from a district office of auxiliary operations. The office had delayed some 4 months before responding to my questions about the Auxiliary. The officer responding did point out, however, that the "good news is . . . the Coast Guard Auxiliary has received authorization to operate in the surf zone. . . ." The letter goes on to point out that, for an Auxiliarist to operate in the surf zone, they must "qualify to active duty standards." The officer who wrote the letter notes the standards "are set by the Coast Guard. However, some stations have more stringent standards because of certain operating conditions and are authorized to impose those standards on Auxiliary as well as active duty personnel, provided the imposition of such standards is uniform to all and not discriminatory." Lastly, the writer says on the topic of Auxiliary personnel being held to the same standards as regular crews, "The most significant barriers are the physical standards that must be met."

If events proceed as they have in the past, headquarters will say that no one is becoming qualified, so we should set up a new set of standards for the Auxiliary, or lower the service's standards. They will point to the minority and say, "See, they can do it. We just need to lower these unreasonable restrictive requirements." Or, as the district Auxiliary letter mentioned, someone will say the standards are discriminatory. In another context, during an interview with a captain in headquarters, I mentioned that there seems to be a perception at the stations that, if a standard is too hard for some members, just lower the standard. His reply: "That's probably correct. Perhaps the standards are too high." Surely, this is the path to disaster.

Next, there is the problem of having Auxiliarists as boat crewmen or even coxswains on Coast Guard boats—an idea now circulating. Recall what headquarters said earlier about crew requirements for Auxiliarist. The office of Auxiliary also adds: "In light of the Team Coast Guard concept[7] and passage of new Auxiliary legislation, which allows an Auxiliarist 'to perform any Coast Guard function, power, duty, role . . .' the policy prohibiting Auxiliary members from serving as coxswains on Coast Guard boats is being reviewed. . . ." Headquarters cares not to comment further on the subject as long as the policy is being reviewed.

If the expanded use of the Auxiliary is such a good idea—and there is merit in using the force to some degree—why has it not been undertaken before this time? While there are numerous reasons put forth by decision-makers, the basic reason can be found in the age and nature of the organization. For years, the Auxiliary has been known among those in the service and in some communities as primarily a social organization for older people. It became, in short, a place for retirees to put on a uniform, replete with medal ribbons, and impress the local community, while having their boat fuel and food provided free. Not all flotillas operated this way, but enough did so that the perception has become well established. In fact, some Auxiliary units are still as just described. It is no wonder they are not taken seriously by many at the small boat stations. As more than one chief related: "The Auxiliary is useful as long as you know how to use them. Let them make their boardings in sheltered waters and give them their coffee and cake and they are happy."

[7]"Team Coast Guard," a favorite phrase now in use, means, according to the Office of Auxiliary Operations, "a concept developed and implemented by the current Commandant of the Coast Guard . . . to denote the complete Coast Guard family—active duty, reserve, civilian, and Auxiliary. Every part of the Team Coast Guard is vital to the successful execution and outcome of each and every Coast Guard Mission, Hence Team Coast Guard."

Some junior crewmen related to me that the only thing Auxiliarists seem interested in is, when is chow?

The expanded use of the Auxiliary and some of the ideas circulating about their use are other examples of the chasm between those at the stations and headquarters. An idea to use the Auxiliary is put forth and suddenly it seems every officer immediately wants to jump on the proposal and offer yet another suggestion. Some of the ideas are the best indication the person really does not know what takes place at the units or has any inkling about small boat rescue work. Unfortunately, as many of these suggestions come from senior officers, they must be tried by the stations. For example, one senior officer told me that the Auxiliary is the same as England's Royal National Lifeboat Institute. Anyone familiar with the two organizations will see this as ludicrous. The members of the RNLI drill constantly and spend many years learning their trade before they can even touch the wheel of one of the RNLI's boats. Compare this to the Coast Guard Auxiliary, which is made up of retirees who can bring their own boat to the flotilla and start to work almost immediately. When I relayed the above comment to headquarters, even other officers were taken aback. The point is, what happens if the officer begins to make plans and implements them, based upon his perceptions? This is exactly how many of the schemes concerning small boat stations go awry.

My comments are not meant to be critical of the Auxiliary. One can appreciate what many members want to do: they want to help. They can perform useful duties. I know Auxiliarists who also agree that no Auxiliarists should be on Coast Guard boats unless they can pass the same qualifications as Coast Guard boat crews.

The expanded use of the Auxiliary is an idea spawned by planners who seem to know nothing about the reality of the work at the stations and by Auxiliarists who, in many cases, know little more.

The reality of this work is simply the deaths at Quillayute River. I recall the comments an Auxiliarist made to me after the deaths of the three Coast Guardsmen: "I didn't know it was so dangerous at the stations." If some in the Auxiliary do not understand the inherent dangers of the work, then they have no business working aboard a unit. Is the Auxiliary ready to help the Coast Guard? Comments such as the preceding make one wonder. If the past is any indication, and so far it has been proven correct time and time again, the planners in the Coast Guard will begin using the Auxiliary without obtaining a proper knowledge of the units.

I will make two forecasts if developments with the Auxiliary proceed as they are now going—and I believe there is no stopping this movement. The Auxiliary will be used in sheltered waters. Then, when the next budget crunch comes, someone will decide the Auxiliary has done a good job in sheltered waters, so we can try putting them to work in all areas. Eventually, some Auxiliarists will be killed and the finger-pointing will begin. Probably the commanding officer or officer-in-charge of the unit will be sacrificed. In fact, almost all of the responses to my questions about the qualifications of Auxiliarists have elicited the headquarters comment: "Each unit commander is required to. . . ." It appears headquarters is setting up the commanding officers for failure to follow orders. That is, the commanding officers will receive heavy pressure from headquarters and the district to employ Auxiliarists and, if they give into this pressure, and someone dies, then the unit commander will be at fault, not headquarters or the district. On the other hand, if commanding officers stand up to the pressure and do not push Auxiliarists onto the boats, they will receive poor officer evaluation reports and thus poor chances of promotion. Joseph Heller wrote a bestselling novel based upon such arrangements.

The other scenario is simpler: someone, either an Auxiliarist or a boater, or both, will be killed on a "routine" SAR mission and the finger-pointing again will begin.

Is the Coast Guard willing to have deaths of Auxiliarists?

One master chief stated rather clearly: "Coast Guard headquarters seems to no longer want the service in the search and rescue business, at least as far as small boat stations are concerned. Search and rescue as performed by cutters and aircraft is a different story, as these units have members of the officer corps attached to them." Unfortunately, I believe this observation appears to be true. Since beginning this project I have heard officers question whether the Coast Guard should even be in the search and rescue business, something I never thought I would hear. The academy officer corps has always seemed to have had an inferiority complex concerning their own service. They desperately want the U.S. Navy and other services to recognize them as a military organization. (Yet they are willing to employ civilians—the Auxiliary—to do some of their work? Does the U.S. Army have volunteer infantrymen to serve without pay? Does the U.S. Navy have a few civilians helping in gun mounts?) The academy officer corps apparently does not see duty aboard a small boat station as duty suitable for Coast Guard personnel, and thus, every so many years, the decision-makers, in the words of one retired captain, "chase butterflies" in their desire for recognition.

In the 1960s, for example, the leadership felt oceanography would save the service. The Coast Guard would lead everyone in the federal government in oceanography. Almost every cutter did some type of oceanography. An oceanographic cutter even reached the design stage. By the 1970s, this "butterfly" stopped fluttering, or, more properly, sank beneath the waves, without reasons for its demise given to the field. Then law enforcement replaced it. The 1990s seem to indicate the new "butterfly" is to make sure the service is known worldwide as a naval force and as a source for training Third World navies. While it can correctly be pointed out that many of the services' "butterflies" began with congressional or executive orders, a great many in leadership positions who should have said "enough" welcomed the assignments.

In the Coast Guard, what program is most completely an enlisted program and therefore expendable? The small boat stations. Yet, the Coast Guard's small boat stations are all the justification the service needs for its existence. But then, this is a view that may lead to someone questioning why there is a Coast Guard academy, large white cutters, and, especially, a large officer corps.

After listening to the people at the small boat stations, living with them, and meeting with the frustrations I encountered in only a small way during this project, it is very easy to feel there is a conspiracy by the leadership in the Coast Guard against the small boat community. To have a conspiracy, however, you must have someone who cares about the outcome. I do not believe there is a conspiracy. It is simply, as many in the small boat community believe, that the leadership of the Coast Guard does not care about the small boat stations, that it sees them only as a means to advance its own agenda, which changes every 4 years with the changing of commandants. If the stations do a good job, fine, the units can be used to justify budgets, but do not ask for resources. If they cannot do the job, this is also fine, as we now can justify doing away with the units. Anyone who spends any amount of time at the stations and listens to the rhetoric on both sides can see this attitude.

Through deliberate actions, or through just the normal military caste system, or just plain neglect, there has always been an unwritten code concerning the stations, which have traditionally been crewed entirely by enlisted personnel. The code says that enlisted people are unlettered and inarticulate. Therefore, there are no stories to tell about the units. It is better to concentrate on those who are articulate. While part of the code in the past may have some truth to it, there have always been a wealth of stories, as this book proves, if someone wishes to take the time to get to know the people and listen to their accounts. What this code has, in effect, accomplished is to make those who serve, or who have served, at the stations forgotten. This is an affront to maritime history and to a group of people that has been willing throughout the years to put their lives on the line for others.

The current Commandant of the Coast Guard's first "vision statement" says Coast Guard personnel should "be professionals and remain proud of our reputation as Lifesavers and Guardians of the Sea." Yet, many of his professionals told me, "We have to train at a higher level than the Commandant's policy. If we trained at his level, there would be more deaths." It seems to this outside observer that all of the personnel policies of the past few years have done everything possible to negate the advancement of professional lifesavers. The most incredulous policy is its rotation policy. How can anyone who claims to be the head of professional lifesavers ever condone a policy whereby large numbers of people are moved during the busiest part of the search and rescue season?

Having said all this, I must also point out that the people at the small boat stations should also shoulder some of the blame. Planners must have information to make decisions. It would be nice if headquarters could go before budget committees and say they saved a certain number of lives and then receive their appropriations. Most congressional hearings want statistics. Traditionally, the commanding officers of the small boat stations never properly document what they do. This needs to be changed. Further, the small boat stations must start advertising what they do. They must write about their accomplishments. They must also recommend their crews for medals, when appropriate.

Small Boats, Small Problems

When I shared these thoughts with officers-in-charge and executive petty officers, I was often met with: "I don't have time" or "I can't write." More than one commanding officer said, "I do put my crew in for awards. It is amazing how many times they become lost at the Group. Of course, the awards for the officers of the Group do not go astray." I can sympathize with them about the lack of time, and I have heard many accounts of lost paperwork concerning awards, but, if a commanding officer feels he or she cannot write, then they should find someone in the crew who can, or they should find a volunteer outside the station who likes to write, or they should start taking writing courses. The best way the American public is going to learn about the stations is through accounts written by the men and women in the boats. Some of the more exciting rescues in this book only rated, at the most, a single paragraph in a press release by some public affairs officer, who did not serve at a station.

The basic problem with the small boat stations can be stated rather simply and should come as a surprise to anyone used to management or military organization. All of both the dangerous and the routine work performed at the stations is accomplished by enlisted people who become experts in small boat operations, while all the decisions that affect their lives, and the lives of others, are made by officers who have rarely, if ever, served at the units. In the U.S. Army or U.S. Marine Corps, on the other hand, a general may be far removed from the troops, but he began in the mud with his troops at the platoon and company levels. I know of no one at the command level in Coast Guard headquarters who has ever worked their way up through the various levels of a small boat station, or even who has commanded a station. In other words, decisions are being made by those who really do not know the field. Even this type of flawed system, however, could work if those in command were willing to listen to the people who are the experts in the field, namely the senior enlisted people and chief warrant officers at the units. The operative word in the previous sentence is "if." At the present time, it appears that very few, if any, of the officers in the command structure, including the Commandant of the Coast Guard, seem really willing to listen to the people in the field. I am amazed, although I should not be, at the amount of bitterness I encountered over this issue and how those in command seem not to notice it. Or perhaps they simply ignore it. The feelings are akin to those of soldiers in the trenches of World War I about staff officers: that they were sent to die by officers who apparently cared little for them, did not understand them, and did not even visit them. One senior chief petty officer asked me: "Why don't officers visit stations more often to learn about our operations?" On the other hand, others have mentioned that some officers come for a few hours and then think they understand everything about a small boat station.

Contributing heavily to the problem is the Coast Guard's desire to be all things to all people. Perhaps the service's leadership is finally awakening to the fact that there is a limit to how much you can stretch a service and a limit to how much you can ask of your people who have to try to carry out the missions. In short, the Coast Guard has too much on its plate. The executive and legislative branches of the government will, largely for political reasons, continue to task the Coast Guard with a myriad of duties. What eventually must happen is for the commandant to say we can no longer do all of our missions unless we are funded and staffed properly. This, however, would not be a career-enhancing move on the part of any admiral. It is now time, in fact it is past the time, for the leadership of the Coast Guard to do what is correct, rather than thinking of careers. If the leadership no longer wants the small boat stations, then they must have the courage to say so and carry out their convictions rather than say "we are lifesavers" and then take actions that seem to contradict everything they are saying. If they want the stations, the leadership should start fighting for more funding to properly staff the units.

Some officers have admitted that no one quite knows how the people at the stations have been able to make do on the limited budgets given to them. From personal experience and observation I can reveal some of the secrets. The crews worked and continue to work hours no one, except in war, should have to work. They listen to the community they live in and help as much as possible. They operate with equipment at times held together with spit and bailing wire and they never fail to go out.

The stations may continue to deteriorate, mainly because one group of people, which has no experience at the units, still chooses to think: small boats, small problems, and the only place for someone in the Coast Guard is at sea on a cutter. What would prevent this deterioration is if the American people chose to say to their elected officials: we want the stations to function properly, and we are willing to shoulder the taxes needed to support them. If this should happen, the American people and their representatives should then demand that the Coast Guard recognize and cure the flawed system now in place.

What is most amazing to me is that, even with their frustrations, their long duty days, being forgotten, and most especially the danger, the men and women of the Coast Guard's small boat stations continue to push out into the cruel sea to save people. Americans should be proud of the work these people have accomplished over the years. It will dishonor their memory if they remain forgotten.

chapter ten

A Willingness to Act

An outsider might well ask: What causes the men and women of the Coast Guard small boat rescue stations to climb aboard small boats, knowing full well they may face death and, in most cases, be completely forgotten by the people they serve? This book is replete with descriptions of mind-numbing boredom, long hours of sometimes tedious work, and the frustrations brought on by senior officers not really understanding what takes place at the stations. Add to this the very real chance of death. Why would anyone want to put out into the cruel sea, only to be forgotten?

There are at least two groups of people that serve at a small boat station. One group is made up of those who see this as just another duty station away from sea duty or from some other type of duty they care more about. They will do their work and are as brave as the other group. The other group thinks small boat stations are the only place to be in the Coast Guard. The latter are the people upon which the traditions of the stations are built. For want of a better term I call these people lifeboat sailors.

One of the traits of most lifeboat sailors is an unwillingness to talk about their feats. In many cases, it is a very difficult task to get more than a few laconic phrases out of the sailors. Do not misunderstand me. There are some who will quickly give you press releases about themselves if they have them handy, and they always seem to have them available. The majority, however, are very reticent about their own rescues, or why they push out into the seas. Even those of the minority, those who like to talk about themselves, hesitate at really trying to verbalize the reasons they go out. It may be refreshing to find modest heroes, but the reluctance means very few people know about their exploits.

Sometimes, even in their frustrations, you can perhaps glimpse why the lifeboat sailors continue in their profession. When complaining about officers thinking they know all about the small boat stations after a single visit of an hour, one senior chief petty officer told me, "Until you've been on a motor lifeboat in heavy seas and have watched as the bow plunges downward in steep swells, and your stomach is tied up in knots because you are not certain you are going to come up again, and all the time the crew is relaxed because the chief is on the wheel, then you don't know what you are talking about."

Public affairs officers would say that the men and women go out into the seas because of their training and traditions. That, of course, is part of the reason. Training and tradition, however, are not the main reasons for pushing off into heavy surf.

Some are "adrenaline junkies." There is no way I can describe the feeling you receive when the alarm rings and you run to the boat and start out toward whatever. Many live for that indescribable feeling. Someone once wrote, "Risk is extra life."

One former instructor at the National Motor Lifeboat School said it very succinctly: "Once you've saved a life, you're hooked."

Comdr. Michael C. Monteith, one of the few commissioned officers to command a small boat station, believes it is "a realization that if you don't go, often no one else will, or can." He went on to tell me, "I suppose firefighters may say something similar, as both types of lifesavers must enter a totally unforgiving environment for which only a few people have the hardware and training and courage to challenge. Knowing that someone may be about to die and you are the only help around is a powerful emotion that can override all other logic and reason. Like Quillayute River, it was not bravado or ego that led the CG-44363 into harm's way; it was just a deep gut passion to help. It's a human trait to help others in need, and the U.S. Coast Guard gives a few of us the joy of experiencing it—and the despair at also failing. Saving a life is a joy that defies description.

"It's a rare moment that, when it's all over, you reflect on just how precious, temporal, and delicate life is. It humbles you, not vice versa. I'm one of the very few officers in the U.S. Coast Guard who has actually reached over the gunwale of a small boat and pulled a person from the sea; and if I could have only one memory in life to cherish, I think that would be it. But even in my short time in lifeboats, there were many calls and sorties where we would not have gone if 'anyone' else could or would have done it. There were times that the only thing that kept us from turning back because we were so cold, wet, sick, and miserable was the fact that we were too damned scared to realize we were all of those other things."

I observed one crew as they came back into the station after pulling someone out of the water. The crewmen are trying to hide a little smile; you do not want to give away the macho image of "just another day." The more senior of the crew could do it better than the boots. A little swagger in their walk, however, really telegraphed their feelings.

The heart of the stations and, in my opinion, the heart of the Coast Guard is this group of people that is dedicated to saving lives. As Commander Monteith put it: "There is nothing that buoys up a crew's morale as a good save." Conversely, recall Petty Officer Clark's feelings of the loss of the *Amber Dawn II* in Chapter 6.

There is also another factor that is best described by Lt. Michael F. White, Jr. The people at the small boat stations are imbued with a sense of "a willingness to act, even at extreme risk . . . particularly when lives are at stake . . . [That] on or off duty, members of our service are Always Ready."

Among many intellectuals and pundits it is now popular to bemoan the fact that "we have no heroes today." If you wish to see heroes—real heroes who have human foibles—find the nearest U.S. Coast Guard small boat rescue station.

epilogue

February 12, 1998

Exactly one year after the tragic events that opened this book, I returned to visit the Quillayute River station. I had visited with the crew many times since that day in 1997, but this day, of course, was special.

The first thing I heard when I parked my car in the visitor's spot in front of the station was: "Mr. Noble, do you want to come look at the bar with us?" In the station's pickup were Petty Officers Brent Cookingham and Albert J. Scholz. We went out to the observation point where Master Chief George A. LaForge and I had sat staring out into the dark, gale-swept night and where we had heard a static-filled "We rolled the boat!" come out of the radio speaker. On this day, a year later, as I watched the waves crashing and talked with Brent and A.J., the weather was eerily similar to last year's. The wind lashed the area, there were occasional showers, and the seas were high.

We drove back to the station, and I talked to Master Chief LaForge and Petty Officer Jon Placido. LaForge commented that things had been a little too weird for him the previous night. The weather had been just as it was the night his men had died. There were gale warnings, high seas, and, to me, the spookiest of all, SN Benjamin F. Wingo had been scheduled for first boat. It seemed like something scripted by Stephen King.

Nothing remains static at a Coast Guard station. Petty Officer Scholz, Bosley's replacement, had arrived 6 months after the incident. He had made BM1 in January 1998 and now he was leaving. The station still did not have the fourth surfman it needed. Of the three people handling communications when I arrived at the operations room that night the previous year, two had departed for school and one was being discharged.

Of the four people aboard Petty Officer Placido's boat that night, only BM3 Marcus M. Martin will be at the station by this summer. One has left for school, and MK2 Thomas L. Byrd will retire before the summer of 1998. Petty Officer Byrd was once stationed at the Coast Guard Loran station on Iwo Jima and is now as knowledgeable on the battle of Iwo Jima as any college history major. BM1 Jon Placido, the XPO and surfman, will leave for a cutter in the Great Lakes. Jon has never stopped talking about how well his crew performed that night a year ago. "I get paid to do that," he has told me more than once. "My crewmembers do not get the extra pay of a surfman. They performed above what could be expected of any crew."

Master Chief George A. LaForge, acting the all-knowing master chief, informed me that he knew when I had arrived on the Quillayute Reservation, even though it is well over 2 miles away. Damned thing is, he probably did. I wish I could say Master Chief LaForge now has enough qualified people to do the job, but he does not. He told me, "I have enough to subsist." He still faces trying to get enough people qualified, just as he did last year. I have visited the station many times, and most of those times the master chief was either on the way to training or just coming off a boat from drilling. After I called him to check a few facts before sending off this manuscript, he ended the conversation, as he has in the past with the comment, "I have to get underway for training." No one at the small boat stations should ever again be put through what Master Chief George A. LaForge went through on the night of February 11–12, 1997.

Benjamin F. Wingo, the only survivor of CG-44363, had departed on leave by the time I arrived at the station. Ben made seaman (E-3) in October and had a request in for aviation machinist's mate school. Like other members of the crew, Ben is besieged with requests for interviews, but he and the rest of the crew almost always refuse to grant them. I feel honored they allow me to talk to them.

Finally, over a year after the incident, the entire crew of

CG-44393 was at last recognized for what they tried to accomplish. They were awarded the Coast Guard Achievement Medal, with "O" device. I know Placido did not wish to receive the award, "because that's my job," but the awards board felt, and I agree, that he deserved the medal.

The crew of the Quillayute River station has always made me feel welcome at each of my visits. I have always received more from them than I could repay. It has been a singular honor to have known the men and women of this small, isolated station on the wild Washington coast. When people of my generation bemoan the state of the younger generation, I remember how some young people performed during the early morning hours of February 12, 1997. As of February 1998, the Coast Guard has not recognized the entire crew of the station, and I suppose there is no appropriate award, but there should be one. They all worked courageously, as a team. Soon, all the people who spent the long night of February 11–12, 1997, and the longer days afterward reliving and thinking about the case and their lost shipmates, will be transferred, retired, or discharged. I will miss them. It is my hope that they do not become forgotten like most of the crews of the small boat rescue stations who have served the American people for so long have been forgotten.

When you stand by the front doors of the Quillayute River station and look past the flag pole, you now see a memorial to those who died on CG-44363: BM2 David A. Bosley, MK3 Matthew E. Schlimme, and SN Daniel P. Miniken. It is a bronze model of CG-44363 rising out of a wave. While I visited with the crew on February 12, 1998, very few people came by to remember events of the previous year. But then the crew of the Quillayute River U.S. Coast Guard Station and I do not need a reminder.

appendix one

Standard Boats at U.S. Coast Guard Small Boat Rescue Stations

Listed below are the standard boats that can be attached to Coast Guard small boat rescue stations. Some stations may have only 44-foot motor lifeboats, some may have only 41-foot utility boats, and some may have a mix of both.

44-Foot Motor Lifeboat

From 1962 the standard motor lifeboat of the Coast Guard, built at the U.S. Coast Guard Yard, Curtis Bay, Maryland. The boat will be

A 44-foot motor lifeboat. *U.S. Coast Guard*

replaced by the 47-foot motor lifeboat. The first major loss of crewmen from the boat occurred on February 12, 1997, at the Quillayute River Station, Washington.

Characteristics

Length, overall:	44 ft 1½ in	Range:	200 nm at 10 kts
Beam, overall:	12 ft 8 in		150 nm at 15 kts
Draft:	3 ft 2½ in	Power plant:	Two GM 6V53 Diesels,
Construction:	Corten Steel		186 HP at 2,000 RPM
Displacement:	36,000 lbs	Propellers:	Two 30 in dia × 25 in
Trial Max. speed:	15.3 kts		pitch × 2 in bore
Cruising speed:	11 kts	Crew:	4
Endurance:	360 degrees of roll motion and recovery	Survivors:	21

47-Foot Motor Lifeboat

The 47-foot motor lifeboat will replace the 44-foot motor lifeboat. It will remain in its aluminum state, with a red slash on the bows and the words "U.S. Coast Guard," breaking with the traditional color of all white. Some of the preproduction prototypes, however, were painted white. Testing of preproduction prototypes began in

A 47-foot motor lifeboat. *U.S. Coast Guard/Dennis Hall*

1993. The first operational boat was delivered to Cape Disappointment, Washington, in 1997. Because the boat is still evolving, the characteristics of the boat will continue to change.

Characteristics

Length, overall:	47 ft 11 in	Range:	200 nm
Beam, molded:	14 ft	Towing cap.:	150 tons
Draft:	4 ft 4 in	Power plant:	Two 6V92TA 425 HP Detroit Diesels
Construction:	Marine aluminum		
Displacement:	40,000 lbs	Propellers:	Two fixed pitch
Max. speed:	27.2 knots	Crew:	4
Cruising speed:	20 knots	Survivors:	Seating for 5
Operational	30 ft seas/20 ft surf/		
Endurance	360 degrees of roll motion and recovery		

41-Foot Utility Boat

The 41-foot utility boat provides a fast boat for inshore work and some offshore work in fair-to-moderate weather. These boats are used extensively in southern waters.

A 41-foot utility boat. *U.S. Coast Guard*

Characteristics

Length, overall:	40 ft 8 in	Max. speed:	22 kts, with 280 HP
Beam, overall:	13 ft 6 in		Cummings
Draft at operating			26 kts, with 320 HP
displacement:	4 ft		Cummings
Construction:	Aluminum hull,	Cruising speed:	18 kts
	fiberglass cabin	Range, at cruising:	300 nm
Displacement,		Power plant:	Two Cummings V903M,
full load:	32,000 lbs		280 HP at 2600 RPM, or
operating	28,000 lbs		Two Cummings VT903M,
Crew:	3		320 HP at 2600 RPM
Survivors:	22	Propellers:	Two 26 in dia. × 28 in pitch
			× 1¾ in bore, 4-blade, or
			Two 26 in dia. × 28 in pitch
			× 2 in bore, 4 blade

30-Foot Surf Rescue Boat

These very fast boats were designed to dash into surf to grab survivors and to dash back out. At one time, they were deployed to both East and West Coasts but now are primarily used on the West Coast.

A 30-foot surf rescue boat. *U.S. Coast Guard*

Characteristics

Length:	30 ft 4 in	Displacement, full load:	11,500 lbs
Beam:	9 ft 4 in	Displacement:	9,200 lbs
Freeboard, Bow:	4 ft 3 in	Engine:	Detroit Diesel 6v92TI, 375 HP
Coxswain flat:	2 ft 10 in	Fuel cap.:	78 gal
Stern:	3 ft 7 in	Max. speed:	31 kts
Draft:	3 ft 7 in	Range@2000 rpm (approx. 20 kts):	130 nm
Min. crew:	2		
Survivors:	7	Hull material:	5/8 in Airex foam-cored fiberglass reinforced plastic; the bottom is solid FRP

Operating limits: 10 ft surf, 40 kt wind
Towing cap: 40 ft or 15 gross tons
Self-righting and Self-bailing

appendix two

Ranks of the U.S. Coast Guard and Other Military Services

Officer

U.S. Coast Guard	Navy	Army	Marine Corps	Air Force
0-11 None	Fleet Admiral	General of the Army	None	General of the Air Force
0-10 Admiral	Admiral	General	General	General
0-9 Vice Admiral	Vice Admiral	Lt. General	Lt. General	Lt. General
0-8 Rear Admiral	Rear Admiral	Maj. General	Maj. General	Maj. General
0-7 Rear Admiral (Lower Half)	Rear Admiral (Lower Half)	Brig. General	Brig. General	Brig. General
0-6 Captain	Captain	Colonel	Colonel	Colonel
0-5 Commander	Commander	Lt. Colonel	Lt. Colonel	Lt. Colonel
0-4 Lieutenant Commander	Lieutenant Commander	Major	Major	Major
0-3 Lieutenant	Lieutenant	Captain	Captain	Captain
0-2 Lieutenant (jr. grade)	Lieutenant (jr. grade)	First Lt.	First Lt.	First Lt.
0-1 Ensign	Ensign	2d. Lt.	2d Lt.	2d Lt.

Warrant

W-4	Chief Warrant Officer	Chief Warrant Officer	Chief Warrant Officer	Chief Warrant Officer	Chief Warrant Officer
W-3	Chief Warrant Officer	Chief Warrant Officer	Chief Warrant Officer	Chief Warrant Officer	Chief Warrant Officer
W-2	Chief Warrant Officer	Chief Warrant Officer	Chief Warrant Officer	Chief Warrant Officer	Chief Warrant Officer
W-1	Warrant Officer	Warrant Officer	Warrant Officer	Warrant Officer	Warrant Officer

Enlisted

Petty Officer/Noncommissioned Officer

E-9	Master Chief Petty Officer	Master Chief Petty Officer	Staff Sgt. Major/ Command Sgt. Major/SPEC9	Sgt. Major/ Master Gunnery Sgt.	Chief Master Sgt/ Chief Master Sgt of the Air Force
E-8	Senior Chief Petty Officer	Senior Chief Petty Officer	1st Sgt/Master Sgt./SPEC8	1st Sgt/Master Sgt.	Senior Master Sgt.
E-7	Chief Petty Officer	Chief Petty Officer	Sgt First Class/ SPEC7	Gunnery Sgt.	Master Sgt.
E-6	Petty Officer First Class	Petty Officer First Class	Staff Sgt/SPEC6	Staff Sgt.	Technical Sgt.
E-5	Petty Officer Second Class	Petty Officer Second Class	Sgt/SPEC5	Sgt	Staff Sgt.
E-4	Petty Officer Third Class	Petty Officer Third Class	Corporal/SPEC4	Corporal	Senior Airman

Nonrated

E-3	Seaman	Seaman	Private First Class	Lance Corporal	Airman 1st Class
E-2	Seaman Apprentice	Seaman Apprentice	Private	Private First Class	Airman
E-1	Seaman Recruit	Seaman Recruit	Private	Private	Basic Airman

U.S. Coast Guard Ratings Assigned to Small Boat Stations

*Boatswain's Mates (BM)

The Coast Guardsman's Manual details the boatswain's mate rating: "Boatswain's Mates are master seamen, people skilled in all phases of seamanship and providing guidance to deck personnel . . . [T]hey must possess strong leadership skills. BMs are capable of performing almost any task associated with the operation of small boats, including navigation, storing cargo, and handling ropes, cables, and lines. Under battle conditions, they are assigned as gun captains, ammunition handlers, or members of damage-control teams. Boatswain's Mates generally 'strike' at their own unit. . . ."

*Machinery Technician (MK)

Personnel assigned as Machinery Technicians operate, maintain, and repair internal combustion engines, steam turbines, and main propulsion power transmission equipment. They perform similar functions on refrigeration, air conditioning, fuel systems, pneumatic systems, and machine shop equipment. Machinery technicians participate in damage-control parties, perform engineering-related administration functions, and read blueprints. Senior MKs organize and lead damage-control parties. Machinery technicians

---

*Rates always assigned to small boat rescue stations.

receive 12 weeks of training at the Reserve Training Center, York-town, Virginia.

Damage Controlman (DC)

Damage Controlmen understand the theory, techniques, and skills of fire-fighting, chemical warfare, carpentry, painting, welding, plumbing, and general damage control aboard ships and have extensive knowledge and understanding of the associated equipment. They maintain and repair damage-control equipment and perform all types of carpentry work. Damage Controlmen receive 13 weeks of training at the Reserve Training Center, Yorktown, Virginia.

Storekeeper (SK)

All shore activities and most ships require storekeepers. Store-keepers procure, stow, preserve, package, and issue clothing, spare parts, provisions, technical items, and all other supplies needed. Storekeepers keep inventories, prepare requisitions, and check incoming supplies. Storekeepers handle the disbursal of funds for logistics. Storekeepers know the principles of the Coast Guard accounting system, which prepares financial accounts and reports. Storekeepers operate equipment ranging from typewriters to computers and forklifts. Storekeeper "A" school is a 9-week course at the Coast Guard Training Center, Petaluma, California. Large units allow personnel to "strike" for this rating.

Food Service Specialist (FS) (Formerly Subsistence Specialists [SS])

Food service specialists work in the food service areas of afloat and ashore Coast Guard dining facilities. Food service specialists know food preparation; the operation of utensils and food service equipment, sanitation, and safety; procurement procedures of food items, equipment, and utensils; receiving and storing subsistence items; menu planning; inventory management; paperwork management; and overall knowledge of food service operations. Food service specialists receive 12 weeks of training at the Coast Guard Training Center, Petaluma, California.

Port Securityman (PS)

The port securityman rating is open only to members of the Coast Guard Reserve. Port securitymen supervise and control the safe handling, transportation, and storage of explosives and other dangerous cargo. They are experts in fire prevention and fire fighting and understand the rules and regulations about the security of vessels, harbors, and waterfront facilities. Port securitymen receive 10 weeks of training at the Reserve Training Center, Yorktown, Virginia.

Jargon

Every profession develops a language of its own, with jargon that can be incomprehensible to outsiders. In the small boat community, those in motor lifeboats have some unique sayings. I have heard some, but not all, of the terms. Here is a good example of the jargon, with the necessary translation.

> Dude! Got to the zone. Slid right into a window. Was crystal, so I jammed inbound. Gave up the wheel to a pig farmer. Told probey to station keep. Rook got us broadside. Took a widowmaker that hammered the turtle. So unsat! Told him to exit. Ended up stern to on the high side. Trashed the snipe. Got inside the bar, said, "Slick! Outta the chair until you get some storm-force. Your mama's gonna be eatin' a lot of kitty litter!" Brother weasel was shakin'.

Translation:

> Dude. Got to the area of surf. Went right into an area of calmer water. It was good, so I motored inward across the bar. Gave up the wheel to a person who wants to be a surfman. Told the probationary surfman to keep the boat in one spot. The rookie got us parallel to the surf or swell. Took a big, nasty

breaking wave that hammered the aft compartment of a 44-foot motor lifeboat. So unsatisfactory! Told him to get out of the surf zone. Ended up with the stern of the boat toward the largest portion of the wave. Injured the rated boat engineer. Got inside the entrance to the bay or river and said, "Idiot! Get out of the coxswain chair until you get some experience in heavy weather. You are a *very* poor coxswain!" I was *very* scared.

I wish to thank BMC Richard Belisle for the jargon and especially for the necessary translation.

Glossary

Aid(s) to navigation   Any device external to a vessel or aircraft that is specifically intended either to assist navigators in determining their position or safe course or to warn them of dangers or obstructions to navigation. Also known as A to N, or ANT.

Aft   To the rear of the boat or ship, as in the aft part of the boat.

Bar   A bank or shoal, usually at the mouth of a river, which makes entry difficult or impossible.

Beach apparatus   All of the equipment used during the U.S. Life-Saving Service era (1878–1915) and into the 1960s for propelling a line from shore to a shipwreck close to the beach. Once a strong line was established, then devices could be used to bring those aboard the wreck to safety.

Beach cart   *See*: Beach apparatus.

Boot   Recruit. Also used to denote a new person.

Breakers (breaks)   Breaking surf or waves.

Broach
A boat or ship that becomes sideways to the sea, surf, or swell. A boat that broaches in heavy surf will usually roll.

Coston signal
A flarelike signaling device used in the U.S. Life-Saving Service.

Detailer
Officer in Coast Guard headquarters who is responsible for the transferring of officers and enlisted personnel.

Dream sheet
A form sent to detailers in which a person expresses his or her choice of duty stations. *See*: Detailer.

Drogue
A baglike device, usually of canvas, used as a drag to steady a boat in heavy seas. Also known as a sea anchor. To use the drogue is referred to as: streaming a drogue.

Float coat
A short jacket that has flotation material and can be used as a life jacket.

Green line
Referring to the left side of channel, returning from sea. Buoys on this side of channel are colored green.

Hash mark
Red diagonal marks on lower left-hand sleeve of the enlisted uniform. Each mark represents 4 years of service. In the Coast Guard, rating badges and hash marks for E-7, 8, 9 are gold.

Kedge the anchor
Move an anchor up a beach to hold a boat in the surf.

Knots (speed)
A knot is slightly higher than 1 mile per hour, as it is based upon nautical miles of 6,080 feet, versus 5,280 feet on land. (1 knot = 1.15 miles per hour)

Medevac
Medical evacuation.

Mustang suit
A coverall type of clothing that protects

the wearer from hypothermia. Usually colored bright orange. The suit also provides flotation.

Red line   Referring to the right-hand side of a channel, when returning from sea. Right-hand side of channel is marked by red-colored buoys.

RHIB   Acronym for rigid-hull inflatable boat.

SAR   Acronym for search and rescue.

Sea anchor   *See*: Drogue

Series   A series of waves, usually followed by a lull.

Screw   Propeller on a boat or ship, also sometimes called a wheel.

Soundings   To come inshore sufficiently to reach the bottom with a hand lead, which is a device to measure depth.

SRB   Acronym for surf rescue boat.

Streaming a drogue   *See* drogue.

Strike   The procedure by which an enlisted man learns his rating by on-the-job training rather than by attending a formal service school. The boatswain's mate rating is learned by striking.

Surf zone   Area of surf.

Turtleback   The top of the aft compartment on the 44-foot motor lifeboat.

Wheel   *See* screw.

Wig-wag   A form of signaling with a single flag. Differs from semaphore, which uses two flags.

Selected Bibliography

Books

Gates, John Humboldt. *Night Crossings*. Eureka, Calif.: Pioneer Graphics, 1986.

Junger, Sebastian. *The Perfect Storm: A True Story of Men Against the Sea*. New York: W. W. Norton & Company, 1997.

Mobley, Joe A. *Ship Ashore!: The U.S. Lifesavers of Coastal North Carolina*. Raleigh, N.C.: Division of Archives and History, Department of Cultural Resources, 1994.

Noble, Dennis L. *That Others Might Live: The U.S. Life-Saving Service, 1878–1915*. Annapolis, Md.: Naval Institute Press, 1994.

Shanks, Ralph, Wick York, Lisa Woo, ed. *The U.S. Life-Saving Service: Heroes, Rescues, and Architecture of the Early Coast Guard*. Petaluma, Calif.: Costano Books, 1996.

Stonehouse, Frederick. *Wreck Ashore: The United States Life-Saving Service on the Great Lakes*. Duluth, Minn.: Lake Superior Port Cities, Inc., 1994.

Webber, Bernard C. *Chatham "The Lifeboatmen": A Narrative by a Seaman Recounting His Life in the Coast Guard on the Southeast Corner of Cape Cod, Massachusetts*. Orleans, Mass.: Lower Cape Publishing Co., 1985.

Articles

Buckley, William F. "On Being Rescued by the Coast Guard." *National Review* (February 16, 1973): 209–211.

Butterworth, W.E., IV. "Surf Patrol." *Boys' Life* (November 1988): 37–39.

Hammett, Cornell M. "There's Nothing More Important . . . Life of a Child." *Compass Point N.W.* (November 1986): 4–5.

Noble, Dennis L. "Incident at Ashtabula." U.S. Naval Institute *Proceedings* 106 (October 1980): 128–129.

———. "Boatswain's Mates Never Cry." U.S. Naval Institute *Proceedings* 123 (August 1997): 40–41.

Parfit, Michael. "They Learn to Work Calmly While Instinct Warns They're About to Die." *Smithsonian* 18, No. 2 (May 1987): 98–102, 104, 106–108.

Sharp, Don. "Passing the Bar Exams." *The Western Boatman* 6, No. 2 (March/April 1988): 36–41, 112–113.

About the Author

Dennis L. Noble entered the U.S. Coast Guard in 1957 and retired as a senior chief marine science technician (E-8) in 1978. His first tour of duty was at a small boat rescue station. After retiring, Noble earned a Ph.D. in history from Purdue University. He has written six books. Three of these books and numerous articles are on search and rescue in the U.S. Coast Guard. Noble has worked as a U.S. Army historian and as a park ranger. He resides in Sequim, Washington.

8/058